ADVANCES IN ACCOUNTING

Volume 14 • 1996

ADVANCES IN ACCOUNTING

Editor: PHILIP M.J. RECKERS
School of Accountancy
Arizona State University

VOLUME 14 • 1996

JAI PRESS INC.

Greenwich, Connecticut   *London , England*

Copyright © 1996 JAI PRESS INC.
55 Old Post Road, No. 2
Greenwich, Connecticut 06836

JAI PRESS LTD.
38 Tavistock Street
Covent Garden
London WC2E 7PB
England

ISBN: 0-7623-0161-9

ISSN: 0882-6110

Manufactured in the United States of America

CONTENTS

vi

LIST OF CONTRIBUTORS

M.J. Abdolmohammadi	Department of Accountancy Bentley College

Barbro Back	Information Systems Science
	Turku School of Economics and
	    Business Administration,
	    Finland

Jesse D. Beeler	Else School of Management Millsaps College
Bruce K. Behn	Department of Accounting and Business Law The University of Tennessee
Bruce Bublitz	Division of Accounting and Information Systems The University of Kansas
B. Douglas Clinton	School of Accounting Central Missouri State University
Cynthia Firey Eakin	Eberhardt School of Business University of the Pacific
Joseph Fisher	Department of Accounting and Information Systems Indiana University
Martin Freedman	School of Management SUNY, Binghamton
Thomas W. Hall	Department of Accounting University of Texas, Arlington

James E. Hunton	School of Accountancy University of South Florida
Bikki Jaggi	Department of Accounting Rutgers University
Eric N. Johnson	Department of Accounting University of Toledo
Teija Laitinen	Department of Accounting and Finance University of Vaasa, Finland
D. Jordan Lowe	Department of Accounting Virginia Polytechnic Institute and State Universiity
Jeffrey J. McMillan	School of Accountancy and Legal Studies Clemson University
Ronald E. Michaels	Department of Marketing University of Central Florida
Hossein Nouri	Area of Accountancy Trenton State College
Robert J. Parker	Department of Accounting and Finance University of Manitoba, Canada
Bethane Jo Pierce	Department of Accounting University of Texas at Arlington
Srinivasan Ragothaman	Department of Accounting University of South Dakota
James E. Rebele	Department of Business Lehigh University
Philip M.J. Reckers	School of Accountancy Arizona State University
William J. Read	Department of Accountancy Bentley College

Jeffrey W. Schatzberg	Department of Accounting The University of Arizona
Kaisa Sere	Department of Computer Science and Applied Mathematics University of Kuopio, Finland
Brian P. Shapiro	Department of Accounting The University of Arizona
Renee Wachter	College of Business Ball State University
Richard A. White	School of Accounting University of South Carolina
Bernard Wong-On-Wing	Department of Accounting and Business Law Washington State University

EDITORIAL BOARD

STATEMENT OF PURPOSE AND REVIEW PROCEDURES

Advances in Accounting (AIA) is a research series publication providing academics and practitioners a forum to address current and emerging issues in accounting. Manuscripts may embrace any research methodology and examine any accounting-related subject. Manuscripts may range from empirical to analytical; timely replications will be considered. Manuscripts must be readable, relevant, and reliable. To be readable, manuscripts must be understandable and concise. To be relevant, manuscripts must be related to problems facing the accounting and business community. To be reliable, conclusions must follow logically from the evidence and arguments presented. For empirical reports, sound research design and execution are critical. For theoretical treatises, reasonable assumptions and logical developments are essential.

REVIEW PROCEDURES

AIA intends to provide authors with timely reviews clearly indicating the acceptance status of their manuscripts. The results of initial reviews normally will be reported to authors within 90 days from the date the manuscript is received. All manuscripts are blind reviewed by two members of the editorial board and an Associate Editor. Editorial correspondence pertaining to manuscripts should be sent to the editor. A $25 submission fee is required.

Editorial correspondence pertaining to manuscripts should be sent to:

> Philip M.J. Reckers
> School of Accountacy
> College of Business
> Arizona State University
> Tempe, Arizona 85287-3606

EDITORIAL POLICY AND MANUSCRIPT FORM GUIDELINES

1. Manuscripts should be typewritten and double-spaced on $8\frac{1}{2}$" by 11" white paper. Only one side of a page should be used. Margins should be set to facilitate editing and duplication except as noted:

   a. Tables, figures, and exhibits should appear on a separate page. Each should be numbered and have a title.

   b. Footnote should be presented by citing the author's name and the year of publication in the body of the text; for example, Schwartz (1989); Reckers and Pany (1990).

2. Manuscripts should include a cover page which indicates the author's name and affiliation.

3. Manuscripts should include on a separate lead page an abstract not exceeding 200 worlds. The author's name and affiliation should not appear on the abstract.

4. Topical headings and subheadings should be used. Main headings in the manuscript should be centered, secondary headings should be flush with the left hand margin. (As a guide to usage and style, refer to William Strunk, Jr., and E.B. White, *The Elements Of Style*.)

5. Manuscripts must include a list of references which contains only those works actually cited. (As a helpful guide in preparing a list of references, refer to Kate L. Turabian, *A Manual for Writers of Term Papers, Theses, and Dissertations*.)

6. In order to be assured of an anonymous review, authors should not identify themselves directly or indirectly. Reference to unpublished working papers and dissertations should be avoided. If necessary, authors may indicate that the reference is being withheld for the reasons cited above.

7. Accepted manuscripts ultimately must be submitted on disk.

8. Manuscripts currently under review by other publications should not be submitted. Complete reports of research presented at a national or regional conference of a professional association and "State of the Art" papers are acceptable.

9. Four copies of each manuscript should be submitted to the Editor-In-Chief. Copies of any and all research instruments should also be included.

10. The author should send a check for $25.00 made payable to *Advances in Accounting* as a submission fee.

VAGUE WORDING EFFECTS ON AUDITORS' COMPLEXITY JUDGMENTS OF RISK-RELATED AUDIT TASKS

Mohammad J. Abdolmohammadi and
William J. Read

ABSTRACT

Task complexity has been a recent topic of interest to many authors in areas of expertise, training, and decision aid development in auditing. An implicit assumption in
much of the prior research is that auditors' judgments of task complexity in experimental settings remain unchanged regardless of the wording used to define audit
tasks. However, the literature on ambiguity and vagueness proposes that the wording
used to define an audit task can significantly influence auditors' judgments of the
nature (e.g., complexity) of the task. More specifically, vague wording will result in
judgments of the same task as relatively more complex than will clear wording. The
objective of this study is to investigate this proposition using a series of risk-related
audit tasks.

Advances in Accounting, Volume 14, pages 1-21.
Copyright © 1996 by JAI Press Inc.
All rights of reproduction in any form reserved.
ISBN: 0-7623-0161-9.

1

Processing

Based on a pilot study, four words ("assessment," "determination," "evaluation," and "identification") were used to describe 30 audit tasks. These wordings were then used to obtained 134 auditors' judgments of task complexity. Sixty-three accounting students then classified the four words as either vague or clear. The overall results indicate that (1) complexity judgments of auditors are significantly affected by the wording used to describe the task, and (2) vague words result in significantly higher complexity judgments than clear words. Implications for behavioral research in areas of decision aid development, experience, and task-specific training are discussed.

INTRODUCTION

The behavioral auditing literature has emphasized the importance of attention to task complexity in recent years (e.g., Abdolmohammadi and Wright 1987; Bonner 1994). The arguments for the importance of attention to task complexity relate to two major developments in the auditing profession. First, decision aid development and staff assignment decisions are influenced by the complexity of the task under consideration. The literature indicates that the accounting profession is moving rapidly in the direction of developing decision aids for use in practice as a means of enhancing audit efficiency and effectiveness and for using less costly, less experienced staff for tasks that normally require audit expertise.[1] As Graham (1990, 15) has observed, "few firms can afford to have their most experienced auditors available for every engagement, yet the expertise and experience of those auditors are really needed to guide every audit." Decision aids, particularly knowledge-based expert systems, can provide such expertise (Abdolmohammadi 1987).

To develop a decision aid for a particular task, there is a need to identify the complexity of the task and to structure the task to the extent possible. Simon (1990, 665) stated that "most realizable artificial intelligence in the near future will be focused on fairly concrete things. Expert systems, for example, do best when there are a zillion specific pieces of knowledge for which they can act as a big recognition memory." The specific pieces of knowledge have to be elicited from experts and structured for the purpose of expert systems development.

The other major development in the auditing profession that underscores the importance of attention to task complexity involves task-specific training. Bonner and Lewis (1990) argued for task-specific training and Bonner and Pennington (1991) provided evidence that auditors' performance on tasks with task-specific instruction was better than for those tasks with minimal or no task-specific training. The authors advocated the development of theories for tasks that lack good instructional material as a means of generating task-specific training material. Task complexity classification and the attributes that affect task complexity assist in the development of such theories and training materials. Also, given that task complexity has been found as an explanatory variable in behavioral research (e.g.,

Abdolmohammadi and Wright 1987), behavioral research will benefit from evidence on task complexity.

Assessment of task complexity is largely dependent on the judgments of the assessor. An implicit assumption in much of the literature is that such judgments remain unchanged regardless of the wording used to describe the tasks under investigation. However, the ambiguity and vagueness literature (discussed in the next section) suggests that the wording used to describe audit tasks may significantly influence auditors' judgments of task complexity. The objective of this study is to investigate whether, in general, different words describing a series of risk-related audit tasks affect auditors' judgments of task complexity. The words used then will be independently classified as vague or clear in order to investigate the effects of vagueness on the results.

The remainder of the paper is organized as follows. The next section provides the background literature on task complexity as well as ambiguity and vagueness and presents the research hypotheses. This is followed by a section on the research method. Next, the results are presented. In the final section, we discuss a summary of the results and their implications for behavioral research.

BACKGROUND AND RESEARCH HYPOTHESES

Task Complexity

The task complexity literature has its roots in organizational settings. Simon (1960) presented a model to classify tasks according to complexity into a continuum ranging from programmable to nonprogrammable. Later, this model was interpreted as a model of task structure for decision aids where categories of "structured," "semi-structured," and "unstructured" replaced the programmable-nonprogrammable continuum (Keen and Scott-Morton 1978). The variables influencing the classification were problem definition, alternative courses of action, and level of expertise and insight needed to make a decision relating to the task under study. According to this model, tasks that are well defined and have only a few courses of action requiring little judgment or insight are defined as simple or "structured." Tasks that are undefined and have infinite or undefined alternative courses of action requiring judgment and insight are defined as complex or "unstructured." "Semistructured" tasks are somewhere in the middle of the "structured-unstructured" categories.

Simon's model is not the only model of task complexity. Bonner (1994) reviews the literature on task complexity in various fields and develops a model for auditing. She discusses task complexity in terms of input, process, and output aspects and classifies task complexity into "inherent" and "perceived" categories. Inherent complexity relates to the task's objective characteristics. However, perceived complexity is the complexity of the task in the judgment of a decision maker and consequently, the cognitive abilities and knowledge of the decision maker influence such a judgment. While no research addresses the relationship between inherent and perceived task complexity, Bonner (1994) speculates that they are very much related because each requires consideration of the same characteristics of the task for its complexity classification. An important aspect of Simon's (1960) and Bonner's (1994) models is that each indicates that task complexity is a task-specific attribute that requires task-specific knowledge. Thus, this study focuses on risk-related audit tasks[2] at a highly detailed level and uses auditor-subjects with varying degrees of experience.

Support for the use of perceived task complexity as an explanatory variable in auditing was provided by Abdolmohammadi and Wright (1987). They furnished evidence that indicates that a task's complexity classification and its experience requirement are major attributes in analyzing the effects of experience on audit judgments. More specifically, while the authors found no experience effect for structured tasks, the judgments of inexperienced auditors differed from those of experienced auditors in semi-structured and unstructured tasks. Their results indicate a value for task complexity classification as a means of better matching the tasks to auditors with varying levels of experience. Furthermore, their findings suggest that decision aid development and task-specific training can benefit from task complexity classifications.

Ambiguity and Vagueness

Interest in understanding the effects of imprecise and inexact language on decision making in various scientific fields increased significantly in the 1960s. For example, Black (1963) discussed several issues regarding reasoning with loose concepts and the MIT Press published a monograph in 1964 dealing with linguistic effects on science and engineering (Katz and Postal 1964). Zadeh (1965) proposed a theory and a precise mathematical model called "fuzzy sets" to handle ambiguous and vague concepts that he called "fuzziness."

Ambiguity relates to the existence of multiple meanings of a word or concept and vagueness relates to the lack of precise boundaries in the meaning of the word or concept (Black 1963). These definitions indicate that ambiguity and vagueness are very much related and are used interchangeably to indicate imprecision and inexactness (Zebda 1991). For this reason, we will use the term vagueness (and its opposite, clarity) in the development and testing of our hypotheses. It is important however, to note that ambiguity and vagueness are different from randomness (i.e., uncertainty) handled by the use of various probabilistic theories.[3] To illustrate the difference, Zebda (1991, 117-118) provides the following example:

> the term "material account error" involves ambiguity and vagueness because of the imprecise meaning of the word material. However, the question about the probability of having an account error of $1,000 involves randomness. The event is well described: either the error is $1,000 or it is not; the uncertainty lies with the occurrence or nonoccurrence of the event.

This difference has motivated research on formulating mathematical models for handling ambiguity and vagueness other than those used in random situations. For example, as mentioned above, Zadeh (1965) coined a mathematical formulation called "fuzzy sets" that allows precise computations using approximations (Armstrong 1990). Zebda (1989) summarizes the literature around fuzzy set theory and its implications for decision making in general and accounting in particular. A major finding in this literature is that ambiguity effects are context-specific (i.e., significant ambiguity effects are found in some contexts but not others (cf. Kahn and Sarin 1988). Given the ambiguous and vague nature of many accounting and auditing tasks, it is likely that ambiguity effects will be present in these tasks and Zebda (1991, 136) calls for ambiguity and vagueness research on auditing applications. For example, auditors' perceptions of task complexity may be affected by the nature of wording (i.e., vague or clear wording) used to define those tasks.

Most of the empirical studies of ambiguity and vagueness have evolved around interpretation of numerical versus verbal probability terms. For example, in a series of experiments, Wallsten and his colleagues have reported wide variability in interpretations of numerical versus verbal probability terms (cf. Wallsten et al. 1986). In the most recent of these experiments, decision makers' rankings (of gambles whose probabilities were provided by other individuals in a numerical or verbal mode) correlated more closely with payoffs when probabilities were expressed verbally rather than numerically (Gonzalez-Vallejo, Erev, and Wallsten 1994). Significant ambiguity effects have also been reported in other choice behaviors. For example, Ghosh and Ray (1992) found that students' choices between two alternative examinations was positively correlated with their attitude toward ambiguity. That is, students with a less (more) favorable attitude toward ambiguity selected a less (more) ambiguous exam.

An implication of these studies is that ambiguity/vagueness has a significant effect on judgment and behavior. However, while there is a general recognition that many audit tasks are ambiguous or vague, research on the effects of ambiguity and vagueness on auditors' judgments is rare. Cooley and Hicks (1983) used fuzzy set theory concepts to formulate a model for aggregation of judgments regarding the evaluation of systems of internal controls. These concepts also were used by Hughes (1980) and Lin (1984) to extend Bayesian models to include ambiguity and vagueness in tests of compliance and account balances and by Kelly (1984) who formulated an analytical model for the ambiguous and vague problem of materiality judgments in auditing.

More recently, researchers have argued, and have provided evidence, that vague wording of professional standards is a source of perception differences among various user groups regarding the numerical meanings of the terms used. For example, building on Chesley's (1986) study on wide variations in interpretations of words such as "probable" and "likely" among students, Reimers (1992) reported perception differences between auditors, engineering managers, marketing managers, and graduate business students regarding the numerical meanings of the terms "probable, "reasonably possible," and "remote." These terms were adopted from Statement of Financial Accounting Standards (SFAS) No. 5, "Accounting for Contingencies" (FASB 1975), and various other expressions. Similar differences were reported by Ponemon and Raghunandan (1994) between auditors, financial analysts, bankers, judges, and legislative staff regarding the meaning of "substantial doubt" used in SFAS 59 and SFAS 64 (AICPA 1994). However, we are not aware of any study investigating the effects of vague wording on auditors judgments of key task variables such as task complexity. We provide evidence regarding the effects of different words, with different levels of vagueness or clarity, used to define audit tasks, on auditors' judgments of task complexity.

Research Hypotheses

The formulation of research hypotheses in this study are preliminary in nature because of the absence of any known research in the auditing area of task wording and complexity judgments. However, the literature reviewed earlier suggests that vagueness has significant effects on judgments in a variety of situations. The literature also indicated that such significant effects are context-specific (Kahn and Sarin 1988, 270). The context of this study is audit risk assessment and the words used to describe various tasks (to be explained later) have different levels of vagueness or clarity (as measured in the study). Thus, in general, we expect to observe an overall significant wording effect on complexity judgments of auditors. Formally:

Hypothesis 1. There is a significant difference between auditors' task complexity judgments under various words used to define these tasks.

The second hypothesis specifically examines the effects of vagueness and clarity. Assuming that different words describing the tasks have different effects on auditors' complexity judgments as expected, does vague wording of task description result in a higher complexity judgment than relatively clear wording? The extant literature on ambiguity and vagueness, as reviewed above, does not explicitly suggest directional hypotheses here—only that vague wording would connote inexactness and imprecision. We posit that vague wording will result in a perception of greater task complexity. Thus, we expect that:

Hypothesis 2. Auditors will perceive as more complex a task defined with vague wording than with clear wording.

METHOD

Data were collected in three phases. In Phase I, a pilot study was conducted with practicing auditors to establish appropriate words for describing audit tasks. In

Phase II, the words identified from Phase I were used to describe 30 risk-related audit tasks. Practicing auditors were then used to judge the complexity of each of these tasks under different wordings. In Phase III, data were collected from accounting students regarding levels of vagueness or clarity of the wording used in Phase II. Detailed information on these phases is presented below.

Phase I: Applicable Words

After consulting several dictionaries of synonyms and antonyms (e.g., Soule 1959; Webster 1973), seven words were selected to describe each task. These terms were "ascertainment," "assessment," "appraisal," "determination," "estimation," "evaluation," and "identification." These words were pilot tested in order to identify their appropriateness for describing each of the audit tasks under study. To accomplish this objective, we sent a questionnaire to 15 auditors from three international accounting firms.

The questionnaire presented each of the audit tasks described by the seven words listed above. The respondents were requested to select the words that they believed appropriate for defining each of the 30 audit tasks. Nine questionnaires were returned.[4] We selected words used by the subjects in a majority of tasks. Four words qualified: "assessment" (selected for 29 tasks), "determination" (selected for all 30 tasks), "evaluation" (selected for 28 tasks), and "identification" (selected for 22 tasks)[5]

Phase II: Complexity Judgments of Tasks Described by Various Words

The four words identified in Phase I formed the four levels of the independent variable: wording. Perceived task complexity of each of the 30 tasks (explained below) was the dependent variable and was measured by a Likert scale that ranged from 1-9 (structured-unstructured).[6] Subjects were 134 practicing auditors from seven international accounting firms. The subjects were procured by contacting audit partners in each of the firms. Each subject was randomly assigned to one of four versions of the task instrument (to be described later). The subjects' overall mean audit experience was 5.71 years, with a 5.12 standard deviation. Virtually all subjects indicated, in a post-experiment questionnaire, that they routinely performed risk-related audit tasks as required by several professional auditing standards [e.g., SAS 39, SAS 47, and SAS 55 (AICPA 1994)] and all but five of them indicated that they had a "working knowledge" of these Statements that was gained from their firms' inhouse training programs.[7]

The 30 tasks used in the study are presented in the Appendix as they appeared in version one of the task instrument. These tasks were identified by consulting audit manuals of three large accounting firms and a leading auditing text as reported in

Table 1.   Experimental Design

Distribution of Tasks by Wording	Version				
	1	2	3	4	Total
Assessment	8	8	7	7	30
Determination	8	7	7	8	30
Evaluation	7	8	8	7	30
Identification	7	7	8	8	30
Total tasks	30	30	30	30	
Subjects assigned	33	33	37	31	134

Abdolmohammadi (1995). While the first 20 tasks relate to engagement risks, the last 10 tasks pertain to inherent risks.

Table 1 presents the Phase II design. As shown, the four words were crossed with four versions of the task instrument where each word appeared in approximately one fourth of the tasks in the experimental material that each subject received. Thus, depending on the version of the instrument, each word was used seven or eight times. For example, in version one, eight tasks were defined by the word "assessment" and eight tasks by "determination," leaving 14 tasks defined by either "evaluation" (seven tasks) or "identification" (seven tasks). The four versions were arranged in a randomized order using a table selected randomly from the table of alternatives in the Latin-Square Random Order Design (Cochran and Cox 1957). Table 1 also shows the number of subjects assigned to each version of the task instrument.

Phase III: Word Vagueness or Clarity Rating

A study was conducted in this phase with accounting students from three accounting courses: two graduate intermediate and advanced courses and a CPA coaching course. This study was conducted to classify the words used in Phase II by their level of vagueness or clarity. We used a generic questionnaire to obtain this information. No accounting or auditing task was involved. For this reason, there was no need for participation of professional accountants. The only requirement was that the participants were fluent in the English language. One of the authors administered a brief questionnaire in his three classes where a total of 63 students participated on a voluntary basis. Of these students, 26 were female and 33 were male; four did not provide demographic or personal information. Only five students indicated that English was not their first language. The remaining students who provided demographic information indicated that English was their first language.

Table 2. Vagueness Ratings by Students
$(n = 63)$
Scale: 3-6 (clear to vague)

Word	Mean	Median	Std. Dev.	Average Rank	Z-value
Panel A: All Words					
Assessment	5.24	6.00	0.96	172.8	5.82
Determination	4.02	4.00	0.94	98.9	−3.48
Evaluation	4.49	5.00	1.15	127.4	0.11
Identification	4.16	4.00	1.18	106.9	−2.46
Overall	4.48	4.00	1.16	126.5	

H-statistic = 41.71, significant at the .000 level

Panel B: Vague versus Clear Words					
Vague[a]	4.87	5.00	1.12	150.1	5.14
Clear[b]	4.09	4.00	1.07	102.9	−5.14
Overall	4.48	4.00	1.16	126.5	

H-statistic = 28.73, significant at the .000 level

W-statistic = 18,912.5, significant at the .000 level

Notes: [a]Assessment and evaluation words;
[b]Determination and identification words;
H-statistic = Chi-square distribution for Kruskal-Wallis test.
W-statistic = Total rank for the Mann-Whitney two-sample test.
Z-statistic = Standardized z-value indicating the degree of deviation of the cell mean rank from overall mean rank. Negative z-value = relatively low complexity; positive z-value = relatively high complexity.

The questionnaire provided the typical dictionary definition of each of the four words and asked that each subject independently judge each word's level of vagueness or clarity in comparison with the other three words (i.e., whether the word was "more vague," "less vague," "about the same, but vague," or "about the same, but clear"). Only six possible pairs of the four words were possible. These six pairs were listed for subjects' consideration. Subject responses were coded as follows: 2 was assigned to a word considered "more vague" and 1 was assigned to a word considered "less vague." While a 2 was also assigned to the words that were judged "about the same, but vague," a 1 was assigned to the words considered to be "about the same, but clear." The codified responses of each subject were summed for each word to form the clarity/vagueness scale of the word. The resulting sum ranged from 3 to 6 (clear to vague). Table 2 presents a summary of these ratings.

Panel A in Table 2 shows descriptive statistics on clarity/vagueness ratings. It also presents the nonparametric Kruskal-Wallis test of the differences between ratings of the four words. The ordinal clarity/vagueness scale lends itself best to nonparametric statistical testing (Gibbons 1976, 22-25). The H-statistic (41.71) is highly significant at the .000 level, indicating significant differences between the four words with regards to their clarity/vagueness ratings. As the average rank column indicates, the average rank of 127.4 for the word "evaluation" is greater, albeit insignificantly from the overall rank of 126.5 (Z-value = 0.11). However, while the clarity/vagueness rating of the word "assessment" is significantly (Z-value = 5.82, significant at the .000 level) more vague than the average, the clarity/vagueness ratings of "determination" and "identification" are significantly (Z-values of −3.48 and −2.46, respectively, and significant at the .001 level) less vague than the average.

In Panel B of Table 2, we have provided data on the vague or clear wording classification. To do this, we considered the overall median in Panel A. The words that had a median of greater than 4 (the overall median) were classified as relatively vague and those that had a median of 4 were classified as relatively clear. Thus, "assessment" (median = 6) and "evaluation" (median = 5) were classified as relatively vague words and "determination" and "identification" were classified as relatively clear words. As the Kruskal-Wallis' H-statistic and Mann-Whitney's W-statistic show, the difference between vague and clear categories was highly significant at the .000 level. The Z-value of 5.14 is also significant at the .000 level indicating that the vague words (median = 5) with an average rank of 150.1 are significantly more vague than the clear words with an average rank of 102.9. We use these categories for the analysis of Hypothesis 2.

RESULTS

The ordinal scale (1-9) used to collect task complexity data lends itself best to nonparametric statistical testing (Gibbons 1976, 22-25). For this reason, only nonparametric tests were performed to test the hypotheses, as reported below.

Test of Hypothesis 1:   Wording Effect

The wording effect hypothesis was tested using the nonparametric Kruskal-Wallis test. This statistic is equivalent to the one-way analysis of variance and provides an H-statistic (equivalent to the F-statistic in parametric ANOVA) and its statistical significance. Table 3 presents the results for each of the 30 tasks and for all tasks combined. The table provides the task complexity mean, median, and coefficient of variation for each task under each of the four words and for the overall data.

In support of Hypothesis 1, the Kruskal-Wallis test of the overall data in the bottom of Table 3 indicates that wording significantly affected auditors' judgments of

Table 3. Kruskal-Wallis Test on the Wording Variable
Complexity Judgment (1-9 Likert Scale) as Dependent Variable

Audit Tasks	Assessment Mean Median (C. of Var)	Determination Mean Median (C. of Var)	Evaluation Mean Median (C. of Var)	Identification Mean Median (C. of Var)	Kruskal-Wallis H-stat.	Sig.
1	4.33 5.00 (0.50)	2.57 2.00 (0.63)	2.88 2.00 (0.68)	2.86 2.00 (0.67)	12.24	.007*
2	3.56 4.00 ((0.60)	5.12 5.00 (0.51)	3.89 5.00 (0.50)	4.60 5.00 (0.49)	7.37	.062**
3	7.49 8.00 (0.23)	7.27 8.00 (0.25)	6.77 7.00 (0.31)	7.94 8.00 (0.17)	7.21	.066**
4	5.30 5.00 (0.39)	5.08 5.00 (0.47)	6.76 7.00 (0.34)	4.69 5.00 (0.57)	14.29	.003*
5	6.93 7.00 (0.24)	6.92 7.00 (0.26)	6.10 6.00 (0.37)	6.64 7.00 (0.27)	2.68	.444
6	5.86 7.00 (0.54)	3.87 2.00 (0.83)	5.16 5.00 (0.56)	3.90 1.00 (0.91)	7.86	.050*
7	7.00 7.00 (0.27)	7.55 8.00 (0.26)	6.22 6.00 (0.33)	6.19 7.00 (0.42)	9.11	.028*
8	4.78 5.00 (0.50)	3.03 2.00 (0.72)	4.45 5.00 (0.62)	3.36 3.00 (0.68)	12.21	.007*
9	5.79 5.00 (0.30)	5.87 5.00 (0.27)	6.52 7.00 (0.32)	5.73 6.00 (0.35)	3.71	.296
10	3.85 4.00 (0.64)	2.61 2.00 (0.74)	3.70 3.00 (0.60)	4.00 5.00 (0.57)	8.36	.040*
11	3.84 4.00 (0.74)	3.61 3.00 (0.69)	5.00 5.00 (0.56)	3.19 2.00 (0.71)	7.22	.066**
12	2.66 2.00 (0.77)	1.30 1.00 (0.49)	3.38 3.00 (0.66)	2.03 1.00 (0.83)	24.17	.000*
13	3.65 3.00 (0.71)	2.57 1.00 (0.89)	3.44 3.00 (0.79)	1.81 1.00 (0.93)	13.44	.004*
14	7.33 9.00 (0.31)	6.36 8.00 (0.41)	7.51 9.00 (0.27)	6.45 7.00 (0.43)	5.82	.121
15	7.03 7.00 (0.25)	6.45 7.00 (0.36)	6.48 7.00 (0.34)	6.28 6.00 (0.35)	1.96	.581
16	4.13 4.00 (0.47)	3.89 3.00 (0.51)	4.03 5.00 (0.52)	3.45 5.00 (0.59)	2.33	.507
17	6.21 7.00 (0.37)	7.48 8.00 (0.23)	6.88 7.00 (0.30)	6.95 8.00 (0.30)	5.71	.128
18	6.51 7.00 (0.34)	6.85 7.00 (0.28)	7.13 8.00 (0.29)	6.09 6.00 (0.34)	4.71	.195

(continued)

Table 3. (Continued)

Audit Tasks	Assessment Mean Median (C. of Var)		Determination Mean Median (C. of Var)		Evaluation Mean Median (C. of Var)		Identification Mean Median (C. of Var)		Kruskal-Wallis H-stat.	Sig.
19	4.16	5.00	3.93	4.00	4.06	3.00	3.78	4.00	.72	.868
	(0.49)		(0.55)		(0.55)		(0.55)			
20	7.32	8.00	7.32	8.00	6.55	7.00	6.64	7.00	5.12	.164
	(0.21)		(0.26)		(0.32)		(0.29)			
21	4.94	5.00	4.74	5.00	4.89	5.00	5.30	5.00	1.16	.762
	(0.46)		(0.48)		(0.44)		(0.41)			
22	7.38	8.00	6.64	7.00	7.13	7.00	7.16	8.00	1.87	.600
	(0.20)		(0.35)		(0.17)		(0.26)			
23	4.75	5.00	5.19	5.00	5.82	6.00	5.92	6.00	6.84	.078**
	(0.47)		(0.40)		(0.36)		(0.35)			
24	4.45	5.00	4.61	5.00	4.94	5.00	5.91	6.00	11.98	.008*
	(0.46)		(0.45)		(0.44)		(0.28)			
25	5.32	5.00	5.52	6.00	4.10	4.00	4.94	5.00	7.36	.062**
	(0.40)		(0.48)		(0.55)		(0.35)			
26	5.65	6.00	5.65	6.00	5.75	5.50	5.30	5.00	.81	.848
	(0.42)		(0.36)		(0.34)		(0.40)			
27	2.85	2.00	2.38	2.00	3.43	3.00	2.61	2.00	5.92	.116
	(0.20)		(0.71)		(0.52)		(0.68)			
28	6.39	7.00	6.67	7.00	5.78	5.00	5.58	6.00	7.97	.047*
	(0.34)		(0.27)		(0.33)		(0.34)			
29	4.72	5.00	4.71	5.00	3.55	3.00	4.44	5.00	7.37	.062**
	(0.35)		(0.42)		(0.54)		(0.42)			
30	6.00	6.00	6.16	6.00	6.32	7.00	6.42	7.00	.43	934
	(0.42)		(0.32)		(0.27)		(0.31)			
Overall	5.37	5.00	5.08	5.00	5.26	5.00	5.03	5.00	9.85	.020*
	(0.47)		(0.53)		(0.48)		(0.52)			
	n = 990		n = 993		n = 999		n = 987			

Notes: H-stat. = H-statistic(chi-square distribution) for Kruskal-Wallis test.
Sig. = Significance level.
C. of Var = Coefficient of variation.
*, ** = Significant at the.05 and.10 levels, respectively.

task complexity (H-statistic = 9.85, significant at the .020 level). In search for the source of this result, we investigated the tasks at the individual level. Table 3 shows 16 significant wording main effects (10 at the .05 level and six at .10) for the Kruskal-Wallis tests. Although the remaining tasks do not show significance, the presence of a significant wording effect in 16 tasks and in the overall data provide support for Hypothesis 1.

Table 4. Kruskal-Wallis Post-hoc Comparison on the
Significant Wording Effects

Audit Tasks	Assessment Z-stat.	Determination Z-stat.	Evaluation Z-stat.	Identification Z-stat.	H-stat.	Sig.
1	3.38*	−1.52**	−0.79	−1.08	12.24	.007*
2	−1.95*	2.03*	−0.89	0.85	7.37	.062**
3	0.34	−0.61	−1.94*	2.15*	7.21	.066**
4	−0.74	−1.19	3.68*	−1.75*	14.29	.003*
6	2.21*	−1.56**	0.69	−1.46**	7.86	.050*
7	0.79	2.44*	−1.74*	−1.40**	9.11	.028*
8	2.56*	−2.38*	1.23	−1.49**	12.21	.007*
10	0.82	−2.81*	0.69	1.31**	8.36	.040*
11	−0.48	−0.75	2.55*	−1.46**	7.22	.066**
12	1.27	−3.78*	3.38*	−1.00	24.17	.000*
13	2.57*	−0.75	1.01	−2.76*	13.44	.004*
23	−2.13*	−0.69	1.07	1.65*	6.84	.078**
24	−1.67*	−1.26	−0.51	3.32*	11.98	.008*
25	1.04	1.51**	−2.45*	−0.21	7.36	.062**
28	1.17	1.95*	−1.30**	−1.86*	7.97	.047*
29	1.36**	0.95	−2.58*	0.31	7.37	.062**

Notes: H-stat. = H-statistic (chi-square distribution) for Kruskal-Wallis test.
Sig. = Significance level.
*, ** = Significant at the .05 and .10 levels, respectively.
Z-stat. = Standardized z-value indicating the degree of deviation of the cell mean rank from overall mean rank. Negative z-value = relatively low complexity; positive z-value = relatively high complexity.

An issue of interest here is whether a clear pattern emerges as to which words resulted in lower or higher complexity judgments. Table 4 lists the 16 significant effects from Table 3 and provides statistics for post-hoc comparisons as reflected in the Z-statistic provided for each wording. The Z-statistic shows the low complexity words (negative Z-values) and the high complexity words (positive Z-values) for these significant main effects.

The data in Table 4 suggest a mixed picture since each word resulted in low complexity judgments in some tasks as well as high complexity judgments in others. A clearer pattern emerges, however, as the relative clarity or vagueness of the words is specifically taken into account, as reported in the test of Hypothesis 2 below.

Test of Hypothesis 2:   Vagueness Effects

In this section, the nonparametric two-sample Mann-Whitney test (also called the two-sample Wilcoxon rank sum test; Gibbons 1976) is used to analyze the effects of the vague and the clear classes of words on auditors' task complexity judgments.

Table 5. Mann-Whitney Test on the Vagueness/Clarity Variable Complexity Judgment (1-9 Likert Scale) as the Dependent Variable

Audit Tasks	Vague Words			Clear Words			Mann-Whitney	
	Mean	(C.o.V)	Median	Mean	(C.o.V)	Median	W-stat	Sig.
1	3.62	(00.60)	3.00	2.73	(00.66)	2.00	4816	.021*
2	3.74	(00.54)	4.00	4.87	(00.50)	5.00	4046	.012*
3	7.16	(00.27)	8.00	7.61	(00.21)	8.00	4291	.170
4	6.06	(00.38)	6.00	4.90	(00.51)	5.00	4754	.009*
5	6.51	(00.31)	7.00	6.79	(00.27)	7.00	3706	.534
6	5.53	(00.55)	6.00	3.88	(00.87)	1.50	4720	.008*
7	6.61	(00.30)	6.50	6.81	(00.36)	8.00	4078	.407
8	4.63	(00.55)	5.00	3.20	(00.69)	3.00	5338	.001*
9	6.15	(00.31)	6.00	5.79	(00.31)	5.00	4670	.329
10	3.77	(00.62)	3.00	3.27	(00.68)	3.00	4985	.178
11	4.46	(00.64)	5.00	3.41	(00.70)	2.50	5040	.055**
12	3.04	(00.71)	2.00	1.66	(00.78)	1.00	5536	.000*
13	3.54	(00.75)	3.00	2.22	(00.92)	1.00	4858	.001*
14	7.43	(00.29)	9.00	6.41	(00.42)	7.50	5235	.018*
15	6.78	(00.29)	7.00	6.37	(00.35)	7.00	4763	.345
16	4.08	(00.49)	4.00	3.69	(00.55)	3.00	4587	.228
17	6.55	(00.35)	7.00	7.19	(00.27)	8.00	4068	.077**
18	6.79	(00.32)	8.00	6.48	(00.31)	7.00	4795	.274
19	4.11	(00.51)	4.00	3.85	(00.55)	4.00	4448	.463
20	6.92	(00.27)	7.00	7.00	(00.28)	7.00	4241	.722
21	4.91	(00.45)	5.00	5.02	(00.44)	5.00	4532	.683
22	7.26	(00.19)	7.50	6.89	(00.31)	8.00	4620	.770

	\(n = 1989 \)			\(n = 1980 \)			W-stat	Sig.
23	5.29	(00.42)	5.00	5.59	(00.37)	6.00	4156	.364
24	4.70	(00.45)	5.00	5.30	(00.37)	6.00	3792	.058**
25	4.78	(00.47)	5.00	5.23	(00.43)	5.00	4208	.255
26	5.70	(00.38)	6.00	5.49	(00.38)	5.00	4346	.570
27	3.16	(00.63)	2.50	2.49	(00.69)	2.00	5102	.056**
28	6.08	(00.33)	6.00	6.14	(00.31)	6.00	4163	.904
29	4.12	(00.46)	5.00	4.57	(00.42)	5.00	4027	.275
30	6.17	(00.34)	7.00	6.29	(00.32)	6.00	4663	.904
Overall	5.32	(00.48)	5.00	5.05	(00.53)	5.00	4054809	.003*

Notes: W-stat = W-statistic (total ranks) for the Mann-Whitney test.
Sig. = Significance level for W-statistic adjusted for ties.
C.o.V = Coefficient of Variation.
*, ** = Significant at the 0.05 and 0.10 levels, respectively.

Table 5 presents the data. The mean, coefficient of variation, and median are provided for each task and the aggregate data under two conditions: vague and clear. The Mann-Whitney W-statistic and its significance are also provided.

In support of Hypothesis 2, the overall data indicate that the vague words resulted in significantly (at the .003 level) higher complexity judgments than did the clear words (means 5.32 and 5.05 respectively). The analysis at the individual-task level in Table 5 shows significant effects in 12 audit tasks (eight at the .05 and four at the .10 level). In nine of these tasks (Nos. 1, 4, 6, 8, 11-14, and 27), the vague words resulted in higher complexity judgments than did the clear words. However, in tasks 2, 17, and 24, clear words resulted in higher task complexity judgments than vague words (task 2 was significant at the .012 level while tasks 17 and 24 were significant at the .10 level). An explanation for these unexpected findings (and the insignificant results) is provided in the final section.[8]

SUMMARY AND IMPLICATIONS

This study provides evidence of an overall significant wording effect on auditors' complexity judgments. Further, the data show that the source of the wording effect is the vagueness of words where relatively vague words resulted in significantly higher task complexity judgments than did the relatively clear words.

Analysis of the data at the individual task level indicated 14 tasks without significant wording effects and 18 without significant vagueness effects. In three of 12 tasks with significant vagueness effects, the direction was counter to that hypothesized. While this evidence may cause concern about the external validity of the overall results, consideration of the nature of the tasks provides a plausible explanation for the unexpected findings. For example, consider task number 17, "the...[wording] of management experience and knowledge." As Table 5 shows, this task unexpectedly resulted in higher task complexity judgments under the clear words (i.e., "determination" and "identification") than under the vague words (i.e., "assessment" and "evaluation"). An explanation for this finding is that the words "determination" and "identification" in this context may have implied a more deterministic or definitive judgment regarding management's level of experience and knowledge than is typically performed in practice. This possibility and similar explanations for many other tasks indicate a need for further investigation taking into account the specific nature of each task.

An implication of the results for behavioral research is that care must be exercised in selecting wording to describe audit tasks in experimental designs where task complexity is of concern (e.g., task-specific experience or expertise). Given the lack of evidence on inherent task complexity, auditors' perceptions of task complexity will play a significant role as the findings from this study indicate. Perhaps a model-based method, similar to Simon's model mentioned in this study, should be used to judge task complexity as a contextual variable in addition to the collection of the main data of concern in future behavioral studies.

A related issue is the research and development of task-specific training materials and decision aids. As argued in prior research, audit task complexity is an important factor in such efforts. Inherent task complexity is of real interest particularly in the area of training, because the nature of tasks for which training is provided plays a major role as compared to the perceived complexity of those tasks. However, as noted earlier, there is a lack of evidence on inherent task complexity in the professional literature. In the absence of such evidence, formal models of task complexity should be utilized in future studies for task complexity judgments using different words related to training and decision aid design.

If it is desirable that tasks be described using wording that reduces perceived task complexity, then one can argue that professional standards should use wording that results in low complexity judgments as well. For example, in a critique of SFAS No. 55, "Consideration of the Internal Control Structure in a Financial Statement Audit" (AICPA 1994), Morton and Felix (1991, 3) stated that "[T]he first and most critical problem we identified is the inconsistent use of the term "control risk assessment" to describe assessments which have fundamentally different interpretations." These authors conclude that "[I]n general, *SAS 55's* obscure reasoning, *imprecise language* and confusing discussions regarding the assessment of control risk make it unlikely that *SAS 55* will achieve its objectives." (p. 10, emphasis added). Perhaps research similar to that reported in this paper is warranted to choose between various words used in the Statements on Auditing Standards. Accounting firms also may benefit from similar studies on the wording of concepts, methods, and procedures in audit manuals as they relate to training, staff assignment, and decision aids.

The context of this study is risk-related audit tasks which is an area that has been of particular interest to behavioral researchers. The significant wording effects found for task complexity judgments indicate opportunities for further study involving tasks in other audit contexts (e.g., tests of controls and substantive tests). However, perhaps fewer tasks should be investigated in order to provide opportunity for a more in-depth classification of wording. The sample for such a study should come from a cross-section of large and small accounting firms to better focus on specific tasks in a variety of audit firm settings. Furthermore, it is desirable to have professional auditors assess the degree of vagueness of the words used in these studies. While the use of student-subjects for vagueness classification of the generic English words used in this study is a reasonable design, the use of professional auditors would mitigate a concern regarding the possibility of differences in such classifications between professional auditors and accounting students.

Finally, investigation of auditors' risk judgments under various wording used to define audit tasks may be an area of future investigation. The "fuzzy set" theory (Zadeh, 1965) discussed earlier is a powerful tool to investigate ambiguity and vagueness in detail. The scope of this study did not allow for collection of data to investigate "fuzzy sets." We suggest this issue as a fruitful avenue for future research.

APPENDIX

Audit Risk Tasks Used in the Study

Engagement Risk Assessment Tasks:

1. The assessment of the profitability of entity relative to its industry.
2. The determination of the sensitivity of operating results to inflation and changes in interest rates.
3. The identification of management aggressiveness in committing the entity to high risk ventures or projects.
4. The evaluation of the rate of change in entity's industry.
5. The evaluation of contentious accounting issues.
6. The identification of the period of relationship with client.
7. The assessment of the expectation of change in ownership or organization structure in the next year.
8. The identification of the degree of regulation of the entity.
9. The assessment of the frequency and significance of hard-to-audit transactions.
10. The determination of projected income error discovered in prior year's audit transactions.
11. The determination of management turnover during the audit period.
12. The determination of the outside debt.
13. The evaluation of the ownership of the entity.
14. The determination of the allegations of improper or criminal behavior against entity or its management.
15. The identification of the management attitude about financial reporting.
16. The evaluation of the degree to which the accounting function is decentralized.
17. The assessment of management experience and knowledge.
18. The identification of the degree of emphasis on meeting earnings projections.
19. The assessment of the centralization of operations.
20. The aggregation of all factors listed above to evaluate engagement risk.

Inherent Risk Assessment Tasks

21. The determination of the complexity of underlying calculations or principles.
22. The identification of the degree to which circumstances (e.g., the financial condition of the company) may motivate management to misstate the account.
23. The assessment of unusual accounting policies and practices (consult the number and significance of audit adjustments and waived audit differences in prior year's audit).
24. The assessment of the difficulty in judging the balance of the account.
25. The identification of the susceptibility of the asset under audit to material fraud or misappropriation.
26. The evaluation of the experience and competence of accounting personnel responsible for the account.

(continued)

Appendix   (Continued)

27. The determination of the mix and size of items comprising the account.
28. The aggregation of all factors listed above to evaluate inherent risk.
29. The assessment of the volume and complexity of transactions flow and control over these flows.
30. The determination of the susceptibility to management override of existing controls.

Source: *Adapted from Abdolmohammadi (1995) and arranged in the order that appeared in experimental task version number 1.

ACKNOWLEDGMENTS

This paper has benefited from accounting workshops at Bentley College, McMaster University, The New England Behavioral Accounting Research Series, and the 1993 annual meeting of the American Accounting Association in San Francisco. The authors appreciate the helpful comments provided by Tom Kida, Larry Klein, Bob Ruland,, Arnie Wright, Awni Zebda, and particularly two anonymous reviewers on earlier drafts of the paper. Debbie Lang and John Schoch have provided able research assistance. The remaining errors are the responsibility of the authors.

NOTES

1.   For detailed reviews of this literature, see Abdolmohammadi (1987), Ashton and Willingham (1988), Messier and Hansen (1987), O'Leary and Watkins (1989), and Messier (1995). For example, Brown (1991) reports that all Big Six accounting firms already are using expert systems and are designing other expert systems for future use.

2.   The selected tasks comprise a complete list of risk-related audit tasks. It is not critically important what tasks are used in the study given its focus (i.e., effects of wording on task complexity). Nevertheless, the risk-related tasks are particularly of interest because auditors are required by professional standards (e.g., *Statements on Auditing Standards* Nos. 39, 47, 55; AICPA 1994) to judge risks of various types and at various levels.

3.   Traditionally, the relative likelihood and the relative payoffs have been investigated in evaluating decisions under uncertainty (Kahn and Sarin 1988). However, Ellsberg (1961) argued that the ambiguity of information affects the degree of confidence in the estimate of relative likelihood rather than affecting the likelihood or payoffs. Recent work has extended the study of ambiguity to choice behavior between nonprobabilistic situations such as the choice between a more or less ambiguous examination (cf. Ghosh and Ray 1992).

4.   The nine auditors who participated in the pilot study possessed, on average, six years of audit experience (range: 2.5-8.0 years). They did not participate in the main study.

5.   "Appraisal" was selected only for 11 tasks, "estimation" for six tasks, and "ascertainment" for five tasks.

6.   Abdolmohammadi and Wright (1987) used a 1-27 Likert scale to measure task complexity. However, the responses in their study were actually centered in the middle of every three-point spread. Consequently, we used a 1-9 Likert scale. This choice also is supported by the extant literature. Reviewing the literature on response alternatives, Cox (1980, 413) showed that gain obtained by using a scale greater than 9 is marginal.

7. This information does not imply that the five subjects did not have any training or "working knowledge" of these Statements. Such knowledge could have been gained from college courses or from self-study but not from in-house training.

8. The data also were analyzed for differences between the junior/senior group versus the manager/partner group of subjects. Overall, no significant results were observed for this experience classification. Similarly, no firm effects were observed when accounting firms were compared individually or in groups (i.e., three groups based on levels of audit structure per Cushing and Loebbecke (1986) and Kinney (1986) firm classification studies).

REFERENCES

Abdolmohammadi, M.J. 1987. Decision support and expert systems in auditing: A review and research directions. *Accounting and Business Research* (Spring): 173-185.

Abdolmohammadi, M.J. 1995. A comprehensive taxonomy of audit task complexity for behavioral research. Working paper, Bentley College.

Abdolmohammadi, M.J., and A. Wright. 1987. An examination of the effects of experience and task complexity on audit judgments. *The Accounting Review* (January): 1-13.

American Institute of Certified Public Accountants (AICPA). 1994. *Codification of Statements on Auditing Standards.* New York: AICPA.

Armstrong, L. 1990. Why "fuzzy logic" beats black-or-white thinking. *Business Week* (May 21): 92-93.

Ashton, R.H., and J.J. Willingham. 1988. Using and evaluating audit decision aids. In *Auditing Symposium IX: Proceedings of the 1988 Touche Ross/University of Kansas Symposium on Auditing Problems*, eds. R.P. Srivastava and J.E. Rebele, 1-25. Lawrence, KS: University of Kansas Printing Service.

Black, M. 1963. Reasoning with loose concepts. *Dialogue* 2: 1-12.

Bonner, S.E. 1994. A model of the effects of audit task complexity. *Accounting, Organizations and Society* 19(3): 213-234.

Bonner, S.E., and B.L. Lewis. 1990. Determinants of auditor expertise. *Journal of Accounting Research* 28(Supplement): 1-20.

Bonner, S.E., and N. Pennington. 1991. Cognitive processes and knowledge as determinants of auditor expertise. *Journal of Accounting Literature* 10: 1-50.

Brown, C.E. 1991. Expert systems in public accounting: Current practice and future directions. *Expert Systems with Applications* 3: 3-18.

Chesley, G.R. 1986. Interpretation of uncertainty expressions. *Contemporary Accounting Research* 2: 179-199.

Cochran, W.G., and G.M. Cox. 1957. *Experimental Designs.* New York: Wiley.

Cooley, J., and J. Hicks, Jr. 1983. A fuzzy set approach to aggregating internal control judgments. *Management Science* 29: 317-334.

Cox, E.P., III. 1980. The optimal number of response alternatives for a scale: A review. *Journal of Marketing Research* XVII(November): 407-422.

Cushing, B.E., and J.K. Loebbecke. 1986. *Comparison of Audit Methodologies of Large Accounting Firms.* Studies in Accounting Research No. 26. Sarasota, FL: American Accounting Association.

Ellsberg, D. 1961. Risk, ambiguity, and the savage axioms. *Quarterly Journal of Economics* 75: 643-669.

Financial Accounting Standards Board (FASB). 1975. *Statement of Financial Accounting Standards No. 5: Accounting for Contingencies.* Stamford, CT: FASB

Gibbons, J.D. 1976. *Nonparametric Methods for Quantitative Analysis.* New York: Holt, Rinehart and Winston.

Ghosh, D., and M.R. Ray. 1992. Risk attitude, ambiguity intolerance and decision making: An exploratory investigation. *Decision Sciences* 23(2, March/April): 431-444.

Ganzalez-Vallejo, G.C., I. Erev, and T.S. Wallsten. 1994. Do decision quality and preference order depend on whether probabilities are verbal or numerical? *American Journal of Psychology* 107(2, Summer): 157-172.

Graham, L.E. 1990. A technological response to the changing audit environment. *The Auditor's Report* (Summer): 10, 155.

Hughes, J. 1980. Optimal auditor decisions with states described as fuzzy sets. Unpublished Working Paper, Duke University.

Kahn, B.E.. and R.K. Sarin. 1988. Modeling ambiguity in decisions under uncertainty. *Journal of Consumer Research* 15(September): 265-271.

Katz, J.J., and P.M. Postal. 1964. *An Integrated Theory of Linguistic Descriptions.* Research Monograph No. 26. Cambridge, MA: M.I.T. Press.

Keen, P.G.W., and M. Š. Scott-Morton. 1978. *Decision Support Systems: An Organizational Perspective.* Reading, Ma: Addison-Wesley.

Kelly, l. 1984. Formulation of the accountant's materiality decision through fuzzy set theory. *TIMS/Studies in the Management Sciences* 20: 489-494.

Kinney, W.R., Jr. 1986. Audit technology and preference for auditing standards. *Journal of Accounting and Economics* (March): 73-89.

Lin, W. 1984. A Bayesian analysis of audit tests with fuzzy sets. *TIMS/Studies in the Management Science on Fuzzy Sets and Systems* 20: 495-510.

Messier, W.F., Jr. 1995. Research in and development of audit decision aids. In *Judgment and Decision Making Research in Accounting and Auditing,* eds. A.H. Ashton and R.H. Ashton. New York: Cambridge University Press.

Messier, W.F., Jr. and J.V. Hansen. 1987. Expert systems in auditing: The state of the art. *Auditing: A Journal of Practice and Theory* (Fall): 94-105.

Morton, J.E., and W.L. Felix, Jr. 1991. A critique of statement on auditing standards no 55. *Accounting Horizons* 5(1, March): 1-10.

O'Leary, D.E., and P.R. Watkins. 1989. Review of expert systems in auditing. *Expert Systems Review for Business and Accounting* (Spring-Summer): 3-22.

Ponemon, L.A., and K. Raghunandan. 1994. What is "substantial doubt?" *Accounting Horizons* 8(2, June): 44-54.

Reimers, J. 1992. Additional evidence on the need for disclosure reform. *Accounting Horizons* 6(1): 36-41.

Simon, H.A. 1960. *The New Science of Management.* New York: Harper and Row.

_____. 1990. Information technologies and organizations. *The Accounting Review* (July): 658-667.

Soule, R. 1959. *A Dictionary of English Synonyms and Synonymous Expressions.* Boston: Little, Brown & Co.

Wallsten, T.S., D.V. Budesco, A. Rappaport, R. Zwick, and B. Forsyth. 1986. Measuring the vague meanings of probability terms. *Journal of Experimental Psychology* General 115: 348-365.

Webster's New Dictionary of Synonyms. 1973. Springfield, MA: Merriam-Webster..

Zadeh, L. 1965. Fuzzy sets. *Information and Control* 8: 338-353.

Zebda, A. 1989. Fuzzy set theory and accounting. *Journal of Accounting Literature* 8: 76-105.

_____. 1991. The problem of ambiguity and vagueness in accounting. *Behavioral Research in Accounting* 3: 117-145.

NEURAL NETWORKS AND BANKRUPTCY PREDICTION:
FUNDS FLOWS, ACCRUAL RATIOS, AND ACCOUNTING DATA

Barbro Back, Teija Laitinen, and Kaisa Sere

ABSTRACT

Studies in predicting bankruptcies have interested accountants for decades and are still of interest because no superior tool has yet been invented for this task. Until recently, alternative classical statistical methods were mainly used. Comparisons of the information content of funds flows versus accruals were conducted by applying multivariate discriminant analysis or logit analysis. As the choice of statistical method can affect the results, the model specification or definition of the variables is also an important factor. Artificial neural networks are a new and promising paradigm of information processing. Several studies have already shown that neural networks outperform classical statistical methods of discriminant analysis, regression analysis, and logit models in predicting bankruptcies. In all these studies, accrual ratios have been used as comparison variables. In this paper, we applied artificial neural networks to compare the information content of funds flows ratios, accrual

Advances in Accounting, Volume 14, pages 23-37.
ISBN: 0-7623-0161-9.

ratios, and absolute numbers from these ratios. We investigated whether it was possible to find different classification results from funds flows-based models compared to those of accrual-based models. We found that the accrual-based models outperformed the funds flows-based models. Furthermore, the ratio-based models performed better than the models based on absolute numbers.

INTRODUCTION

In 1983, Gombola and Ketz (1983) assessed the impact of cash flow measurement upon the classification patterns of financial ratios. They developed classification patterns using factor analysis in 119 firms with 40 ratios during the 19-year period 1962-1980. Their results indicated that cash flow ratios loaded on a separate and distinct factor. This result, as Gombola and Ketz state, suggests that cash flow ratios may contain some information not found in profitability ratios. Furthermore, the authors concluded that the omission of cash flow ratios in earlier bankruptcy prediction studies may have been inappropriate. This generated several studies concerning the information content of cash flows versus accruals in failure prediction.

Casey and Bartczak (1984) found that accrual-based multivariate discriminant models forecasted corporate bankruptcy more accurately than any single operating cash flow ratio. One year later, Casey and Bartczak (1985) studied the marginal predictive content of operating cash flow variables when used in combination with accrual-based ratios. They found that expanding the accrual-based model with cash flow ratios did not improve the accuracy of failure prediction. Furthermore, Gentry, Newbold, and Whitford (1985a) attempted to predict failure using eight cash flow variables. Using logit analysis, they were able to correctly classify 70 percent of distressed firms and 74 percent of nondistressed firms in a holdout sample one year before failure. Even though classification accuracy was quite high, only one variable—dividends to total cash flow—was statistically significant at the 0.05 level. The study was later modified by the authors (1985b), by replacing a working capital ratio variable with five working capital components, each divided by cash flow. Using probit analysis, they were able to classify 83 percent of the 66 failed and nonfailed firms accurately. Unfortunately, the results are difficult to evaluate, because the authors did not report on prediction accuracy for a holdout sample.

In these as in most previous studies, the comparison of the information content of cash flows versus accruals has been conducted mainly by applying multivariate discriminant analysis or logit analysis. As the choice of statistical method can affect the results, the model specification or definition of the variables is also an important factor.

Artificial neural networks are a new and promising paradigm of information processing. The most attractive characteristic of these networks is that they are able to learn the pattern of a system from a given set of examples. They are suitable for a set of applications such as classification, prediction, control, and inference. Several studies have recently shown that neural networks outperform classical statistical methods—often discriminant analysis, regression analysis, and logit models—in predicting bankruptcies (Bell et al. 1989; Koster et al. 1990; Odom and Sharda 1990; Tam and Kiang 1992; Wilson and Sharda 1994). In all these studies, accrual ratios were used as comparison variables. For surveys on using neural networks in business applications, including bankruptcy prediction, see also Wong et al. (1994) and Back and Sere (1993)

A study conducted by Serrano-Cinca and colleagues (1993) differs from the above-mentioned studies, in that the authors used neural networks to compare accrual-based financial absolute numbers and accrual ratios as predictors of Spanish bank bankruptcies. The found only minimal differences in the results between these different predictors.

In this paper, we apply artificial neural networks to compare the information content of funds flows ratios, accrual ratios, and absolute numbers from these ratios. Contrary to previous studies, we use not only cash flow variables as a funds flow measure but also the revenue-expenditure flow from operations and the working capital flow from operations. We wish to investigate whether we can find different classification results from funds flows models compared to those of accrual-based models. The models are specified with Finnish financial practice in mind.

The paper is organized as follows. In the next section, we describe the possible failure processes. The third section specifies four different models for bankruptcy prediction. The fourth section offers a brief description of neural networks and the main ideas behind them. We take a closer look at a particular type of neural network, the multilayered feedforward network, and at the backpropagation algorithm, which we have used in our experiments in this study. In the fifth section, we present the data and the empirical results of the study. The last section concludes the paper.

FAILURE PROCESSES

Two Possible Failure Processes

In Finland, the failure of a limited firm can be the consequence of two different juridical processes stated in the Finnish Companies Act (1978) and the Finnish Bankruptcy Act (1868). First, if losses incurred cause the stockholders' equity on the balance sheet to fall below one-third of the stock capital, the firm goes into liquidation. This means that all claims against the firm are settled. However, if the value of the company's debts is less than the value of its assets, the company can continue its operations. Even though this process does not always lead to the failure of a liquidated firm, it is an obvious sign of continuing unprofitable operations.

If, on the other hand, the company is in liquidation and the company's debts exceed the value of its assets, the company is declared bankrupt. In the present study, a failure of this type is called *solidity bankruptcy*. The second type of failure occurs if a firm cannot pay its debts when they fall due—that is, *liquidity bankruptcy*.

Both types of failure have been discussed in previous studies, where both failure types have been approached through various theoretical frameworks. This body of theoretical literature constitutes the basis for the selection of financial ratios. Naturally, these failure processes are not mutually exclusive; that is, decreased liquidity may be connected with solidity bankruptcy, or signals indicating the preconditions for solidity bankruptcy may surface in the context of liquidity bankruptcy.

Solidity Bankruptcy

The basis for solidity bankruptcy theory is the gambler's ruin model of probability theory (see, e.g., Feller 1968). If this approach is applied with respect to Finnish legislation and the failure process of a firm, it can be written as follows:

$$K + EBIT - (T + I + D + R) < 1/3 \, S \qquad (1)$$

where: K = stockholders' equity before profit for the current period;
$EBIT$ = earnings before interest and taxes;
T = taxes;
I = interests;
D = dividends;
R = change in reserves;
S = stock capital.

The probability of failure—or, more precisely, liquidation—thus increases when the value of the left-hand side of Equation (1) decreases, provided that the amount of stock capital (S) remains constant. This increased probability of failure thus depends on three factors measured in absolute terms. The first factor (K) is a measure of *solidity*; the second factor ($EBIT$) is a measure of *profitability*; and the third factor ($T + I + D + R$) is a measure of *profit sharing* (Laitinen 1993). This study focuses on the first two essential concepts. Factors that describe solidity and profitability have also proved to be important in empirical studies (see, e.g., Beaver 1966; Altman 1968; Prihti 1975; Altman et al. 1977).

Liquidity Bankruptcy

The liquidity bankruptcy problem concerns insolvent firms. Beaver (1966, 80) discusses the theory of ratio analysis in failure prediction and defines liquidity bankruptcy. According to Beaver, the firm should be seen as having a reservoir of liquid assets, which is supplied by inflows and drained by outflows. The reservoir serves as a buffer against variations in the flows. The solvency of a firm is defined in terms of the probability that the reservoir will be exhausted, with the result that the firm becomes unable to meet its obligations as they mature. This definition is consistent with liquidity failure as defined in the Finnish Bankruptcy Act. Thus, the third economic dimension to be considered in this study—in addition to solidity and profitability—when constructing the failure prediction models is *liquidity*.

MODEL SPECIFICATION

We have built four different models which all include the fundamental economic dimensions essential in failure prediction as described previously, namely solidity, profitability, and liquidity. Tables 1 and 2 summarize all four models as now presented.

Accrual-based Ratio Model (Model 1)

For the accrual-based ratio model (Model 1), the absolute measures of solidity and profitability as presented in Equation (1) are changed into relative measures by dividing them by the firm's total assets. The first and second financial ratios in Model 1 are total debts [corresponds to K in Equation (1)] to total assets, and operating income [corresponds to *EBIT* in Equation (1)] to total average assets, respectively. For the latter ratio, operating income was arrived at by deducting depreciations, other expenses, and taxes from the operating margin and by adding dividend revenues, interest revenues, and other revenues. The result was divided by the average of total assets of the beginning and end of the year.

The numerator of the financial ratios describing liquidity in Model 1 is selected to be that portion of financial assets that can be used when short-term debts fall due. Furthermore, while the amount payable can at the most be the size of short-term debts, it is logical to relate these two concepts together. Thus, in this study, the liquidity aspect is considered in Model 1 by including the ratio of financial assets to current liabilities. Financial assets include cash, accounts receivable, loans receivable, advances paid, deferred assets, and other financial assets.

Funds-Flows-based Ratio Model (Model 2)

For the funds flows-based model (Model 2), the corresponding variables measuring solidity and profitability are revenue-expenditure flow from operations to total debts and working capital flow from operations to sales, respectively. Note that the denominators of these ratios are free from depreciation effects. The exact calculation for numerators of funds flow variables is presented in the Appendix.

Table 1.   Ratio-based Models

Model	Solidity Variable	Profitability Variable	Liquidity Variable
Model 1	Total debts/ Total assets	Operating income/ Average assets	Financial assets/ Current liabilities
Model 2	Revenue-expenditure flow from operations/ Total debts	Working capital flow from operations/ Sales	Cash flow from opera-tions/ Sales revenue in cash

Table 2.   Models Based on Absolute Numbers

Model	Variables
Model 3	Total debts Total assets Operating income Average assets Financial assets Current liabilities
Model 4	Revenue-expenditure flow from operations Total debts Working capital flow from operations Sales Cash flow from operations Sales revenue in cash

The liquidity aspect is considered in Model 2 by including variable cash flow from operations to sales revenue in cash. The model is summarized in Table 1 and the exact calculation of both numerator and denominator is presented in the Appendix.

Component or Absolute-Figures-based Models (Models 3 and 4)

In Models 3 and 4 in Table 2, we have included the components that were used in the two previous models when constructing the ratio variables; that is, Model 3 includes the numerators and denominators of financial ratios in Model 1 (absolute figures) separately. Similarly, Model 4 is formed by using the numerators and denominators of the funds flows-based ratios of Model 2 separately.

NEURAL NETWORKS

An (artificial) *neural network* consists of a large number of processing elements, *neurons*, and connections between them. Originally, these computing devices were developed to serve as a computer analogue to the human brain. They have been successfully used in many classification and optimization problems, among others (Hecht-Nielsen 1990).

A neural network implements some function f that maps a set of given input values x to some output values y: $y = f(x)$. If the function f is simple, we do not need a neural network at all. However, if we wish to perform a complicated mapping where we do not know how to describe the functional relationship, but we do know of examples of the correct mapping, we could use a neural network. In this situation, the network will discover its own algorithms to carry out the mappings.

A neural network tries to find the best possible approximation of the function f. This approximation is coded in the neurons of the network using weights that are associated with each neuron.

A formal *neuron* is the basic element of any neural network. A neuron is a simple processing element that as inputs takes an n-dimensional vector $[\mathbf{x_1}, \ldots, \mathbf{x_n}]^T$, extended with a constant component $x_0 = 1$. The neuron forms the weighted sum:

$$w^T x = w_0 + \sum_{1 \leq i \leq n} w_i x_i \qquad (2)$$

where $\mathbf{x} = [1, x_1, \ldots, x_n]^T$ and where $\mathbf{w} = [w_0, \ldots, w_n]^T$ is the weight vector stored in the neuron. In the simplest case, the output of a neuron is the sign of this expression, $y = \text{sgn}(w^T x)$. Such a neuron can classify n-dimensional vectors into two different classes when the weights are determined so that $y = 1$ for class 1 vectors and $y = -1$ for class 2 vectors.

Most neural networks are built up by composing together such simple processing elements as described above. However, the elementary *sgn* function is usually replaced with more sophisticated *activation functions*.

Learning

The weights of a neural network are *learned* using an iterative procedure during which examples of correct input-output associations are shown to the network, and the weights get modified so that the network starts to mimic this desirable input-output behavior. Learning in a neural network thus means finding an appropriate set of weights. This ability to learn from examples—and, based on this learning the ability to generalize to new situations—is the most attractive feature of the neural network paradigm.

We distinguish between two types of learning: *supervised learning* and *unsupervised learning*. In supervised learning, a network learns the weights from a set of correct input-output pairs of data, the *training set*, which is provided by the user. In unsupervised learning, there are no correct output data present. Only the input pattern is provided, and the network has to figure out by itself which categories to form from the data. In this paper, we concentrate on supervised learning and the most popular learning algorithm for this type of learning, the backpropagation algorithm.

The architecture of a network is also of importance. The architecture used in connection with the backpropagation algorithm is the *feedforward layered network*. Excellent surveys of this and other network models can be found in any standard textbooks on neural networks (see, e.g., Hecht-Nielsen 1990; Hertz et al. 1991; Kohonen 1989).

Feedforward Layered Networks

In a feedforward layered network the neurons are divided into disjoint subsets, called *layers*. All processing elements in one layer have essentially the same activation functions.

Figure 1 shows a typical feedforward network. In this case, the network has two layers, the output layer that delivers the result $y_1, \ldots y_m$, and one so-called *hidden layer*. Sometimes the inputs form a layer of their own, called the *input layer*. The input data $x_1, \ldots , x_n$ flows through the network from the hidden layer forward toward the output layer. The number of hidden layers in a feedforward network can be arbitrary, but two successive layers are fully connected using unidirectional connections. Each neuron on the hidden and output layers has a weight (V respective W) for each of its incoming connections. The more complex the network, the more complex the functional mapping implemented by the network.

Backpropagation Algorithm

The backpropagation algorithm provides an implementable way for weights to be learned in a feedforward layered network using the *gradient descent* method. Here, the weights are changed adaptively toward their optimal values using only

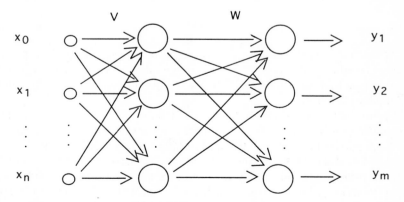

Figure 1. A Feedforward Network with One Hidden Layer

one vector pair (x_i, y_i) at a time. The most popular activation function is the sigmoid function $g(t) = (1 - e^{-t})^{-1}$.

The backpropagation algorithm first causes an input vector x_i to be propagated through the network generating the output. Then the error in this output is determined with respect to the desired output y_i for the input x_i. Thereafter, the observed error is propagated backwards through the network starting from the neurons in the output layer. Each neuron updates its weights using its share of the error as a basis, applying the so-called generalized delta rule. The procedure is repeated for each vector pair in the training set. When the error is acceptably small for each of the training vector pairs, the training stops.

The performance of the generated network is then tested using an additional set of correct input-output pairs, the *test set*. If the results are acceptable, the network can be used in real applications; otherwise, more training is needed, perhaps with a modified network structure. The trained network should be able to generalize to new situations where no correct output data is present anymore.

The backpropagation algorithm has two important parameters, *learning rate* and *momentum*. The learning rate effects the speed at which the network settles to a solution, by allowing us to regulate how much the error decreases on each iteration. Momentum is another way to increase the speed of convergence: when calculating the weight change at each iteration, we add a fraction of the previous change. This additional term tends to keep the weight changes moving in the same direction. Normally, the raw input data to a network is somehow preprocessed— for example, normalized—so that each variable takes values between 0 and 1. This makes the network learn faster and more easily. The details of the backpropagation algorithm are described in standard textbooks on neural networks (see, e.g., Hecht-Nielsen 1991; Hertz et al. 1991).

EMPIRICAL RESULTS

Data

The data comprised the annual financial statements of 76 firms: 38 randomly selected failed Finnish companies and their nonfailed matched pairs. Each failure had occurred between 1986 and 1989. We did not differentiate between solidity and liquidity failures.

The firms in the sample represented different industries, most of them operating in manufacturing (see Table 3). Furthermore, the sample consisted mainly of small and medium-sized companies. The lack of larger companies is explained by the fact that the number of large firms that in those years failed was very small in Finland. In 1988, for instance, only three firms employing more than 200 people failed (*Bankruptcy Bulletin* 1989). The use of a matched-pair sample made it possible to mitigate the potentially disruptive effects of industry, size, and time on classification accuracy.

Table 3. The Distribution of the Firms in the Sample by Industry

Industry	Frequency
Manufacture of textiles	2
Manufacture of clothing	4
Footwear except rubber and plastic	5
Manufacture of wood products, except furniture	3
Manufacture of furniture and fixtures	1
Manufacture of fabricated metal products	4
Manufacture of machinery	3
General housing contractors	4
Special trade contractors	3
Wholesaling of food and beverages	1
Other wholesaling	2
Agency	1
Textiles, clothing, and footwear shops	2
Automobile retailing and service	2
Services allied to transport	1
Total	38

Training the Networks

The data were randomly split into a training set and a test set. Each set consisted of 38 companies. In these sets, there were 19 nonbankruptcy and 19 bankruptcy companies with data stretching back one year before the bankruptcy. Then the data was preprocessed to make the network's learning task easier, using histogram equalization. This is a way of mapping rare figures to a small part of the target range and spreading out frequent figures so that it becomes easier for the network to discriminate among frequent figures.

Four different feedforward networks were built, one for each model described in Tables 1 and 2. The input layer consisted of 3, 3, 6, and 6 nodes, respectively. The output layer had only one node in each network, with an output value of 0 for bankruptcy and 1 for nonbankruptcy. Several different hidden layer architectures were tested for each model, keeping track of the error in order to be able to find the best generalizing network in each experiment. For each network, one hidden layer—consisting of 3, 3, 9, and 9 neurons, respectively—was finally chosen.

In training the neural networks, supervised learning and the backpropagation algorithm described in the previous section were used. The sigmoid function served as activation function. The momentum parameter was set after considerable experimentation, to 0.9. The best learning rate was found to be 0.01 for Model 1 and 0.03 for the other models.

Table 4. Classification Results

Model	Type I Error		Type II Error		Total error		Percentage Correct
	n	%	*n*	%	*n*	%	
Model 1	2	10.5	0	0	2	5.3	94.7
Model 2	4	21.0	1	5	5	13.2	86.8
Model 3	2	10.5	2	10.5	4	10.5	89.5
Model 4	4	21.0	2	10.5	6	15.8	84.2

Testing the Networks

Using the test set, the four networks created were tested for their classification capabilities. The results from the testing data runs using these optimal networks are presented in Table 4, which shows the observed classification errors per model together with the percentage correct classifications.

The observed classification errors are split in Table 4 into Type I and Type II errors. A Type I error occurs when a company that the network classifies as a non-failed firm is a failed firm and a Type II error occurs when a company that the network classifies as a failed firm is in fact a nonfailed firm. It is generally agreed that it is worse to classify a failed firm as a nonfailed firm than vice-versa; that is, it is worse to make a Type I error than a Type II error (Watts and Zimmerman 1986).

In the experiments, three models (Models 1, 2, and 4) resulted in more Type I errors than Type II errors and one model (Model 3) had equal occurrences of both.

The columns "Total Error" and "Percentage Correct" in Table 4 show that the best classification results came from using Model 1, which included just three accrual-based ratios. The correctly classified firms totalled 94.7 percent. Interestingly, the second-best result came from Model 3, where accrual-based absolute numbers were used. Further, Model 2 (funds-flows-based ratios) is slightly better than Model 4 (funds-flows-based absolute numbers).

Analyzing the Results

To be able to assess whether there is a statistical difference between the results of different models, the results were tested against each other using the normal distribution for proportions as test statistics; that is, the test hypothesis is that there is no difference between the models. None of the correct proportions differ statistically from another at a level of significance less than 0.134, which indicates that there is no clear statistically significant difference in the classification abilities between the models. These negative results could be partly explained by the small sample size in the experiment.

Our results support earlier studies carried out using statistical methods (see, e.g., Gentry, Newbold, and Whitford 1985a, 1985b) in that we cannot state that funds-flows-based data (Models 2 and 4) would improve classification accuracy.

Considering the advantages in using ratios (Models 1 and 2) versus absolute numbers (Models 3 and 4), we were unable to find statistically significant differences at conventional levels. In their study, Serrano-Cinca and colleagues (1993) stated that there was a minimal difference observed. However, they do not indicate whether this difference was statistically significant or not.

In this study, we have not considered the relative costs of each type of error of misclassification (see, e.g., Hsieh 1993; Koh 1992). We pointed out above that it is generally agreed that a Type I error is worse than a Type II error. In training the network, we chose that network which minimized the Type I error given a high level of accuracy of total correctness. However, for Model 1, doing so has at the same time resulted in zero Type II errors, which can be regarded an ideal result, especially when considering rare phenomena. Bankruptcies are in reality a rare phenomena and a high rate of Type II errors leads to a large absolute number of unwanted misclassifications.

In analyzing our results, we should also observe that the training and testing of our data was done on the same periods; that is, for prediction purposes the accuracy received holds only under the assumption that the external conditions are similar to those of the training period.

CONCLUSIONS

We have compared the classification capability of neural networks using four different models for bankruptcy prediction. Two of the models were based on accrual data, and two were based on on funds-flow data. In this study, the accrual-based models (Models 1 and 3) outperformed the funds-flows-based models (Models 2 and 4) in classifying a company as bankrupt or nonbankrupt. Moreover, the ratio-based models performed better than those based on absolute numbers. However, when testing whether the differences can be considered statistically significant, enough evidence was not found.

Furthermore, we have looked for the best feedforward networks to perform the classification tasks. The results reported here are based on several test runs, using many different network architectures with different numbers of hidden layer nodes, momentums, and learning rates. In this study, we kept the input data fixed for each model. In the future, we want to focus more on this and try to identify those input variables that have the best information value in building the networks. It may also be of interest to combine the different models.

APPENDIX

Revenue-Expenditure Flow from Operations

Sales
- materials
- wages
- rents
- other short-term production expenses
+ production for own use
- other expenses
+ other revenues
- interests
- taxes
- dividends

= Revenue-expenditure flow from operations

Working Capital from Operations

Revenue-expenditure flow from operations
- decrease in inventory
+ increase in inventory

= Working capital from operations

Cash Flow from Operations

Revenue-expenditure flow from operations
- increase in accounts receivable
+ decrease in accounts receivable
- increase in advances paid
+ decrease in advances paid
- increase in accrued income and deferred expenses
+ decrease in accrued income and deferred expenses
+ increase in accounts payable
- decrease in accounts payable
+ increase in advances received
- decrease in advances received
+ increase in deferred income and accrued expenses
- decrease in deferred income and accrued expenses

= Cash flow from operations

Sales Revenue in Cash

Sales
+   decrease in accounts receivable
-    increase in accounts receivable
+   increase in advances received
-    decrease in advances received

=   Sales revenue in cash

ACKNOWLEDGMENTS

The authors wish to thank Guido Osteroom, Michiel van Wezel, and Teemu Seesto for training and for testing the neural networks. We are also grateful for the comments received on an earlier version of this paper at the 17th annual Congress of the European Accounting Association. The research reported here was carried out within the AnNet project. We also wish to thank *Liikesivistysrahasto* for funding this project.

REFERENCES

Altman, E.L. 1968. Financial ratios, discriminant analysis and the prediction of corporate bankruptcy. *The Journal of Finance* 23 (September): 589-609.

Altman, E., R. Haldeman, and P. Narayanan. 1977. ZETA analysis: A new model to identify bankruptcy risk of corporations. *Journal of Banking and Finance* (June): 29-54.

Back, B., and K. Sere. 1993. Neural networks in accounting applications. Paper presented at the 16th Annual Congress of the European Accounting Association, Turku, Finland, April 1993. [Also available as a publication of the Turku School of Economics and Business Administration, Series Discussion and Working Papers 9.]

Bankruptcy Bulletin. 1989. No. 2. Helsinki, Finland: Statistical Office of Finland.

Beaver, W. 1966. Financial ratios as predictors of failure. *Journal of Accounting Research* 5(Supplement): 71-111.

Bell, T., G. Ribar, and J. Verchio. 1984. Neural nets vs. logistic regression. Paper presented at the Second International Symposium on Expert Systems in Business, Finance and Accounting, November.

Casey, C., and N. Bartczak. 1984. Cash flow—It's not the bottom line. *Harward Business Review* (July-August): 60-66.

Casey, C., and N. Bartczak. 1985. Using operating cash flow data to predict financial distress: Some extensions. *Journal of Accounting Research* (Spring): 384-401.

Feller, W. 1968. *An Introduction to Probability Theory and its Applications.* New York: Wiley.

Finnish Bankruptcy Act. 31/1868. Helsinki, Finland: Valtion Painatuskeskus.

Finnish Companies Act. 734/1978. Helsinki, Finland: Valtion Painatuskeskus.

Gentry, J., P. Newbold, and D. Whitford. 1985a. Classifying bankrupt firms with funds flow components. *Journal of Accounting Research* (Spring): 146-159.

———. 1985b. If cash flow is not the bottom line, what is? *Financial Analysts Journal* (September-October): 47-56.

Gombola, M., and J. Ketz. 1983. A note on cash flow and classification patterns of financial ratios. *The Accounting Review* (January): 105-114.

Hecht-Nielsen, R. 1991. *Neurocomputing.* Reading, MA: Addison-Wesley.

Hertz, J., A. Krogh, and R. Palmer. 1991. *Introduction to the Theory of Neural Computing*. Reading, MA: Addison-Wesley.

Hsieh, S.J. 1993. A note on the optimal cut-off point in bankruptcy prediction models. *Journal of Business Finance and Accounting* 20(April): 457-464.

Koh, H.C. 1992. The sensitivity of optimal cut-off points to misclassification costs of type I and type II errors of the going concern prediction context. *Journal of Business Finance and Accounting* 19(January): 187-197.

Kohonen, T. 1989. *Self-Organization and Associative Memory*. Berlin: Springer-Verlag.

Koster, A., N. Sondak, and W. Bourbia. 1990. A business application of artificial neural network systems. *The Journal of Computer Information Systems* 31: 3-10.

Laitinen, T. 1983. The information content of alternative income concepts in predicting corporate failure. *Acta Wasaensia* No 35, University of Vaasa, Finland.

Odom, M., and R. Sharda. 1990. A neural network model for bankruptcy prediction. *Proceedings of the 1990 IJNN* 2: 163-168.

Prihti A. 1975. *The Prediction of Bankruptcy with Published Financial Data* [in Finnish]. Helsinki: Painomies Oy.

Serrano-Cinca, C., B. Martin, and J. Gallizo. 1993. Artificial neural networks in financial statement analysis: Ratios versus accounting data. Paper presented at the 16th Annual Congress of the European Accounting Association, Turku, Finland, April.

Tam, K.Y., and M.Y. Kiang. 1992. Managerail applications of neural networks: the case of bank failure predictions. *Management Science* 38(7): 926-947.

Watts, R.L., and J.L. Zimmerman. 1986. *Positive Accounting Theory*. Englewood Cliffs, NJ: Prentice-Hall.

Wilson, R.L., and R. Sharda. 1994. Bankruptcy prediction using neural networks. *Decision Support Systems* (11): 545-557.

Wong, B.K., T. Bodnovisch, and Y. Selvi. 1995. A bibliograpyhy of neural networks business application research: 1988-September 1994. *Expert Systems* 12(3): 253-262.

ACCOUNTABILITY AND ESCALATION OF COMMITMENT: THE EFFECTS OF COMPENSATION AND DISCLOSURE

Jesse D. Beeler and James E. Hunton

ABSTRACT

This study examines compensation method and disclosure level as two antecedent accountability factors believed to exacerbate the escalation of commitment phenomenon. This research also addresses the theoretical linkage between escalation of commitment and justification needs. It has been theorized that these two psychological processes are inextricably linked but little empirical research has been conducted to support this contention. This research reports the results of an experiment using 111 practicing certified public accountants (CPAs) as subjects. The experiment employed a 2 (compensation method: salary and contingent) by 2 (disclosure level: public and private) fully crossed, randomized design. Experimental results show that in light of negative feedback concerning performance results of an investment portfolio, CPA subjects whose compensation was contingent on such performance, demonstrated stronger escalation of commitment than did subjects who were paid a

Advances in Accounting, Volume 14, pages 39-59.
ISBN: 0-7623-0161-9.

salary. Escalation of commitment was also greater when investment choices were made public. Findings further revealed that the linkage between accountability and escalation of commitment is moderated by self-justification needs.

INTRODUCTION

Rational decision making calls for considering only future costs and benefits when allocating organizational resources. Unrecoverable (sunk) costs should not affect future resource allocation decisions. However, prior research has shown that, in light of negative feedback, decision makers who feel personally responsible for a decision tend to increase their commitment to that decision (Brockner 1992; Northcraft and Wolf 1984; Staw 1976; Teger 1980; Thayler 1985). In essence, sunk costs seem to exert a psychological influence on future allocation decisions. This behavioral phenomenon has been broadly labeled *escalation of commitment* or the *sunk cost effects* (Arkes and Blummer 1985).

Staw and Ross (1987) suggest that a binding of belief to behavior, such as that seen in the foot-in-the-door (Freedman and Fraser 1966) and low-balling (Cialdini et al. 1978) studies, may partially account for the escalation phenomenon. Kanodia and colleagues (1989) provided a mathematical model suggesting that when a given set of decision rules are applied, escalation of commitment can be explained in terms of reputation and information asymmetries. Other research literature suggests that escalation of commitment may result from a tension-producing psychological state referred to as cognitive dissonance (Brockner 1992). This state is said to occur when there is a discrepancy between beliefs and behaviors or outcomes (Festinger 1957). It is widely believed that cognitive dissonance may create a need for decision makers to justify past decisions. Fox and Staw (1979) provide a model suggesting that an important process variable in the escalation phenomenon is the motivation to justify past decisions to oneself or to others. Although the relationship between escalation of commitment and a need to justify past actions has often been hypothesized, the linkage between these two constructs has not been empirically validated.

Escalation of commitment and antecedent factors contributing to this phenomenon may have important implications for accountants. It is not uncommon for company stakeholders (e.g., management, investors, creditors, and customers) to presume that accounting information and financial advice provided by public and private accountants is unbiased. In fact, Ijiri (1975) called for accountants to remain unbiased providers and users of accounting information. However, in certain decision scenarios, advice given by accountants may be unknowingly biased due to a need to justify past decisions. It is important for accountants to understand the conditions under which increased accountability and the resulting need to justify past decisions may affect their preferences regarding future resource allocations. Increased understanding of such antecedent conditions may allow accountants to better deal with situations where the sunk cost effect is likely to bias judgment and behavior.

Many antecedent factors have been identified that tend to exacerbate the escalation of commitment phenomenon. For example, Staw (1976) demonstrated that high levels of personal responsibility lead to high levels of escalation. Fox and Staw (1979) found that job insecurity and the degree of corporate resistance to change also impact the extent of escalation. Prior accounting research in this area has been limited. However, recently, the topic has gained increased attention in the accounting literature. Jeffery (1992) found that when there is personal responsibility for a series of judgments, such as the audit of bank loans, escalation of commitment to an initial audit classification decision is more likely if detection of a troubled loan is perceived as a negative outcome by the auditor. Because loan evaluations are documented in working papers, any reclassification is likely to be noticed. This creates increased accountability for the auditor and may require subsequent justification of the initial decision. Other related accounting research is found in Kennedy's (1993, 1995) work on debiasing the curse of knowledge in relation to auditors' going concern evaluations and analytical review judgments.

Kennedy (1995) reported that auditors who thought they would likely be held accountable for audit decisions expended more effort in arriving at their audit judgments than did auditors who believed accountability was not likely. Interestingly, the extra effort seemed to worsen the curse of knowledge effect. Intuitively, increased accountability seems to be a desired outcome; however, it may lead to an increased need to justify past behavior. The need to justify past decisions can lead to negative consequences such as an increase in escalation of commitment and, as in Kennedy's studies, an increase in the curse of knowledge effect. This study extends the accounting literature on justification and accountability by explicitly exploring sources of accountability and their effect on the escalation phenomenon.

Accountability for Behavior

Two sources of accountability, (1) public disclosure of allocation decisions and (2) the decision maker's method of compensation, are important factors for they operate within the context of business organizations and may exert significant influence on a prime determinant of escalation of commitment—the need to justify prior actions (Arkes and Blummer 1985). This study investigated the impact of public disclosure of resource allocation decisions and compensation method on subsequent commitment to an initially chosen, but failing, course of action. Subjects made two investment allocation decisions. The first decision was based on information provided through case material. The second allocation decision was made after subjects received negative feedback about the outcome of the first decision. The decision process used in this study is analogous to the process accountants and financial analysts use daily. For example, accountants are often involved in treasury functions (i.e., investment of corporate and trust funds) and capital budgeting decisions. When provided with feedback concerning the performance of prior resource allocation decisions, accountants frequently advise or decide whether to continue to hold an investment at the current level, increase the investment, or invest in alternative opportunities.

Accountability Factors

The first factor, public disclosure of the allocation decision, concerns the degree to which resource allocations are known to others (Davis and Bobko 1986). Kanodia and colleagues (1989) suggest that escalation may be explained as the result of a rational choice of managers who seek to protect their public position or reputation. Salanick (1977) and Kiesler (1971) provide evidence that individuals are likely to become more committed to a behavior when the act is public or visible to others. Frey (1986) reported that when individuals are publicly committed to a position they selectively seek supportive information for their position. Theory and empirical evidence suggest that public disclosure of allocation decisions, which subsequently lead to failure, may create undesirable psychological and behavioral outcomes such as a need to justify past behavior and escalation of commitment.

The degree of private/public disclosure of resource allocation decisions made by accountants can vary. For example, management or clients might rely heavily on the advice of an individual accountant or team of accountants regarding the level of initial and subsequent resource allocations in the management of pension or other funds. In this scenario, the individual accountant's investment recommendations may be offered to only one person (i.e., a treasurer or client) or to many people (i.e., an investment oversight board or board of directors). Where a team of accountants offers investment advice, individual accountants within the group may make their positions known to other group members or their advice may be anonymous (i.e., some sort of Delphi technique). In other scenarios, an accountant may be directly responsible for managing an investment trust for a family estate where only a few individuals are aware of the portfolio's performance or an accountant may be investing employee pension funds where many affected individuals are monitoring performance. Similar scenarios can be conceived in the context of capital budgeting decisions. The degree of public disclosure in making these recommendations may be important if public disclosure of investment strategy exacerbates the escalation of commitment phenomenon.

The second factor, method of compensation, concerns the extent to which outcomes of initial and subsequent allocations are linked to external monetary rewards. Where an initial course of action is framed as a loss, individuals may suffer from cognitive dissonance associated with making a bad decision. Additional dissonance may also result from the consequential loss of performance-based monetary rewards. Increased cognitive dissonance, in turn, may exacerbate the sunk cost effect thereby influencing future behavior (Arkes and Blummer 1985; Brockner

1992). Additional theory and empirical evidence regarding the influence of compensation method and escalation of commitment is presented in the next section.

To continue with the example above, accountants might be paid a bonus based on investment yields of pension or other funds being managed or the accountants could be paid a salary where investment performance has no direct affect on compensation. The extent to which accountants' compensation is linked to the investment yield may influence the sunk cost effect. If under certain conditions these two antecedent factors (disclosure level and compensation method) create a biasing effect, it is important to understand the nature of conditions creating the effect and the extent of such an effect in order to better anticipate and control their influence on escalation of commitment.

The major purpose of this study is to examine the extent to which public disclosure of allocation decisions and the accountants' method of compensation influences the escalation of commitment phenomenon. These issues are important to accountants who make resource allocation decisions characterized by failure, public disclosure of decision strategies, and compensation for making such decisions.

THEORY AND HYPOTHESES

Researchers such as Staw (1981) and Brockner (1992) rely on Festinger's (1957) theory of cognitive dissonance to explain the sunk cost effect. Dissonance theory focuses on the effects of inconsistency between behavior and cognitions. Festinger (1957) argued that dissonance can occur as a result of perceiving an inconsistency between one's beliefs and the outcomes of one's behavior based on these beliefs.

Authors such as Aronson (1968) and Nel and colleagues (1969) suggest that dissonance is created by occurrences that threaten one's self-esteem where the occurrences arise from freely chosen behaviors. These authors believe that dissonance is created by a need to maintain a certain image, either a self-image or public-image. Cooper and colleagues (1974), in a study requiring students to deceive other students, found that dissonance occurred only when subjects believed they had personal responsibility for some aversive consequence. Goethals and colleagues (1979) found that the outcome of one's action has to be a foreseeable unwanted event in order for cognitive dissonance to occur. Scher and Cooper (1989) provided evidence that an outcome has to be seen as irrevocable in order for dissonance arousal to occur. Under these circumstances, once decision makers take personal responsibility for their actions, cognitive dissonance can occur. When dissonance is aroused, individuals tend to engage in dissonance reducing behaviors such as self-justification and escalation of commitment (Brockner 1992).

Disclosure, Justification, and Escalation

Of interest in this study is the extent to which public disclosure of an investment position affects the need to justify past actions and escalation of commitment when the position becomes publicly discredited. Davis and Jones (1960) contend that, under conditions of failure, public disclosure of a position causes an increase in cognitive dissonance. This provides the basis for suggestions by Salanick (1977) and Kiesler (1971) that individuals are likely to become bound to a behavior when the act is public or visible to others.

Consistent with a dissonance theory explanation, Frey (1986) reported that when individuals are publicly committed to a position, they selectively seek supportive information for their position. Similar conclusions regarding attention to supportive information were reached by Kernan and Lord (1989). Steele and Liu (1981, 1983) provide evidence that self-justification may be based on a need for internal consistency. They argue that persons may change their attitude so that their behaviors are seen as an affirmation of their internal beliefs.

Hypotheses 1 and 2

In this experiment, subjects were asked to make an initial investment decision. In the public disclosure condition, subjects were asked to tell other subjects in the room the names of the companies in which they had invested. In the private condition, subjects did not reveal the names of their companies. After receiving negative feedback about the initial investment, subjects had a chance to review a forecast of general economic conditions for the upcoming year. Subjects were then asked to make a subsequent investment decision. After the subsequent investment, subjects were requested to provide a written explanation (justification) of their overall investment strategy. Escalation of commitment and cognitive dissonance literature indicates that individuals in the public disclosure condition, as opposed to those in the private condition, should be more committed to their initial investment strategy. This leads us to Hypothesis 1, stated in the alternative form:

Hypothesis 1.   Escalation of commitment will be greater when the disclosure level is public rather than private.

Fox and Staw (1979) suggested that a need to justify past decisions to others may occur when there is "public surveillance of one's decisions." Hypothesis 2 is, therefore, stated as:

Hypothesis 2.   Objective measures of justification behavior will be higher when the disclosure level is public rather than private.

Compensation, Justification, and Escalation

Incentives are often classified as internal or external. Internal incentives include any intrinsic reward that people receive for performing a task well. For example, people often have an internal need to show mastery of a task or they may perform a task because it is enjoyable (Deci and Ryan 1985). External contingent incentives are explicit rewards such as money, the receipt of which is dependent on performance. This research investigates the impact of external contingent rewards on escalation of commitment behavior.

Individuals seem to attend to a relatively small set of cues when incentive compensation is offered. This phenomenon is known as cognitive narrowing or attending to a cognitively narrow field. Under high drive states, people consider only limited cues and fail to attend to new information (Wood et al. 1990). This tendency has been shown to decrease performance on certain types of complex cognitive tasks such as allocating organizational resources (McCullers 1978; McGraw 1978). Assuming that the personal salience of incentives causes a state of arousal, a complimentary explanation of why incentives may be ineffective in increasing performance in certain conditions is found in Zajonc's (1965) work on social facilitation. He suggests that when people are aroused they will be more likely to respond to stimuli with the emission of a dominant response. On complex tasks, or tasks that are not learned well, the dominant response may not be the "best" response. Social scientists such as Humphreys and Revelle (1984), Kanfer and Ackerman (1989), and Wood and colleagues (1990) suggest that the presence of incentives acts to direct attention to how well one is doing, and away from how to do the task. This may mean that while people want to perform well, they may be too preoccupied with keeping score to focus on performing the task at hand. This tendency may inhibit successful performance of cognitively difficult tasks.

In the context of dissonance theory, contingent monetary incentives (e.g., performance-based rewards) may increase cognitive dissonance when people commit to a failing course of action. Loss of monetary incentives may increase aversiveness of the decision outcome. That is, individuals may suffer from dissonance associated with making a bad decision and, at the same time, suffer additional dissonance as a result of the consequential loss of monetary incentives. In Staw's (1981) terms, this may result in a stronger need to justify one's behavior.

Hypotheses 3 and 4

Based on the review of compensation literature, there are several reasons why contingent monetary rewards may heighten escalation of commitment. Cognitive narrowing, emission of the dominant response, actual or perceived loss of contingent external rewards, and the need to justify previous behavior may each act singularly or in combination to enhance the tendency to continue with a previously chosen behavior, even in the face of a negative outcome. Thus, the following hypothesis is formulated (alternate form):

Hypothesis 3. Escalation of commitment will be greater when compensation is contingent on performance than when compensation is salary based.

Individuals who are paid for making a decision which leads to a failing course of action may engage in justification behaviors to a greater extent than those who are not paid for making the same decision (Deci 1972). Relying on the work of Staw and Fox (1979), which related dissonance and escalation of commitment to a need for both internal and external justification of failure, it was hypothesized that subjects whose compensation was contingent on performance (where performance was insufficient to earn compensation) would likely exhibit a greater degree of justification behavior than would salaried individuals. That is, subjects in the contingent compensation condition may suffer from a need to justify past decisions to others and, at the same time, may also have a need to self-justify why they did not earn compensation. Based on this reasoning, Hypothesis 4 is formulated as follows:

Hypothesis 4.   Objective measures of justification behavior will be greater when compensation is contingent on performance than when compensation is salary based.

Justification and Escalation

Fox and Staw (1979) developed a model of the escalation process in which a motivation to justify past decisions acts as a mediating variable between negative consequences and escalation of commitment (see Figure 1); however, the theoretical model has not been empirically tested. Demonstration of the need to justify past behavior has generally been inferred from escalation of commitment. Research by Brockner and Rubin (1985) and Strube and Lott (1984) provide support for a self-justification explanation. As reported by Brockner and colleagues (1987), subjects, more often than not, explained that self-justification was a dominant reason for their escalation of commitment behavior. For example, subjects were quoted as saying "I had invested so much that I had to continue, it seemed foolish not to continue." Similar results were reported by Strube and Lott (1984) regarding the importance of self-justification motives in the escalation of commitment behavior. There have been some exceptions where more direct methods have been employed to measure self-justification. Conlon and Parks (1987), using Staw's (1976) basic research protocol, gave subjects the opportunity to request information prior to making the second investment decision. Information that could be selected varied in the extent that the information could be used to justify past decisions. Conlon and Parks (1987) reported that information that could be used to justify past decisions was more likely to be examined when previous allocation decisions lead to failure. This is consistent with a self-justification explanation for escalation of commitment. Data from Bobocel's (1994) study suggest that justification of past decisions is a necessary condition for escalation of commitment to occur. The current study was designed to allow direct testing of the relationship between a motivation to justify past behavior and escalation of

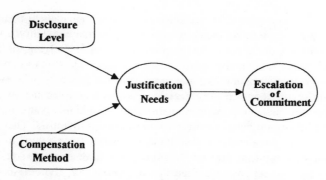

Note: In Fox and Staw's (1979) model, Disclosure Level and Compensation Method would be termed "Attributions of Responsibility."

Figure 1. Proposed Model Linking Justification Needs to Escalation

commitment. Therefore, based on the theoretical relationship proposed by the Fox and Staw (1979), the alternate form of Hypothesis 5 is presented below:

Hypothesis 5. A need to justify past decisions mediates the escalation of commitment created by public disclosure and contingent compensation.

METHOD

Subjects

Volunteer subjects were practicing CPAs attending a continuing professional education (CPE) seminar. The sample size was 111. The mean (standard deviation) age was 34.4 (9.1), and the sample consisted of 69 males (62%) and 42 females (38%).

Experimental Design

This study employed a 2 (compensation method) by 2 (disclosure level) fully crossed, randomized design. The two levels of compensation method were salary and contingent. The two disclosure levels were private and public. The experiment was conducted over eight trials, each lasting about one-and-a-half hours. The compensation method manipulation was randomized within each trial via a computer program. The experimenter did not know who was exposed to which treatment. Due to the nature of the disclosure level manipulation, only one level was manipulated in any given trial. Trials were randomized over three consecutive weekdays.

Procedure

Participants reported to a dedicated conference room equipped with 15 notebook computers. The group sizes ranged from 10 to 15. Subjects were randomly seated around the room and the distance between subjects was sufficient to avoid any one subject viewing the computer screen of another subject. Where possible, the instructions, manipulations and response measures were administered through the use of computer software.

After a greeting and introduction, subjects were told that the purpose of the experiment was to determine the decision cues or important factors people consider when they make investment decisions (the cover story). Subjects were asked to play the role of corporate controller responsibe for investing $200,000 of pension funds. They were told that the board of directors would like the funds allocated evenly among four prespecified, diversified industries ($50,000 each) but that the subjects could use their discretion in investing the $50,000 in one of three companies within each industry. Compensation method was then manipulated.

Compensation Method Manipulation

Two compensation levels were manipulated (salary and contingent). These manipulations were introduced via computer software. Subjects in the salary condition read that as compensation for participating in the experiment, they would be given 10 drink or dinner tickets, valued at one dollar each, redeemable at the hotel restaurant. This treatment was designed to simulate a salary compensation method. Subjects in the contingent compensation condition read that they could earn dinner or drink tickets, valued at one dollar each, based on their success in picking profitable companies in which to invest. The computer displayed a schedule of the incentive program. To keep expectations similar across conditions, subjects were told that most people would earn about 10 drink or dinner tickets worth a total of 10 dollars. Because the success of the investment was controlled by the experimenter, all subjects were given 10 dinner or drink tickets worth a total of 10 dollars at the end of the experiment.

Subjects next read qualitative and quantitative data concerning the 12 companies relative to the past five years. To add experimental realism to the task, subjects were informed that the data represented actual cases but that the company names were changed. In fact, the data was created by the experimenter. The four industries represented were: (1) investment banking, (2) insurance, (3) mining and timber, and (4) computer manufacturing. Subjects were provided with magic markers and were asked to highlight important cues or factors about each company that they felt were important in making this investment decision. This was done to lend credibility to the cover story. After reading the background material, subjects chose one company per industry in which to invest $50,000 each. The public disclosure manipulation was then introduced. Immediately thereafter, failure feedback was manipulated.

Public Disclosure Manipulation

This variable was introduced at two levels: public or private. In the public treatment condition, the experimenter asked each subject to stand up and tell the other participants the names of the companies in which he or she invested. In the private condition, subjects were not asked to reveal their initial investment decisions.

Failure Feedback Manipulation

Subjects were given false feedback about the first year's performance of each company in their portfolio. Three companies showed losses and one company posted a small gained. Overall, their investment portfolio had declined in value by approximately 7 percent. This failure feedback manipulation was held constant across all conditions. The subjects were also told that the stock market had experienced an overall 3.2 percent growth rate in stock prices for this time period. This was done to provide subjects with a positive earnings expectation for the stock market in general in order to heighten their sense of failure.

Following the failure manipulation, subjects were asked to invest another $200,000 ($50,000 per industry) for the upcoming year. The subjects could allocate the funds between the three companies within each industry in any combination they desired, as long as the total allocation to each industry was $50,000.

To assist subjects in making the subsequent investment decision, they were provided with a computer screen describing the general economic outlook for the upcoming year. The forecast provided some slightly optimistic and slightly pessimistic forecasts about the upcoming year. Overall, the forecast was neutral, meaning that the economy would likely remain as it was in the prior year. After making the subsequent allocation, subjects were presented with a blank word processing screen. They were asked to take no more than 15 minutes to write a statement about the factors they used in deciding which stocks to invest in during the second investment allocation (measurement of justification behavior). Finally, all subjects responded to manipulation check questions and general demographic questions. Subjects were then debriefed.

Measurement of Dependent Variable

The dependent variable was the amount of money subsequently invested in the initially chosen companies that had declined in value. The additional investment in losing stocks was used to gauge the subject's escalation of commitment to a failing course of action. This was measured by summing the amount each subject invested during the subsequent investment allocation in those stocks that had incurred a market loss after the initial investment. This is called the escalation of commitment (EC) variable and follows the methodology used in many escalation studies (e.g., Brockner and Rubin 1985; Garland 1990; Staw 1976).

Measurement of Process Variable

A process variable measured in this study was the amount of overt justification behavior (JB) exhibited by the subjects. For all groups, JB was measured after a second allocation decision was made. To measure justification behavior, subjects were asked to provide an explanation of the factors they considered in arriving at their investment decision. Berelson (1952) suggested that content analysis of such explanations can be used "to reveal the focus of individual, group, institutional, or societal attention." Hence, the researchers used two content analysis techniques to quantify JB.

First, the length of the explanation was measured. This variable, hereafter called JB1, was measured by counting the number of keystrokes that subjects made when asked to provide an explanation of their investment decision. This is similar to the technique used by Kaplan and Pany (1992), who used a word count form of content analysis The second justification variable (JB2) was measured by performing a more sophisticated content analysis on the explanations provided by the subjects. The explanations were scored by identifying and counting the number of discrete arguments or reasons given by each subject for their investing behavior. Aires (1977) classified text into categories and used higher category counts to infer higher concern with the category. Explanations were scored separately by both researchers of the current study. Following procedures used by Christ (1993), Libby (1985), and Tubbs (1992) an independent third party also scored the explanations. During scoring, the scorers remained blind to the treatment conditions. The scores were compared on a subject-by-subject basis to gauge interrater reliability. The overall interrater reliability was .897. Differences in scoring were discussed on a case-by-case basis and resolved to the satisfaction of all three raters.

RESULTS

Manipulation Checks

Manipulation check items were assessed regarding: (1) compensation method, (2) disclosure level, and (3) perceived failure of the initial investment. Subjects responded to multiple items for each experimental manipulation to allow reliability measurement. Inter-item correlation for the manipulation check items, respectively, were .89, .91, and .83. Due to the relatively high estimates of reliability, related items regarding each manipulation check were combined into single indexes. ANOVA models were used to test the success of each manipulation.

There were significant main effects for compensation method index (F-ratio = 897.07, p-value $\leq$ .0001). As expected, subjects in the salary condition did not believe their compensation was related to performance of their investments, whereas subjects in the contingent condition did believe their incentive was performance-based. There were also significant main effects for the disclosure level index (F-ratio = 446.52, p-value $\leq$ .0001). Analysis of disclosure manipulation responses predictably indicated that subjects in the private condition did not believe they announced their initial investment decisions to other group members while subjects in the public condition responded that they did announce their initial investment decisions to the group.

For the sunk cost effect to be operationalized, subjects had to perceive that their initial course of action was unsuccessful (e.g., they received negative feedback). This was a constant manipulation across all treatment conditions. Three questions relating to the subjects' perceptions of success of their initial investments were asked. These questions were designed to determine if subjects perceived their initial investments as having failed in an absolute sense and to determine if any of the treatments created a difference in the sense of failure between conditions. A 9-point scale was used where a 1 indicated that the initial investment was extremely unsuccessful and 9 indicated that the initial investment was extremely successful.

There were no significant main or interaction effects on perceived failure for compensation method (F-ratio = .02, p-value $\geq$ .8803) or disclosure level (F-ratio = .01, p-value $\geq$ .9588). The mean value of the perceived failure index ranged from 3.08 (salary by private condition) to 2.81 (contingent by private condition). Individual scores on the failure questions range from a low of 1 to a high of 4. The relatively low individual scores (4 or less) indicate that all subjects perceived that their initial investment strategy was unsuccessful.

Hypothesis Testing

Hypothesis 1

The first hypothesis predicted that escalation of commitment would be greater when the disclosure level was public rather than private. Results of ANOVA testing on the escalation of commitment (EC) measure is presented in Table 1. ANOVA calculations (Table 1, Panel A) show significant main effects for disclosure level (F-ratio = 40.57, p-value $\leq$ .0001) on the EC variable. As shown in Table 1, Panel B, the mean number of dollars invested in the losing companies was $98,780 and $80,924 in the public and private disclosure levels, respectively.

Hypothesis 2

Hypothesis 2 posited that objective measures of justification behavior would be higher in the public disclosure condition than in the private condition. Table 2 shows the results of ANOVA on the JB1 (Panel A) and JB2 (Panel B) measures. The ANOVA models reveal significant main effects for disclosure level on both JB1 (F-ratio = 99.68, p-value $\leq$ .0001) and JB2 (F-ratio = 74.71, p-value $\leq$ .0001). Analysis of Table 2, Panel C, shows that subjects in the public condition wrote longer explanations and provided more discrete arguments for their investment strategy than did subjects in the private condition. Subjects in the public condition entered an average of 586 keystrokes and 5.8 discrete arguments whereas those in

Table 1. ANOVA Results: Escalation of Commitment (EC)

Panel A. *ANOVA Results of Escalation of Commitment (EC)*

Source	D.F.	M.S.	F-ratio	P-value
Disclosure level (A)	1	7.24×10^9	40.57	.0001
Compensation method (B)	1	8.96×10^{10}	502.60	.0001
Interaction term (AB)	1	1.43×10^8	0.80	.3725

Panel B. *Mean responses for EC*

	Mean EC
Disclosure Level	
Private	80,924
Public	98,780
Compensation Method	
Salary	58,427
Contingent	121,276

the private condition entered an average of 456 keystrokes and 4.2 discrete arguments.

Hypothesis 3

Hypothesis 3 predicted that escalation of commitment would be greater when compensation was contingent on performance. The ANOVA calculations presented in Table 1, Panel A, show significant compensation method main effects (F-ratio = 502.60, p-value $\leq$ .0001) on the EC measure. As shown in Table 1, Panel B, the average number of dollars subsequently invested in losing companies was $58,427 (salary) and $121,276 (contingent).

Hypothesis 4

The fourth hypothesis posited an increase in overt justification behavior as the compensation level changed from salary to contingent. Examination of the ANOVA models shown on Table 2 (Panels A and B) indicate significant main effects for compensation method on both JB1 (F-ratio = 421.93, p-value $\leq$ .0001) and JB2 (F-ratio = 251.46, p-value $\leq$ .0001). Subjects in the salary condition entered fewer characters (387) and offered fewer discrete arguments (3.5) than did subjects in the contingent condition (654 and 6.4, respectively), as presented in Table 2, Panel C.

Table 2. Results of Justification Behavior Testing

Panel A. *ANOVA Results of Justification Behavior (JB1)*

Source	D.F.	M.S.	F-ratio	P-value
Disclosure level (A)	1	393,924	99.68	.0001
Compensation method (B)	2	1,625,148	421.93	.0001
Interaction term (AB)	2	2,503	0.65	.4223

Panel B. *ANOVA Results: Justification Behavior (JB2)*

Source	D.F.	M.S.	F-ratio	P-value
Disclosure level (A)	1	66.02	74.71	.0001
Compensation method (B)	2	222.21	251.46	.0001
Interaction term (AB)	2	2.68	1.02	.1847

Panel C. *Mean Responses for JB1 and JB2*

	Mean JB1	Mean JB2
Disclosure Level		
Private	456.00	4.20
Public	586.00	5.80
Compensation Method		
Salary	387.00	3.50
Contingent	654.00	6.40

Hypothesis 5

The fifth hypothesis suggested that the need to justify past decisions mediates the antecedent factors manipulated in this study (i.e., disclosure level and compensation method) and resulting escalation of commitment (see Figure 2 for results of path analysis). The correlation between JB1 (number of keystrokes) and JB2 (discrete arguments) was .92 (p-value $\leq$ .01). These variable were not readily collapsible into a single index since they were measured using different scales. Figure 2 presents path analysis using JB2; however, similar results were obtained using JB1 as the justification variable. Using a chi-square index to test the goodness of fit, it was concluded that the proposed model fit the data ($X2 = 1.52$, $d.f. = 5$, p-value $\leq$ .91).

There were significant (p-value $\leq$ .01) direct and indirect paths from the manipulated variables to escalation of commitment. Disclosure level appeared to heighten justification needs ($b = .48$) as did compensation method ($b = .65$). In

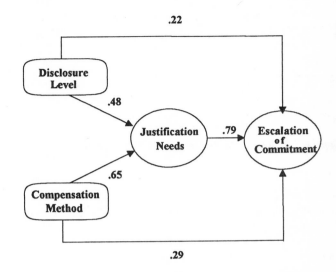

All paths are significant at p-value less than or equal to .01

Path	Indirect Effect	Direct Effect	Residual
Disclosure Level to Escalation of Commitment	.38	.22	.02
Compensation Method to Escalation of Commitment	.51	.29	.01
Justification Needs to Escalation of Commitment		.79	.03

Figure 2. Results of Path Analysis on Proposed Model Linking Justification Needs to Escalation of Commitment

turn, it seems that a need to justify past behavior positively influenced escalation of commitment (b = .79). There were, however, significant direct paths from disclosure level to escalation of commitment (b = .22) and from compensation method to escalation of commitment (b = .29). The direct paths suggest that other psychological variables may be operating between the antecedent factors operationalized in this study and escalation of commitment. The evidence strongly suggests that a need for justifying past decisions acts as an important link in the escalation cycle; however, it may not be a necessary condition to escalation of commitment as suggested by Bobocel (1994). Rather than a mediating variable as suggested by Fox and Staw (1979), self-justification needs may be more appropriately categorized as a moderator variable since justification behavior appeared, in this study, to strengthen the relationship between the antecedent factors and escalation of commitment.

DISCUSSION

The primary objective of this research was to investigate the impact of two accountability factors, public disclosure of allocation decisions and compensation method, on subsequent commitment of resources to an initially chosen, but failing, course of action. To empirically investigate the research objective, hypotheses relating to escalation of commitment and self-justification behavior were proposed. These propositions were tested in a laboratory experiment using an interactive computer exercise. The exercise was designed to simulate decision making involving the allocation of resources among alternative investment opportunities. Subjects were 111 practicing CPAs attending a CPE seminar.

This research posited that public disclosure of an initial course of action, which later becomes discredited, increases a need for self-justification and subsequently increases escalation of commitment. The results of this study support this conjecture. Public announcement of initial investments led to (1) increased self-justification behavior as measured by two behavioral justification variables and (2) increased commitment to a previously chosen course of action as measured by the behavioral escalation of commitment variable.

This study also suggested that the presence of incentive compensation may cause an increased self-justification need which may lead to escalation of commitment. On the basis of this reasoning, it was hypothesized that justification behavior and escalation of commitment would be greater in the incentive compensation condition than in the salary condition. Research results provide support for this reasoning. Compared to subjects in the salary condition, subjects in the incentive compensation condition: (1) engaged in more self-justification behavior and (2) exhibited greater escalation of commitment.

A secondary objective of this research was to test the theoretical linkage between escalation of commitment and justification of past decisions. The evidence provides empirical support for the idea that a need to justify past behavior is an important link between attributions of responsibility and escalation of commitment.

Theoretical and Practical Contributions

The linkage between self-justification needs and escalation of commitment had been theorized but not tested. The current study provides empirical support for the notion that a need for justification of past decisions is an important factor associated with escalation of commitment. The current research provided two objective, behavioral measures of justification behavior. Research evidence did not fully support the theory that a need to justify past decisions acts as a mediator between antecedent accountability factors (e.g., disclosure level and compensation method) and escalation of commitment. However, justification needs do appear to moderate the antecedent-consequence relationship.

Empirical examination of the posited relationship between accountability and escalation of commitment enhances our understanding of the escalation of commitment phenomenon. It is possible that justification needs are a necessary condition to escalation of commitment, as suggested by theory. Perhaps the self-justification behavior examined in this study did not fully capture the justification need construct. It is also possible that other psychological variables moderate the antecedent-consequence relationship investigated in this study. Future research should attempt to advance and reconcile these conceptual and theoretical issues.

Gibbins and Newton (1994) report that most public accountants "feel strong accountability pressure" in most situations. The current study provides evidence that disclosure of an allocation decision, a source of accountability, increases justification behavior and subsequent escalation of commitment. Another source of accountability, incentive compensation, also resulted in enhanced self-justification and escalation of commitment. In order to avoid deleterious effects of accountability, accountants should be: (1) aware of the escalation of commitment phenomenon and its relevance to certain accounting functions, (2) cognizant of antecedent conditions giving rise to the sunk-cost effect, (3) mindful of situations where they might be personally susceptible to escalation of commitment in their professional roles, and (4) trained to develop and implement procedures designed to mitigate the sunk-cost effect. The latter suggestion should be the focus of future research in this area. It may be possible to develop decision/recommendation procedures that avoid negative consequences associated with the need to justify past decisions, such as group decision making. For example, in face-to-face group meetings, procedures could be developed that require group members to examine and consider a broad range of contemporary, relevant information thereby increasing spanning activities and mitigating cognitive narrowing. Electronic forums could also be considered. Certain group decision support software allows for anonymous discussions over a computer network. Perhaps such anonymity can lessen or eliminate the need to self-justify and thereby mitigate escalation of commitment. Another possible solution strategy is to develop a system of peer reviews over accountants' advice or decisions in situations where the escalation of commitment phenomenon may be operating.

Judgment and decision-making issues are relevant to accountants, as such cognitive processes are integral to many accounting functions. Findings from this study call for more research regarding the theoretical and practical aspects of accountability, cognitive dissonance, and escalation of commitment.

REFERENCES

Aires, E. 1977. Male-female interpersonal styles in all male, all female, and mixed groups. In *Beyond Sex Roles,* ed. A.G. Sargent. St. Paul, MN: West.

Arkes, H., and C. Blummer. 1985. The psychology of sunk costs. *Organizational Behavior and Human Decision Processes* 35: 124-140.

Aronson, E. 1968. Dissonance theory: Progress and problems. In *Theories of Cognitive Consistency,* eds. R. Abelson, E. Aronson, W. McGuire, T. Newcombe, M. Rosenberg, and P. Tannenbaum. Chicago: Rand McNally.

Berelson, B. 1952. *Content Analysis in Communications Research.* New York: Free Press.

Bobocel, D.R. 1994. Escalating commitment to a failing course of action: Separating the roles of choice and justification. *Journal of Applied Psychology* 79(3): 360-363.

Brockner, J. 1992. The escalation of commitment to a failing course of action: Toward theoretical progress. *Academy of Management Review* 17: 39-61.

Brockner, J., and J.Z. Rubin. 1985. *Entrapment in Escalating Conflicts: A Social Psychological Analysis.* New York: Springer-Verlag.

Brockner, J., J.Z. Rubin, and E. Lang. 1987. Face-saving and entrapment. *Journal of Experimental Social Psychology* 17: 68-79.

Cialdini, R.B., J.T. Cacioppo, R. Basset, and J. Miller. 1978. Low-ball procedure for producing compliance: Commitment then cost. *Journal of Personality and Social Psychology* 36: 463-476.

Conlon, E.J., and J.M. Parks. 1987. Information requests in the context of escalation. *Journal of Applied Psychology* 72: 344-350.

Cooper, J., M.P. Zanna, and G.R. Goethals. 1974. Mistreatment of an esteemed other as a consequence affecting dissonance reduction. *Journal of Experimental Social Psychology* 10: 224-233.

Christ, M.Y. 1993. Evidence on the nature of audit planning problem representations: An examination of auditor free recall. *Accounting Review* 68 (2): 304-322.

Davis, K.E., and E.E. Jones. 1960. Changes in interpersonal perception as a means of reducing cognitive dissonance. *Journal of Abnormal and Social Psychology* 61: 402-410.

Davis, M., and P. Bobko. 1986. Contextual effects on escalation processes in public sector decision making. *Organizational Behavior and Human Decision Processes* 26: 121-138.

Deci, E.L. 1972. The effects of contingent and noncontingent rewards on intrinsic motivation. *Organizational Behavior and Human Performance* 8: 217-229.

Deci, E.L., and R.M. Ryan. 1985. Intrinsic Motivation and Self-determination in Human Behavior. New York: Plenum.

Festinger, L. 1957. *A Theory of Cognitive Dissonance.* Stanford, CA: Stanford University Press.

Fox, F.V., and B.M. Staw. 1979. The trapped administrator: Effect of job insecurity and policy resistance upon commitment to a course of action. *Administrative Science Quarterly* 24: 449-471.

Freedman, J.L., and S. Fraser. 1966. Compliance with out pressure: The foot-in-the-door technique. *Journal of Personality and Social Psychology* 4: 195-202.

Frey, D. 1986. Recent research on selective exposure to information. In *Advances in Experimental Social Psychology,* Vol. 19, ed. L. Berkowitz, 41-80. New York: Academic Press.

Garland, H. 1990. Throwing good money after bad: The effect of sunk cost on the decision to escalate commitment to an ongoing project. *Journal of Applied Psychology* 755: 728-731.

Gibbins, M., and J.D. Newton. 1994. An empirical exploration of complex accountability in public accounting. *Journal of Accounting Research* 32(2): 165-186.

Goethals, G.R., J. Cooper, and A. Naficy. 1979. Role of foreseen, foreseeable, and unforeseeable behavior consequences in the arousal of cognitive dissonance. *Journal of Personality and Social Psychology* 37: 1179-1185.

Humphreys, M.S., and W. Revelle. 1984. Personality, motivation and performance: A theory of the relationship between individual differences and information processing. *Psychological Review* 74(4): 153-184.

Ijiri, Y. 1975. Theory of accounting measurement. Studies in Accounting Research No. 10, American Accounting Association.

Jeffery, C. 1992. The relation of judgment, personal involvement, and experience in the audit of bank loans. *Accounting Review* 67(4): 802-819.

Kanfer, R., and P.L. Ackerman. 1989. Motivation and cognitive abilities: An integrative/aptitude-treatment approach to skill acquisition. *Journal of Applied Psychology* 74(4): 657-690.

Kanodia, C., R. Bushman, and J. Dickhaut. 1989. Escalation errors and the sunk cost effect: An explanation based on reputation and information asymmetries. *Journal of Accounting Research* 27(1): 59-77.

Kaplan, S., and K. Pany. 1992. A study of public comment letters on the auditor's consideration of the going concern issue (SAS 59). *Research in Accounting Regulation* 6: 3-23.

Kennedy, J. 1993. Debiasing audit judgment with accountability: A framework and experimental results. *Journal of Accounting Research* 31(2): 231-245.

Kennedy, J. 1995. Debiasing the curse of knowledge in audit judgment. *Accounting Review* 70(2): 249-273.

Kernan, M.C., and R.G. Lord. 1989. The effects of explicit goals and feedback on escalation processes. *Journal of Applied Psychology* 19: 1125-1143.

Kiesler, C.A. 1971. *The Psychology of Commitment.* New York: Academic Press.

Libby, R. 1985. Availability and the generation of hypotheses in analytical review. *Journal of Accounting Research* 23(2): 648-667.

McCullers, J.C. 1978. Issues in learning and motivation. In *The Hidden Costs of Reward,* eds. M.R. Lepper and D. Greene, 5-18. Hillsdale, NJ: Erlbaum.

McGraw, K.O. 1978. The detrimental effects of reward on performance: A literature review and a prediction model. In *The Hidden Costs of Reward,* eds. M.R. Lepper and D. Greene, 33-60. Hillsdale, NJ: Erlbaum.

Nel, E., R. Helmreich, and E. Aronson. 1969. Opinion change in the advocate as a function of the persuasibility of his audience: A clarification of the meaning of dissonance. *Journal of Personality and Social Psychology* 12(2): 117-124.

Northcraft, G.B., and G. Wolf. 1984. Dollars, sense, and sunk cost: A life-cycle model of resource allocation decisions. *Academy of Management Review* 9: 225-234.

Salanick, G.R. 1977. Commitment and the control of organizational behavior and belief. In *New Directions in Organizational Behavior,* eds. B.M. Staw and G.R. Salanick. Malabar, FL: Robert E. Krieger.

Scher, S.J., and J.L. Cooper. 1989. Motivational basis of dissonance: The singular role of behavioral consequences. *Journal of Personality and Social Psychology* 56(6): 899-906.

Staw, B.M. 1976. Knee deep in the big muddy: A study of escalating commitment to a chosen course of action. *Organizational Behavior and Human Performance* 16: 27-44.

———. 1981. The escalation of commitment to a course of action. *Academy of Management Review* 6: 577-587.

Staw, B.M., and J. Ross. 1987. Commitment to a policy decision: A multi-theoretical perspective. In *Research In Organizational Behavior,* Vol. 9, eds. B.M. Staw and L.L. Cummings, 39-78. Greenwich, CT: JAI Press.

Steele, C.M., and T.J. Liu. 1981. Making the dissonance act unreflective of self: Dissonance avoidance and the expectancy of a value-affirming response. *Personality and Social Psychology Bulletin* 7: 393-397.

———. 1983. Dissonance processes as self-affirmation. *Journal of Personality and Social Psychology* 45: 5-19.

Strube, M.W., and C.L. Lott. 1984. Time urgency and the type A behavior pattern: Implications for time investment and psychological entrapment. *Journal of Research in Personality* 18: 395-409.

Teger, A. 1980. *Too Much Invested to Quit.* New York: Pergamon Press.

Thayler, R. 1985. Mental accounting and consumer choice. *Marketing Science* 4: 199-214.

Tubbs, R.M. 1992. The effect of experience on the auditor's organization and amount of knowledge. *Accounting Review* 67(4): 783-803.

Wood, R., A. Bandura, and T. Bailey. 1990. Mechanisms governing organizational performance in complex decision-making environments. *Organizational Behavior and Human Decision Processes* 46: 181-201.

Zanjonc, R.B. 1965. Social facilitation. *Science* 149: 269-274.

VALUE IMPLICATIONS OF UNFILLED ORDER BACKLOGS

Bruce K. Behn

ABSTRACT

This study uses a returns-earnings framework to model unfilled order backlogs as a predictor of future earnings to theoretically demonstrate that this information source, along with current earnings, can be useful in explaining contemporaneous equity returns. This perspective differs from previous research in that information other than past earnings or stock prices is used to formulate earnings expectations. To test this model empirically and to examine the incremental value relevance of unfilled order backlogs over current earnings, two tests were employed: (1) a firm-specific time-series test using mandatory disclosures in the 10-K, and (2) a cross-sectional test using voluntary disclosures in the 10-Q. The findings from these tests suggest that the equity markets are valuing firm-specific unfilled order backlog information supplied on a consistent basis and are valuing more timely UOB information as disclosed voluntarily in the 10-Q. These findings are consistent with the AICPA's Special Committee recommendation that more forward-looking information be disclosed and that, from an investment perspective, more timely and consistent disclosure may be warranted.

Advances in Accounting, Volume 14, pages 61-84.
Copyright © 1996 by JAI Press Inc.
All rights of reproduction in any form reserved.
ISBN: 0-7623-0161-9.

INTRODUCTION

There is substantial anecdotal evidence that unfilled order backlogs (UOBs) are used by market participants to value stock (e.g., Byrne 1991, 33; Barrett 1991, 18; Dubashi 1988, 12). This study empirically investigates whether information about UOBs is used by market participants to value common stock. I provide a numeric example and analytic model which yield a testable hypothesis regarding the incremental utility of UOBs vis a vis earnings in company valuation. The hypothesis is empirically examined using: (1) annual firm-specific regressions which exploit the mandatory 10-K UOB information, and (2) an endogenous switching regression model (ESRM) which exploits the more timely information contained in voluntary 10-Q disclosures.[1] Results of the study indicate that changes in UOBs provide information to equity participants beyond that contained in earnings alone. This conclusion holds for firms which have provided consistent 10-K reporting of UOBs over a 20-year period and firms which voluntarily disclose the information in their 10-Qs.

Lev and Thiagarajan (1993) found that changes in unfilled order backlogs provided incremental information to equity investors relative to changes in earnings considered alone. This paper provides the following incremental contribution relative to Lev and Thiagarajan. First, this paper provides a formal model of the relation between changes in order backlogs and returns, which hinges on the ability of changes in UOBs to signal changes in future earnings. Second, the paper estimates firm-specific time-series regressions which provide more powerful tests of the return backlog association than Lev and Thiagarajan's cross-sectional tests. If the fundamental relationships among equity returns, earnings, and UOBs are firm specific, individual time-series regressions should provide better assessments of the associations because cross-sectional approaches inherently constrain all firms' fundamental processes to be the same. Third, the paper uses the more timely quarterly disclosures in cross-sectional tests to address the potential attenuating effects of self-selection bias on the relation Lev and Thiagarajan observed between returns, earnings, and UOBs. This requires methodological refinements not contemplated by Lev and Thiagarajan.

In addition to these contributions, the findings support the American Institute of Certified Public Accountants Special Committee's (1994) recommendation that more forward-looking information be disclosed, and from an investment perspective, more timely and consistent UOB disclosure may be warranted. These results can also have implications for audit policy makers. Although users are divided over expanding the scope of audits to include new types of supplemental information not currently audited, the Special Committee did recommend that the auditing profession should be prepared to lend assurances to such disclosures. If investors rely on these unfilled order backlog numbers to make investment decisions, auditors may need to expand their audit scope and lend assurances to the accuracy and validity of this currently unaudited information source.[2] In addition, this forward-looking information could possibly assist auditors in evaluating going-concern problems or in predicting bankruptcy.

The remainder of this paper is organized as follows. In the second section, the theoretical relationships among unfilled order backlogs, earnings, future earnings, and equity returns are developed. In the third and fourth sections the models are described, sample selection procedures are outlined, and results for the firm-specific time-series and cross-sectional tests are discussed. In the final section, the findings are summarized and the implications for accounting research and the study's limitations are addressed.

THEORY AND HYPOTHESIS DEVELOPMENT

This section theoretically derives the relationship among unfilled order backlogs, earnings, future earnings, and equity returns. Using an ARIMA (0,1,1) time-series model based only on the earnings series as a proxy for the market's expectation of future earnings, it has been demonstrated that the fundamental relationship between earnings and returns for individual firms is as follows:

$$\frac{P_t - P_{t-1}}{P_{t-1}} = Ret_t = \left[\frac{\theta E(X_t)}{P_{t-1}E(R)} - 1\right] + \left[1 + \frac{1-\theta}{E(R)}\right]\frac{X_t}{P_{t-1}}, \qquad (1)$$

where P_t and P_{t-1} are values of the firm's equity at time t and $t-1$, respectively; Ret_t is the firm's raw equity return during period t; θ is the moving-average parameter of the ARIMA (0,1,1) time-series model; $E(R)$ is expected return; and X_t is the firm's earnings during period t.

Using an ARIMA (0,1,1) time-series model as a proxy for the market's expectation of future earnings, however, excludes any information that is not directly related to current accounting earnings. Therefore, as the following example suggests, expectations of future earnings can potentially be improved by incorporating information not contained in current earnings, such as UOBs.

	$Period_t$	$Period_{t+1}$	$Period_{t+2}$	$Period_{t+3}$
Beginning UOB	330	390	260	340
Orders received	260	200	270	350
Orders shipped	200	330	190	220
Ending UOB	390	260	340	470
Shipments (price/unit = $1)	200	330	190	220
Fixed costs	50	50	50	50
Variable costs (cost/unit = $.6)	120	198	114	132
Earnings	30	82	26	38
Change in UOBs		−130	+80	+130
Change in earnings		+52	-56	+12

In this simplified example, when UOBs decrease in $Period_{t+1}$ (−130), future earnings in $Period_{t+2}$ (−56) also decrease. On the other hand, when UOBs increase, as in $Period_{t+2}$ (+80), future earnings in $Period_{t+3}$ (+12) also increase. Hence, there is a direct relationship between current changes in UOBs and future earnings, although each firm-specific relationship may be quite different.

These scenarios illustrate that an important piece of leading information, UOBs, is excluded from the standard returns-earnings model when market expectations are calculated using the earnings stream alone (i.e., ARIMA (0,1,1) model). Therefore this UOB information is incorporated in the market expectation of future earnings as follows:

$$E(X_{t,\,t+1,\,...,\,\infty}|X_{t-1},B_{t-1},B_{t-2}) = X_{t-1} + (\delta_2(B_{t-1} - B_{t-2}) - \theta_2\alpha_{t-1},) \quad (2)$$

where E is the expectations operator; B is UOBs; t is time subscript; δ is the autoregressive parameter on differenced UOBs; and θ is the moving average parameter on the error term. For this study, it is assumed that the market's reaction to UOB information is incorporated in the coefficient δ. If the market perceives that the change in UOBs contains measurement error (e.g., a number of orders were canceled), this knowledge would be incorporated in the δ coefficient. In addition, it is assumed that prior years' UOB changes have no influence on investor expectations. Using this formulation with a few additional assumptions and manipulations, a formal relationship between returns, earnings, and UOBs is established as follows:

$$Ret_t = \left[\frac{\theta E(X_t)}{P_{t-1}E(R)} - 1\right] + \left[1 + \frac{1-\theta}{E(R)}\right]\frac{X_t}{P_{t-1}} + \left[\frac{\delta}{E(R)}\right]\frac{B_t - B_{t-1}}{P_{t-1}}, \quad (3)$$

with all variables as previously defined.[3]

The third term on the right-hand side of this model predicts that changes in unfilled order backlogs are also relevant to firm value, and leads to the following hypothesis:

Hypothesis 1.   Changes in the level of unfilled order backlogs provide incremental information beyond the level of current earnings when explaining equity returns.

This formulation is used to examine the value equity investors place on consistent 10-K reporting of UOB disclosures by performing annual firm-specific time-series regressions for firms meeting the data demands. The specifics of this test are discussed in the next section.

THE TIME-SERIES ANALYSIS

Firm-specific regressions provide the most powerful test of the returns, earnings, and unfilled order backlog association because coefficients generated from these regressions are not averages of multiple firm relationships. In addition, many of the cross-sectional econometric problems (e.g., cross-sectional correlation) are not encountered. Since the minimum number of continuous quarterly observations to meet the statistical requirements are not obtainable, annual data are used to test this relationship. Equation (3) is used to test this relationship by incorporating the following changes.

In contrast to cross-sectional regressions, the variables included in time-series regressions must be stationary; otherwise, OLS parameter estimates are biased and inconsistent. Lipe (1986), among others, has shown that earnings levels are nonstationary and, therefore, must be first-differenced.[4] Since prior research has not examined the stationarity of UOBs, this variable was tested to determine if further differencing was required. Stationarity was tested for all 90 firms meeting the selection criteria described in the following section and further differencing of UOBs was not required. The following firm-specific time-series model is used

$$Ret_t = \beta_0 + \beta_1\, Earnch_t + \beta_2\, Backch_t, + \varepsilon_t \qquad (4)$$

where Ret_t is the firm's raw return for year t, calculated as the continuously compounded return from the end of March of year t to the end of March of year $t{+}1$; $Earnch_t$ denotes the change in the firm's annual earnings available to common shareholders and is measured as earnings for year t minus earnings for year $t{-}1$, scaled by the market value of equity at the end of March of year $t{-}1$; $Backch_t$ is the change in the firm's UOBs, measured as the difference between UOBs at December 31 of year t minus UOBs at December 31 of year $t{-}1$, scaled by the market value of equity at the end of March of year $t{-}1$; and ε_t is the error term with ordinary least-squares (OLS) properties. To calculate the market value of equity at time $t{-}1$, the price of common stock is multiplied by the number of shares outstanding at time $t{-}1$, adjusting the outstanding shares for stock dividends and splits.[5]

Sample Selection and Data Sources

To meet the requirements for the time-series analysis, firms must have a December 31 year-end, 20 consecutive years of earnings (item number 18), and unfilled order backlog information (item number 98) on the 1991 Compustat Industrial File, and complete price, shares outstanding, and returns information on the 1992 Center for Research in Security Prices (CRSP) Daily Returns NYSE/AMEX File. Earnings available to common stockholders was measured as earnings (Compustat, item number 18) less preferred dividends (Compustat, item number 19).

Table 1. SIC Distribution of Sample Firms and
Variable Descriptive Statistics

Panel A. Distribution of Firms Included in Time-Series Regressions for Years 1972-1991, by One-Digit SIC Code

SIC	SIC Description	Firms	%
1000-1999	Mining, building construction, heavy construction	5	5.56
2000-2999	Food products, textile mill products, apparel, lumber, furniture and fixtures, paper products, publishing	6	6.67
3000-3999	Plastic and rubber products, leather products, stone products, primary metals, metal fabrication, commercial machinery, electronics, transportation equipment	73	81.11
4000-4999	Railroad, water, and motor freight, transportation	2	2.22
5000-5999	Durable goods, nondurable goods, food stores, auto dealers, home furniture	1	1.11
7000-7999	Hotels, personal services, motion pictures, recreation services	1	1.11
8000-8999	Health services, educational services, engineering services	2	2.22
		90	100.00

Panel B. Descriptive Statistics for Raw Returns, Earnings Changes, and Unfilled Order Backlog Changes for all Sample Firms, Years 1972 1972-1991, N = 1,710

	Mean	Std.Dev.	Minumum	Median	Maximum
Ret_t	.1828	.4646	−.7334	.1043	6.6851
$Earnch_t$	.0089	.1848	−1.7687	.0051	2.9867
$Backch_t$	.0958	.9313	−6.6262	.0211	13.8549

Notes: Ret_t = The firm's raw return for year t, calculated as the continuously compounded return from the end of March of year t to the end of March of year $t+1$.

$Earnch_t$ = The change in the firm's annual earnings available to common shareholders, measured as earnings for year t minus earnings for year $t-1$, scaled by the market value of equity at the end of March of year $t-1$.

$Backch_t$ = The change in the firm's UOBs, measured as the difference between UOBs at December 31 of year t minus UOBs at December 31 of year $t-1$, scaled by the market value of equity at the end of March of year $t-1$.

All other variables have been defined previously. The SIC distribution of the 90 firms meeting these selection criteria is shown in the Panel A of Table 1. SIC grouping 3000-3999 contains 81.11 percent of the firms.

Statistics for raw returns, earning changes, and unfilled order backlog changes for these firms are summarized in the Panel B of Table 1. Unfilled order backlog changes have a larger standard deviation than raw returns or earnings changes. In

Table 2. P-Value Classifications for Partial F-statistics for Firm-Specific Time-Series and Two-Way Fixed Effect Pooled Regression Results

Panel A. *P-Value Classifications for Partial F-statistics of Incremental Explanatory Power of Unfilled Order Backlogs, N = 90*

	$p > .20$	$.20 \geq p > .15$	$.15 \geq p > .10$	$.10 \geq p > .05$	$.05 \geq p$
UOBs	67	7	1	3	12
%	74.4%	7.8%	1.1%	3.3%	13.4%

Panel B. *P-Value Classifications for t-statistics of Earnings in Firm-Specific Time-Series Regressions of Returns on Earnings, N=90*

	$p > .20$	$.20 \geq p > .15$	$.15 \geq p > .10$	$.10 \geq p > .05$	$.05 \geq p$
EARN	54	3	11	9	13
%	60.0%	3.3%	12.2%	10.0%	14.5%

Panel C. *Pooled Time-Series and Cross-sectional Regressions of Raw Returns on Earnings Changes and Unfilled Order Backlog Changes with Firm and Time-Specific Dummy Variables, N = 1,710*

	Int	*Earnch*	*Backch*	*Adj. R^2*	*Model F*	*Partial F*
Coefficient	.173	.533	.052	.296	7.54	24.21
t-statistic	18.248	10.182	4.925			
p-value	(<.001)	(<.001)	(<.001)			

Notes: UOBs = The number of firms meeting p-value classifications using the raw return metric calculated from March 31 of year *t* to March 31 of year *t+1*.

EARN = The number of firms meeting p-value classifications using the raw return metric calculated from March 31 of year *t* to March 31 of year *t+1*.

% = The percentage of firms in each category based on a total of 90 firms.

p = The corresponding p-value.

The correlation between earning changes and backlog changes is .121. All other variables are -defined previously.

addition to these statistics, the correlation between earnings changes and backlog changes for the combined sample is .0795.

Time-Series Results

To determine whether changes in UOBs provide incremental information beyond that of earnings in these firm-specific regressions, the sum of squared errors of the "full model" [see Equation (4)] was compared with that of the "reduced form" model [see Equation (5)] and partial *F*-statistics were calculated for each firm.[6] The *p*-value classifications of partial *F*-statistics are presented in Panel A of Table 2.

$$Ret_t = \beta_0 + \beta_1 \ Earnch_t + \varepsilon_t \qquad\qquad (5)$$

Although the majority of firms have p-values in excess of .20, the hypothesis being tested here is whether the observed number of firms with p-values less than .05 is greater than one would expect in nature. Using the information from the partial F-statistics in Panel A of Table 2, this assertion was investigated by performing the following two tests. First, a binomial test is used to observe whether or not the observed proportion of significant partial F-statistics is greater than the expected proportion at a .05 level.[7] Comparing the observed proportion of significant F-statistics (12/90, or 13.4%) with the expected proportion (4.5/90, or 5.0%), a z-score of 1.94 was calculated, which is significant at approximately the .03 level. Second, the sum of squared errors across firms was pooled and a grand F-statistic was calculated.[8] Using the pooled information, a grand F-statistic was calculated as 3.02, which is also significant at less than the .01 level.

Based on these statistical tests, it appears that UOBs do provide incremental information beyond that of earnings; however, taken alone, this evidence does not appear to be economically significant since only a few firms appear to contribute to the statistical result.[9] To determine the relative magnitude of the UOB results, the partial F-statistics in Panel A of Table 2 are compared with the results of the reduced form firm-specific time-series regressions of returns on earnings shown in Panel B of Table 2. Surprisingly, for 60 percent of firms in this sample, earnings are not significant at conventional levels.[10] For p-values less than or equal to .05, the number of firms with a significant earnings variable is similar to the number of firms with significant UOB information. It appears, at least for these sample firms, that UOBs are valued as much as earnings.

Pooled Two-Way Fixed Effect Model Results and Overall Conclusions

Hsiao (1989) has suggested that panel data approaches have several advantages over conventional time-series or cross-sectional analyses—namely, providing more efficient parameter estimates and controlling for such econometric problems as omitted variable bias and multicollinearity. One of these methods, called a two-way fixed effect model, contains both firm- and time-specific dummy variables to control for firm-specific factors which remain constant across time and economic factors which influence all firms contemporaneously. Since these methods control for factors that remain constant across firms, this test should provide further evidence on the dynamic relationships among equity returns, earnings, and UOBs. The results for the two-way fixed effect model are presented in Panel C of Table 2. Earnings and UOB changes as well as the partial F-statistic are all significant at less than the .001 level.

Taken together, the results of binomial statistics, grand F-statistics, and the two-way fixed effect test all suggest that for firms that have consistently disclosed UOBs, changes in UOBs have statistically significant explanatory power for equity returns beyond that of earnings. However, care must be taken in generalizing these results because only firms meeting the stringent data demands are included in these tests (survivorship bias) and certain industries are systematically excluded.

CROSS-SECTIONAL ANALYSIS

The SEC mandates that firms provide quarterly financial statement information in accordance with Rule 10-01 of Regulation 10-K, and it requires management's discussion and analysis of financial condition in accordance with Item 303 of Regulation S-K. Because these quarterly guidelines are not as extensive as the 10-K disclosure requirements, disclosures such as UOBs are not specifically required. Therefore, companies are allowed discretion over whether or not to disclose this information in their 10-Qs. This situation offers a unique opportunity to investigate whether or not the relationship among returns, earnings, and UOBs holds for firms that voluntarily decide to disclose this information to investors in their 10-Qs. If firms use the 10-Q as an important source of information dissemination a positive relationship might be expected between UOB changes and equity returns.

However, it could be argued that since quarterly UOB disclosures are voluntary, companies that choose to disclose this information self-select into this particular disclosure regime. This self-selection process can cause the following statistical problems. First, the independent variables used to explain returns may be conditioned on the disclosure choice of the firm. Second, the potential difference in returns from disclosing and not disclosing may be related to the choice of disclosure (i.e., firms may consider the return effect before deciding to disclose UOBs). In econometric terms, these self-selection issues can create omitted variables and endogeneity problems which lead to biased and inconsistent OLS parameter estimates. To control for these potential econometric problems and test hypothesis one using these quarterly disclosures an endogenous switching regression model (ESRM) was employed that was developed by Heckman (1979) and Lee (1978).

The following sections outline this two-stage approach, describe the sample selection procedures, and summarize the results. In the first section, the ESRM model is described, highlighting how the disclosing and nondisclosing groups are modeled as two different functional relationships and how the model allows the for the possibility that the dependent variable, returns, may influence the firm's decision to disclose UOBs. The second section describes how the model controls for the possibility that factors "not in the hypothesized model" contributed to the firms disclosure choice. The ESRM model requires that information related to this choice be incorporated into the model by using a probit procedure and estimating the inverse Mills ratio. The next sections discuss the sample selection procedures, the ESRM results, and the OLS findings using the discloser group.

The Endogenous Switching Regression Model

The ESRM is composed of the following two equations, which represent the fundamental relationships of the 10-Q disclosing group and the 10-Q nondisclosing group

$$Ret_{1i,1t} = \beta_0 + \beta_1\, Earn_{1i,1t} + \varepsilon_{1i,1t} \tag{6}$$

and

$$Ret_{2i,2t} = \beta_0 + \beta_1\, Earn_{2i,2t} + \varepsilon_{2i,2t}. \tag{7}$$

For these formulations, $Ret_{1i,1t}$ and $Ret_{2i,2t}$ are the market-adjusted return for a UOB disclosing and UOB nondisclosing firm i, respectively, for quarter$_t$, calculated as the continuously compounded return on firm i's common stock from quarter$_{t-1}$ to quarter$_t$, minus the value-weighted market return over the same period. $Earn_{1i,1t}$ and $Earn_{2i,2t}$ denote firm i's earnings for the disclosing group and nondisclosing group, respectively, for quarter$_t$ scaled by the market value of firm i's equity at the end of quarter$_{t-1}$. Since the two equations are based on disclosure mode (i.e., UOBs are only observed for the first group), the change in UOBs is not included as an independent variable in either group.

Using these two equations, the entire population of firms that have UOBs (whether disclosed or not) is represented. However, the firms in each of these regimes have self-selected themselves into a particular disclosure mode and, thus, are nonrandom groups. To obtain unbiased and consistent parameter estimates in this situation, the ESRM requires an indicator function for disclosure choice. The propensity for firm i to disclose UOBs, $Disclose_{i,t}{}^*$, is represented as a function of the potential difference in returns, a vector of other explanatory variables $W_{i,t}$, and an error term $\mu_{i,t}$:

$$Disclose_{i,t}^* = \gamma_0 + \gamma_1\, (Ret_{1i,1t} - Ret_{2i,2t}) + \gamma_{2'}\, W_{i,t} + \mu_{i,t}. \tag{8}$$

The problem with this model is that the theoretical construct $Disclose_{i,t}{}^*$ is unobservable; thus, a proxy is required, which is labeled $Discback_{i,t}$. Since a firm's unfilled order backlog is only observed if it chooses to disclose this information, $Discback_{i,t}$ equals 1 if UOBs are disclosed for firm i at time t and $Discback_{i,t}$ equals 0 otherwise.

Thus, if firm i has disclosed unfilled order backlog in its 10-Q, and the quarterly return is conditioned on the unfilled order backlog being disclosed ($Ret_{1i,1t} \mid Discback_{i,t} = 1$) is observed. If $Disclose_{i,t}{}^* \le 0$, then firm i has not disclosed UOBs in its 10-Q and the quarterly return conditioned on UOBs not being disclosed ($Ret_{2i,2t} \mid Discback_{i,t} = 0$) is observed. The differential effect between $Ret_{1i,1t}$ and $Ret_{2i,2t}$ is included because this potential expected benefit (i.e., higher return) may be associated with the firm's decision to disclose UOBs.

To estimate the probability of disclosure, probit estimation is used on the following equation

$$Disclose_{i,t}^* = \xi \,' Z_{i,t} + v_{i,t}, \tag{9}$$

where all the exogenous variables in Equations (6), (7), and (8) are included as independent variables; Z_i, ξ_i are the theoretical coefficients; and v_i is the error term. Using this reduced form model, the inverse Mills ratios (IMRs) can then be calculated using the following representations:

$$Y_{1i,1t} = \left(\frac{\phi \xi' Z_{i,t}}{\Phi \xi' Z_{i,t}} \right), \tag{10}$$

and

$$Y_{2i,2t} = \left(\frac{-\phi \xi' Z_{i,t}}{1 - \Phi \xi' Z_{i,t}} \right), \tag{11}$$

where Φ is the cumulative distribution of the standard normal function, and ϕ is the standard normal probability density function. The inverse Mills ratios are calculated for each observation in the sample for both the disclosure and nondisclosure groups.

By including the IMRs as additional explanatory variables, Equations (6) and (7) become:

$$E(Ret_{1i,1t} \mid Discback_{i,t} = 1) = \beta_1 \, Earn_{1i,1t} + \sigma_{1,\eta}^* \, Y_{1i,1t}, \tag{12}$$

and

$$E(Ret_{2i,2t} \mid Discback_{i,t} = 1) = \beta_2 \, Earn_{2i,2t} + \sigma_{2,\eta}^* \, Y_{2i,2t}, \tag{13}$$

where $\sigma_{1\eta}^* = Cov(\varepsilon_{1i,1t}, \eta_{i,t})$ and $\sigma_{2\eta}^* = Cov(\varepsilon_{1i,1t}, \eta_{i,t})$, theoretically. The empirical counterparts of these models are:

$$(Ret_{1i,1t} \mid Discback_{i,t} = 1) = \beta_0 + \beta_1 \, Earn_{1i,1t} + \sigma_{1,\eta} \, Y_{1i,1t} + \Gamma_{1i,1t}, \tag{14}$$

and

$$(Ret_{2i,2t} \mid Discback_{i,t} = 0) = \beta_0 + \beta_2 \, Earn_{2i,2t} + \sigma_{2,\eta} \, Y_{2i,2t} + \Gamma_{2i,2t}, \tag{15}$$

where the coefficients $\sigma_{1,\eta}$ and $\sigma_{2,\eta}$ are empirical realizations for $\sigma_{1,\eta}^*$ and $\sigma_{2,\eta}^*$ respectively; and $\Gamma_{1i,1t}$ and $\Gamma_{2i,2t}$ are random error terms with mean zero.

OLS parameters can now be consistently estimated. However, the error terms are still heteroscedastic (Lee 1978, 422) and the standard errors used to calculate the t-tests are incorrect because the empirical realizations of $\sigma_{1,\eta}$ and $\sigma_{2,\eta}$ are not equal to their theoretical counterparts $\sigma_{1,\eta}^*$ and $\sigma_{2,\eta}^*$. To correct for the heteroscedasticity problem, the procedure outlined in Lee (1978) is used.[11]

To determine if the potential expected benefit in equity returns, $Ret_{1i,1t} - Ret_{2i,2t}$, is a determinant in a firm's decision whether or not to disclose UOBs (the endogeneity problem), $Ret_{1i,1t}$ and $Ret_{2i,2t}$ need to be estimated for each firm. These estimates can be generated using Equations (14) and (15). The resulting approximations of $Ret_{1i,1t}$ and $Ret_{2i,2t}$ can then be used on the right-hand side of the structural probit model, Equation (8), to ascertain whether or not this differential is associated with returns. γ_1 is a measure of this effect.

A Model of Unfilled Order Backlog Disclosure Choice

In order to use the ESRM, a formal model of disclosure choice is required. This section identifies and describes several factors that may contribute to the firm's propensity to disclose unfilled order backlog. Unfilled order backlog disclosure choice is modeled as follows:

Disclosure Choice = f (changes in sales, inventory, and earnings; the level of sales, inventory, and earnings; management ownership; competition; government contracts; institutional ownership; and analysts' following),

where disclosure choice is 1 if UOBs are disclosed, and 0 otherwise. All variables and predicted signs of coefficients are defined and explained in Table 3.

The coefficients on the variables *Salch* (change in sales) and *Earnch* (change in earnings) can be positive or negative depending on the firm's current operating environment. Several empirical studies on voluntary management forecasts (see King, Pownall, and Waymire 1990 for a summary) find that managers tend to disclose good news more frequently than negative information. Therefore, if these variables are negative, firms may want to disclose UOBs to offset this "bad news" by demonstrating to the market its future earnings potential—a predicted negative coefficient. Second, if these variables are positive, firms may want to disclose UOBs to demonstrate to the market that the current earnings and sales changes are sustainable. Regardless of the direction of the coefficient's sign, it is predicted that the greater the magnitude of the change becomes in either direction, the more likely it is the firm will disclose UOBs. Consequently, the absolute value of these variables is included as the metric and a positive coefficient is predicted for both variables.

In addition to changes in sales, management could decide to disclose UOBs to demonstrate to the market that the current level of revenues is sustainable. Accord-

Table 3. Definitions and Predicted Signs of Coefficients for Variables
Included in the Disclosure Choice Model

Predicted Sign	Variable Name		Description (Compustat item numbers shown in parenthesis)
+	Salch	=	The absolute value of the dollar change in sales from period$_{t-1}$ ($V2_{t-1}$) to period$_t$ ($V2_t$), scaled by market value of equity at period$_{t-1}$.
+	Invch	=	The absolute value of the dollar change in inventory from period$_{t-1}$ ($V38_{t-1}$) to period$_t$ ($V38_t$), scaled by market value of equity at period$_{t-1}$.
+	Earnch	=	The absolute value of the dollar change in earnings from period$_{t-1}$ ($V25_{t-1}$) to period$_t$ ($V25_t$), scaled by market value of equity at period$_{t-1}$.
+	Sal	=	The current level of sales ($V2_t$), scaled by market value of equity at period$_{t-1}$.
+	Inv	=	The current level of inventory ($V38_t$), scaled by market value of equity at period$_{t-1}$.
−	Earnd	=	1 if the current level of earnings ($V25_t$) is positive, 0 otherwise.
−	Own	=	The percentage of stock owned by managers to the total number of common shares outstanding for the company at period$_{t-1}$.
+	Comp	=	The percentage of firms in its own four-digit SIC code that disclose unfilled order backlog at period$_t$.
+	Gov	=	1 if the firm has any governmental contracts, 0 otherwise, at period$_t$.
?	Inst	=	The percentage of common stock owned by institutional investors at period$_{t-1}$.
−	Anlyst	=	The number of analysts forecasting earnings of the firm one period in advance at period$_{t-1}$.

ingly, *Sal* (current year sales level) is included. As the level of *Sal* increases, the more likely it is that management will disclose UOBs; therefore, a positive coefficient is predicted for this variable.

Bernard and Stober (1989) suggest that inventory can be an important contextual variable when trying to explain whether cash flows are good news or bad news. If management is building inventory levels to convey information about future sales prospects, UOBs could be used to prevent investors from getting concerned about these unusual buildups. Management may disclose UOBs to substantiate high inventory levels and demonstrate that this buildup is not from management ineptitude or declining demand but from the potential for increased sales. Here, the variables *Invch* (change in inventories) and *Inv* (current level of inventory) are included to isolate these effects and accordingly a positive coefficient for *Inv* and *Invch* are predicted.

Current year earnings can also influence the decision to disclose backlogs. Similar to the earnings change story above, if current years' earnings are negative, management may want to disclose UOBs to offset this negative news. The variable *Earnd* (current earnings level) is used to capture this effect and a negative coefficient is predicted for this variable.

Ruland, Tung, and George (1990) find that ownership structure, measured by the percentage of stock held by officers and directors, is the most important factor distinguishing disclosing and nondisclosing firms for management earnings forecasts. Thus an ownership variable, *Own*, is included in this study. It is predicted that as the percentage of stock held by management decreases, the need for disclosing unfilled order backlog will increase because investors require more information to monitor managers. A negative coefficient is predicted for *Own*.

The full disclosure principle posits that nondisclosure of information, even if good news, will be penalized by investors because they will assume the worst. The variable, *Comp* (competition), is included to proxy for nondisclosure. It is predicted that as the percentage of firms in the same four-digit SIC grouping that disclose UOBs increases, more pressure will be put on the individual firm to disclose its own unfilled order backlog in order to avoid the full disclosure penalty. A positive coefficient is predicted for *Comp*.

Gov (government contracts) is included to isolate the effects of public disclosure. Since government contracts awarded are public information, firms that receive such contracts are more likely to disclose UOBs. As Darrough (1993) points out, in competitive environments such as Cournot or Bertrand, if competitor firms can determine information on firm A's demand data, firm A will disclose this information voluntarily. A positive coefficient is predicted for *Gov*.

The last two variables capture investor sophistication, fiduciary responsibility, and private information structure. Based on Indjejikian's (1991) study, it appears that less sophisticated investors benefit from better quality disclosure. Therefore, Indjejikian's model predicts that as the level of sophisticated investors rises, measured by institutional investors (*Inst*), the quality of disclosures (as measured by UOB disclosure) will decrease. On the other hand, as O'Brien and Bhushan (1990) suggest, institutions must satisfy standards of fiduciary responsibility, exercising the care and judgment of a "prudent person" in dealing with investment decisions. Having firms disclose sensitive information, such as UOBs, provides institutions with a "quality" number that can be relied on for its fiduciary responsibility. In this scenario. a positive sign would be predicted for *Inst*. Due to the conflicting arguments, no sign is predicted for the coefficient on *Inst*. Bushman (1991) posits that as private information structures increase, the amount of disclosure needed decreases. Using the number of analysts (*Anlyst*) following the firm as a proxy for private information structure, this study predicts that as the number of analysts following a firm increases, the number of disclosures decreases.

Sample Selection and Data Sources

Selecting firms with UOBs directly from the 10-Qs eliminates many firms that have recorded UOBs but have chosen not to disclose this information in the 10-Q. Therefore, in order to use the ESRM model, a population of firms that have UOBs must be gathered. In this study, I limit the sample to calendar year-end companies on the 1990, 1991, and 1992 Compustat Industrial File that have recorded annual UOBs in each of the following years: 1990, 1991, and 1992. In addition, the terms *bookings, orders,* and *backlogs* were searched using LEXIS to find any additional firms not listed on Compustat. Although several firms were located, there were no firms that had unfilled order backlogs for all three years.

The sample was selected using the following criteria: (1) all firms with UOBs less than 10 percent of sales were removed in order to concentrate on firms with significant UOBs; (2) all firms not included in one-digit SIC codes 2000 and 3000 were eliminated in order to concentrate on manufacturing industries; (3) security prices and outstanding share information must be available in the 1992 Center for Research in Security Prices (CRSP) Daily Returns NYSE/AMEX File in order to calculate quarterly compounded returns and market value of equity; and (4) all firms must have inventory, sales, and earnings information on the 1992 Compustat Quarterly File, institutional and managerial ownership information in the firms' proxy statements, and analyst information from Zacks Investment Service or I/B/E/S Inc. in order to gather information for the ESRM disclosure choice model.

Since the number of days between the release of the annual 10-K and the release of the first quarter 10-Q is minimal, it is difficult to isolate the informational effects of the two reports; therefore, as a final screen, only the second and third quarters of 1991 and 1992 were examined. This selection procedure resulted in a total sample of 566 firm-quarter observations, 214 for disclosing firms and 352 for nondisclosing firms. Unfilled order backlog information was obtained by reviewing individual 10-Qs. If a firm's 10-Q could not be found using LEXIS, the 10-Q was located using Q-files from Arizona State University's Hayden library. The dates for the return compounding period were gathered from LEXIS and, if not found on LEXIS, the stamp date on the 10-Q was used.

The original sample of disclosing firms of 214 was reduced to 190 for the following three reasons: (1) using UOB changes, rather than disclosed amounts, decreased the sample by 15; (2) any observation more than five standard deviations away from the mean was removed, reducing the sample by three; and (3) any observed residual that was more than three standardized residuals away from the mean was eliminated, reducing the sample an additional six observations.

Endogenous Switching Regression Results

The pooled sample and individual quarter results for the reduced form probit are summarized in Table 4. For the pooled sample, only the coefficients on variables

Table 4. Pooled and Quarterly Reduced Form Probit Results

	Pooled	1992		1991	
		Qtr #3	Qtr #2	Qtr #3	Qtr #2
Int	−1.112	−1.485	−1.202	−1.642	−.961
	[−3.66][a]	[−2.54][b]	[−2.25][b]	[−2.94][a]	[−1.80][c]
Salch	−.248	−2.954	−.201	−.880	2.060
	[−.363]	[−1.38][c]	[−.098]	[−.670]	[1.446][c]
Invch	−.149	−2.6290	.919	2.847	.038
	[−.133]	[−.843]	[.547]	[.873]	[.126]
Earnch	1.015	5.407	.133	1.462	−10.375
	[.665]	[1.436][c]	[.042]	[.411]	[−1.67][b]
Sal	−.039	−.096	−.105	.065	−.121
	[−.254]	−.240]	[−.342]	[.190]	[−.414]
Inv	.285	1.209	.161	.271	.246
	[1.65][c]	[2.297][b]	[.442]	[.751]	[.752]
Earn	.904	5.07	−.228	−.613	−2.314
	[.646]	[1.377][c]	[−.092]	[−.216]	[−.686]
Earnd	−.230	−.988	−.213	.225	−.671
	[−1.27][d]	[−1.78][c]	[−.578]	[.559]	[−1.47][d]
Own	.002	−.191	.009	.068	.177
	[.057]	[−.244]	[.013]	[.094]	[.252]
Comp	.820	.778	.662	1.132	.548
	[3.43][a]	[1.538][c]	[1.405][c]	[2.308][a]	[1.14][d]
Gov	.026	−.117	.196	.009	−.025
	[.228]	[−.480]	[.856]	[.042]	[−.114]
Inst	1.42	1.665	1.85	1.312	1.143
	[3.761][a]	[1.986][b]	[2.455][b]	[1.756][c]	[1.529][d]
Anlyst	−.036	.006	−.009	−.004	−.007
	[−.297]	[.239]	[−.373]	[−.199]	[−.324]
Log-likelihood (LL)	−353.36	−78.499	−89.725	−87.053	−91.046
Restricted LL	−375.33	−88.521	−96.228	−95.278	−96.197
Chi-squared (12)	43.944[a]	20.043[b]	13.005	16.451[d]	10.301
CA disclosers	69%	69%	67%	66%	70%
CA nondisclosers	67%	69%	64%	68%	64%

Notes: [a,b,c,d] Statistically significant at the .001, .05, .10, and .20 alpha levels, respectively.
CA is defined as classification accuracy.

Comp (competition) and *Inst* (institutional ownership) are significant at the .001 level. It appears that specific industry disclosure practices and fiduciary responsibility are important determinants of UOB disclosure. The coefficient on *Inv* is significant at the .10 level, indicating that management may want to disclose UOBs

Table 5. Pooled and Individual Quarter ESRM Results for UOB Disclosing and UOB Nondisclosing Firms

	Int	Earn	Lambda	Adjusted R^2	F-statistic
Pooled Sample (D)					
Coefficient	−.074	.774	.022	.137	17.98[a]
Het-Adjusted *t*-statistic	−2.034[c]	5.650[a]	.592		
Pooled Sample (ND)					
Coefficient	−.051	.932	.015	.143	30.31[a]
Het-Adjusted *t*-statistic	−1.332[d]	7.748[a]	.432		
1992 Qtr#3 (D) (N=50)					
Coefficient	−.014	.968	.055	.062	2.62[c]
Het-Adjusted *t*-statistic	−.220	2.292[b]	.803		
1992 Qtr#3 (ND) (N=84)					
Coefficient	.049	1.451	-.052	.173	9.69[a]
Het-Adjusted *t*-statistic	755	4.228[a]	-.930		
1992 Qtr#2 (D) (N=56)					
Coefficient	−.144	.804	.053	.071	3.11[c]
Het-Adj t-stat	−2.346[b]	2.316[b]	.829		
1992 Qtr#2 (ND) (N=88)					
Coefficient	−.115	1.605	.047	.249	15.43[a]
Het-Adj t-stat	−1.691[c]	5.518[a]	.744		
1991 Qtr#3 (D) (N=55)					
Coefficient	−.074	.502	.013	.136	5.26[a]
Het-Adj t-stat	−1.230	2.707[b]	.215		
1991 Qtr#3 (ND) (N=88)					
Coefficient	−.080	1.05	.039	.084	5.02[b]
Het-Adj t-stat	−1.170	3.010[a]	.641		
1991 Qtr#2 (D) (N=54)					
Coefficient	−.091	1.420	.011	.170	6.42[a]
Het-Adj t-stat	−1.523[d]	3.497[a]	.189		
1991 Qtr#2 (ND) (N=92)					
Coefficient	−.056	1.025	.029	.055	3.66[b]
Het-Adj t-stat	−.715	2.491[b]	.412		

Notes: [a,b,c,d] Statistically significant at the .001, .05, .10, and .20 alpha levels, respectively.
Het-Adjusted is the *t*-statistic adjusted for hetereoskedasticity and (D) and (ND) are disclosers and nondisclosers, respectively.

to support growing inventory levels. The overall model is significant at the .001 level.

The quarterly results are much weaker. Only the models for quarter three of 1992 and quarter three of 1991 are significant at conventional levels. Although the coefficients on *Comp* and *Inst* are significant at least at the .20 level in all quarters examined, few of the other coefficients are significant at conventional levels. The classification accuracy remains relatively constant throughout the quarters examined. The structural probit results, not displayed, mirror the reduced form findings. The potential expected benefit in equity returns, $Ret_{1i,1t} - Ret_{2i,2t}$, is not significant, suggesting that this difference is not influencing the firm's decision to disclose UOBs. The model's significance and groups' classification accuracy are similar to the reduced form results.

The results for the ESRM model are shown in Table 5. None of the λ coefficients are significant at any level, suggesting that the omitted variables bias from self-selection is not biasing the results. The coefficient on earnings and the models are significant at least at the .20 level in every period and with the pooled sample.

Quarterly OLS Regressions of Disclosing Firms

Based on the ESRM results, it appears that although certain firms are voluntarily disclosing UOBs, there appears to be no systematic bias associated with this act. Therefore, to determine whether changes in UOBs provide information beyond earnings in explaining stock returns for only the firms that voluntarily decide to disclose this information in their 10-Qs, OLS regression was performed using the following adaptation of Equation (3):

$$Ret_{i,t} = \beta_0 + \beta_1 Earn_{i,t} + \beta_2 Back_{i,t} + \varepsilon_{i,t} \tag{16}$$

Here, $Ret_{i,t}$ is the market adjusted return for firm i for quarter t calculated as the continuously compounded return on firm i's common stock from quarter$_{t-1}$ to quartert, minus the value-weighted market return over the same period. $Earn_{i,t}$ denotes firm i's earnings for quarter t scaled by the market value of firm i's equity at quartert-1. $Back_{i,t}$ is the change in firm i's UOBs from quarter$_{t-1}$ to quartert, scaled by the market value of firm i's equity at quarter$_{t-1}$, and $\varepsilon_{i,t}$ is the regression's error term with ordinary least squares (OLS) properties.

Cross-sectional correlation and heteroscedasticity can cause severe problems in cross-sectional studies using return information. Bernard (1987) finds that the bias from cross-sectional dependence can be significant in cross-sectional regressions using quarterly (or annual) returns and recommends a procedure by Froot to correct for these problems. Froot's (1989) general method of moments correction procedure exploits information in the residuals in small samples to account for heteroscedasticity and cross-sectional dependence. In simulation studies, Froot finds that, even in small samples, the estimated variance (using OLS) is significantly downwardly biased and that his correction procedure appears to achieve

Table 6. Cross-Sectional Regressions of Market Adjusted Returns on Earnings and Changes in Unfilled Order Backlogs for UOB Disclosing Firms

	Intercept	Earn	Back	Adjusted R^2	Model F	Partial F
1992 Quarter 3 (N=50)						
Coefficient	.027	.713	.191	.113	4.03	6.225^a
OLS t-statistic	1.449^d	2.607^a	2.495^a			
Froot t-statistic	1.498^d	2.362^b	1.553^d			
1992 Quarter 2 (N=46)						
Coefficient	-.087	1.635	.180	.215	7.17	3.104^c
OLS t-statistic	-5.148^a	3.773^a	1.762^c			
Froot t-statistic	-7.540^a	4.952^a	1.772^c			
1991 Quarter 3 (N=47)						
Coefficient	-.072	.4986	.108	.201	6.78	1.548
OLS t-statistic	-4.309^a	3.573^a	1.244^d			
Froot t-statistic	-5.884^a	8.365^a	2.208^b			
1991 Quarter 2 (N=47)						
Coefficient	-.078	1.641	.099	.298	10.79	2.049^d
OLS t-statistic	-5.083^a	3.945^a	1.432^d			
Froot t-statistic	-9.920^a	4.897^a	2.037^b			
Pooled (N=190)						
Coefficient	-.047	.704	.156	.163	19.45	14.930^a
OLS t-statistic	-5.160^a	5.828^a	3.864^a			
Froot t-statistic	-10.735^a	7.708^a	3.241^a			

Notes: [a,b,c,d] Statistically significant at the .001, .05, .10, and .20 alpha levels, respectively. All variables are defined previously.

asymptotic efficiency. Two-digit SIC codes are used as the grouping variable for industry classifications for the Froot test.

Table 6 presents the results of the cross-sectional OLS regressions along with the Froot corrected *t*-statistics. The coefficients on *Earn* and *Back* are positive and significant for all periods examined, using either the OLS *t*-statistics or the Froot corrected *t*-statistics. The partial *F*-statistics for each year, which measure the increased explanatory power of UOBs beyond that of earnings, are also significant at least at the .20 level in all quarters, except for the third quarter of 1991. Overall, the results of the cross-sectional tests suggest that changes in unfilled order backlog do provide additional information beyond earnings for firms in this sample.

Cross-sectional Conclusions

Overall, the results of the cross-sectional tests suggest that changes in unfilled order backlog provide additional information beyond earnings for firms in this sample and this finding does not appear to be influenced by the omitted variables or endogeneity problems. However, this conclusion must be interpreted in light of the following concern. A limitation of this cross-sectional design is that changes in UOBs cannot be used as the selection criterion for the ESRM model. Using disclosure choice (probit 0 or 1) as the selection criterion may not capture the fundamental relationships being modeled (i.e., there could be other variables that are only associated with UOB changes that are not accounted for in this ESRM model).

In addition, since return is a change variable, the ESRM should be capturing the effects of the change from the disclosing group to the nondisclosing group and vice-versa. In this sample, most of the firms did not change from disclosing status to nondisclosing status. It appeared that once in a particular group, the firms tended to remain in the same disclosing or nondisclosing group. Therefore, the disclosure model may have been capturing the effects of cross-sectional differences in two stable groups, not determinants of disclosure choice. A stronger test of this relationship would be to collect a number of firms (if available) that switched from disclosing UOBs to not disclosing UOBs, and vice-versa, then use the ESRM to capture the determinants of that change.

CONCLUSIONS, EXTENSIONS, AND LIMITATIONS

This paper investigates how unfilled order backlog (UOB) information is used by market participants to value common stock. By modeling UOBs as a predictor of future earnings, it demonstrated that this supplemental accounting disclosure can be useful in explaining contemporaneous equity returns. The empirical results suggest that unfilled order backlogs do provide information to the equity markets beyond that of earnings alone. Although these results are not generalizable beyond these particular samples, this evidence is consistent with the AICPA Special Committee's suggestion that investors require more forward-looking information such as UOBs in financial reports. Providing evidence that investors use quarterly UOB information suggests that, from an investment context, more timely and consistent disclosure may be warranted.

Finding that this supplemental information source, UOBs, is valued by the equity markets, can have implications for audit policy makers and other academic researchers as well as for financial policy makers. If investors rely on these numbers to make investment decisions, auditors may need to expand their audit scope and lend assurances to the accuracy and validity of currently unaudited information such as UOBs. In addition, this information could possibly assist auditors in evaluating going-concern problems or detecting fraudulent activities.

If firms' order cancellations reduce ending unfilled order backlog substantially, this information may be critical in evaluating whether or not these firms have the ability to continue as a going concern. Also, if companies are continually making substantial adjustments to their backlog, it could indicate that an aggressive sales force is booking more orders than the company can ship. Aggressive booking of orders is a problem highlighted in a recent *Wall Street Journal* article which asked "When Is a Sale Really a Sale?" (Miller 1993). For instance, as competition increased, IBM took a more liberal interpretation of its sales return policies and, thus, recorded as sales items normally classified as merely orders. Examining unfilled order backlog changes may have provided earlier evidence of this problem.

Unfilled order backlogs may also provide additional contextual information needed to predict whether cash flows or accruals are more important in valuation (e.g., Bernard and Stober 1989). For example, if UOBs increase along with inventories, the scenario is consistent with the statement that companies are building inventories for future sales (good news). Previous studies have not included information relating to UOBs or order intake, even though a majority of the sample firms were manufacturing entities.

One limitation of this study is that the firm's internal decision process of disclosing UOBs is unknown. Therefore, the fundamental relationships developed in this study are incomplete. For example, Gibbons, Richardson, and Waterhouse (1990) point out that a firm's decision to disclose information may be due to internal organizational factors such as management personality, extent of internal agreement, or internal organizational structure. Identifying reasonable proxies for such factors is difficult. Even if there were a method to accurately collect this information, these factors may influence individual firm's decisions in different ways. Modeling such individual behavior influences is beyond the scope of this paper. One other qualification that requires highlighting is that certain industries are systematically excluded from this study; therefore, care must be taken in generalizing the results.

82 BRUCE K. BEHN

ACKNOWLEDGMENTS

This paper is based on the author's dissertation, which was completed at Arizona State University. I am grateful to my dissertation committee members, Jim Boatsman (Chair), Mike Hertzel, Stuart Low, Phil Regier, and Hal Reneau for their guidance and comments. This paper has also benefited from comments from Dick Riley, Marty Loudder, and Carol Johnson; the participants of National Chengchi University's Second Annual International Conference of Contemporary Accounting Issues; and the workshop participants at the following universities: Arizona State, Boston, Florida State, George Mason, Georgetown, Tennessee, Tulane, Colorado at Denver, Virginia Polytechnic Institute and State, and Washington State.

NOTES

1. The Securities and Exchange Commission S-K Subpart 229.101(c)(viii) does mandate disclosure of unfilled order backlogs in the 10-K (when material); however, there is no such mandate for the 10-Q.
2. Monroe (1995) points out one of the most common methods firms use to enhance financial performance is to record contingent contracts (UOBs) as sales. A similar situation is documented by Schiff (1993), who demonstrates that McDonnell Douglas failed to remove four MD11s from its order books in the first quarter of 1992 even though Guiness Peat Aviation stated in its own IPO prospectus that it had canceled these orders.
3. The first term on the right-hand side of this model and the slope of the second term (earnings response coefficient) have been the subject of extensive theoretical and empirical work over the past 10 years and were not specifically analyzed in this paper. See Cho and Jung (1991) for a summary of the literature. In addition, this study does not address the differential roles of the autoregressive parameter, δ, or expected returns $E(R)$.
4. Although the theoretical model posits that earnings, not earnings changes, is the variable of interest, earnings changes must be employed in the OLS to obtain statistical validity. This change not only creates a weaker proxy for the theoretical construct earnings but also results in the loss of information due to differencing the data.
5. The return window of March 31 $_{t-1}$ to March 31 $_t$ should be wide enough to capture the equity adjustments caused by information released between issuances of the firms' 10-Ks.
6. The partial F-statistics were calculated as follows:

$$Partial\ F-statistic = \frac{\frac{(RSSE_i - USSE_i)}{1}}{\frac{USSE_i}{(19-3)}},$$

where $RSSE_i$ = restricted sum of squared errors and $USSE_i$ = unrestricted sum of squared errors for each firm-specific regression. The numerator and denominator for these partial F-statistics have 1 and 16 degrees of freedom, respectively.
7. Yamane (1973, 732) specifies the one-tailed z-statistic as:

$$z = \frac{(p_1 - p_2)\sqrt{n_0}}{\sqrt{(p_1 + p_2)\left(1 - \frac{p_1 + p_2}{2}\right)}},$$

where the sample size $n_0 = n_1 = n_2$, p_1 is the actual proportion of significant F-statistics, and p_2 is the expected proportion of significant F-statistics.

    8.   The grand F is calculated as follows:

$$Grand\ F-statistic = \frac{\left(\sum_1^{90} RSSE_i - \sum_1^{90} USSE_i\right)}{90*1} \Bigg/ \frac{\sum_1^{90} USSE_i}{((90*19)-(90*3))}$$

where $RSSE_i$ = restricted sum of squared errors and $USSE_i$ = unrestricted sum of squared errors for each firm-specific regression (see Lipe 1986, 47). The numerator and denominator for these partial F-statistics have 90 and 1,440 degrees of freedom, respectively.

    9.   In order to rule out potential specification problems, all the firm-specific regressions were rerun after correcting for first-order serial autocorrelation, adjusting returns for market movements, recalculating returns for various compounding periods, and eliminating the effects of influential data points. All the results were qualitatively the same as shown in Table 2.

    10.   This result is quite similar to what Kormendi and Lipe (1987) found in their earnings persistence paper. They find that earnings is significant at the 10 percent level in 50 percent (74/145) of the firm-specific regressions.

    11.   The *Limdep* statistical routine accounts for the fact that IMRs are estimated (see Green 1991).

REFERENCES

American Institute of Certified Public Accountants, Special Committee of Financial Reporting. 1994. *Improving Business Reporting—A Customer Focus: Meeting the Information Needs of Investors and Creditors.* New York: AICPA.

Barrett, A. 1991. McDermott: Betting on that backlog. *Financial World* (April 16): 18-19.

Bernard, V. 1987. Cross-sectional dependence and problems in inference in market based accounting research. *Journal of Accounting Research* (Spring): 1-48.

Bernard, V., and T. Stober. 1989. The nature and amount of information reflected in cash flows and accruals. *The Accounting Review* (October): 624-652.

Byrne, H. 1991. Foster Wheeler Corp.: Swelling backlog sets stage for a surge in earnings. *Barron's* (August 19): 33-34.

Bushman, R. 1991. Public disclosure and the information structure of private information markets. *Journal of Accounting Research* (Autumn): 261-276.

Cho, J., and K. Jung. 1991. Earnings response coefficients: A synthesis of theory and empirical evidence. *Journal of Accounting Literature* 10: 85-166.

Darrough, M. 1993. Disclosure policy and competition: Cournot vs. bertrand. *The Accounting Review* (July): 534-561.

Dubashi, J. 1988. Gruman's shares: What price for backlog? *Financial World* (June 28): 12.

Froot, Kenneth A. 1989. Consistent covariance matrix estimation with cross-sectional dependence and heteroscedasticity in financial data. *Journal of Financial and Quantitative* Analysis (September): 333-355.

Gibbons, M., A. Richardson, and J. Waterhouse. 1990. The management of corporate financial disclosures: Opportunism, ritualism, policies, and processes. *Journal of Accounting Research* (Spring): 121-143.

Greene, W. 1991. Limdep Version 6.0—User's Manual and Reference Guide. Bellport, NY: Econometric Software Inc..

Hsiao, C. 1989. *Analysis of Panel Data.* New York: Cambridge University Press.

Heckman, J. 1979. Sample selection bias as a specification error. *Econometrica* (January): 153-161.

Indjejikian, R. 1991. The impact of costly information interpretation on firm disclosure decisions. *Journal of Accounting Research* (Autumn): 277-301.

King, R., G. Pownall, and G. Waymire. 1990. Expectations adjustment via timely management forecasts: Review, synthesis, and suggestions for future research. *Journal of Accounting Literature*: 113-114.

Lee, L. 1978. Unionism and wage rates: A simultaneous equation model with qualitative and limited dependent variables. *International Economic Review* (June): 415-433.

Lev, B., and R. Thiagarajan. 1993. Fundamental information analysis. *Journal of Accounting Research* (Autumn): 190-215.

Lipe, R. 1986. The information contained in the components of earnings. *Journal of Accounting Research* (Supplement): 37-64.

Miller, M. 1993. Softer numbers: As IBM's wows grew, its accounting tactics got less conservative. *Wall Street Journal* (April 7): A4.

Monroe, A. 1995. After the fall. *CFO* (April): 24-30.

O'Brien, P., and R. Bhushan. 1990. Analyst following and institutional ownership. *Journal of Accounting Research* (Supplement): 55-76.

Ruland, W., S. Tung, and N. George. 1990. Factors associated with the disclosure of manager's forecast. *The Accounting Review* (July): 710-721.

Schiff, D. 1993. The dangers of creative accounting. *Worth* (March): 92-94.

Yamane, T. 1976. Statistics—An introductory analysis. New York: Harper & Row.

PERCEPTIONS OF SUPERVISOR/ SUBORDINATE TASK-SPECIFIC EXPERTISE AS A MODERATOR OF PARTICIPATIVE BUDGETING OUTCOMES

B. Douglas Clinton, Thomas W. Hall,
James E. Hunton, and Bethane Jo Pierce

ABSTRACT

A laboratory setting was used to test whether subordinates' perceptions of relative supervisor/subordinate task-specific expertise moderate participation outcomes. Based on the Vroom-Yetton leadership model a high (low) level of participation was expected to produce better outcomes when subordinates perceived a low (high) difference in supervisor/subordinate task-specific expertise. Study results for three attitudinal measures generally confirm the hypothesized relationships between participation outcomes and subordinates' perceptions of relative supervisor/subordi-

Advances in Accounting, Volume 14, pages 85-106.
Copyright © 1996 by JAI Press Inc.
All rights of reproduction in any form reserved.
ISBN: 0-7623-0161-9.

nate expertise. Results for a performance measure were inconclusive. A methodological implication of these findings is that a lack of control for subordinates' perceptions of relative expertise in earlier participation studies may partially account for the mixed results reported. Hence, accounting researchers planning further study in the participation area should consider the need to control subjects' perceptions of relative supervisor/subordinate task-specific expertise. Also, managers of accounting personnel should consider the level of this moderator before deciding on the appropriate degree of employee participation in decision making.

INTRODUCTION

Early participative budgeting studies concluded that a positive association exists between the level of employee participation in the budgetary process and employee motivation and performance (Argyris 1952; Becker and Green 1962). In the intervening decades researchers have found it difficult to consistently produce positive effects attributable to participation. For example, a meta-analysis by Locke and Schweiger (1979) disclosed that approximately equal numbers of studies reported positive and negative consequences associated with participation. In a review of 28 studies published in accounting journals between 1970 and 1991, Shields and Young (1993) found that the effects of participation were not significant or were negative for approximately 60 percent of the tests performed.

In trying to reconcile these inconsistent findings several authors have noted the difficulty in making comparisons across participative decision making studies due to confoundings created by the use of different settings (Chalos and Haka 1989; Locke and Schweiger 1979; Wagner and Gooding 1987). However, a recent meta-analytic study of the participative budgeting literature by Greenberg et al. (1994) found little evidence that methodological moderators contribute to the reported inconsistencies. Shields and Young (1993) argue that the mixed findings result from a narrow focus on the consequences of participation without linking these consequences to the antecedents of participation. To resolve this problem, they suggest that researchers develop theories tying together the antecedents and consequences of participation. Similarly, Greenberg et al. (1994) suggest that researchers focus more effort on theoretical moderators identified in the organizational behavior and psychology literatures.

The current study uses a contingency model approach coupled with an experimental task[1] to test a conjecture that antecedent subordinate perceptions of relative supervisor/subordinate task-specific expertise[2] can produce positive or negative participation outcomes depending on the perceptions held. This is an important avenue of investigation given the increased use of employee participation in recent years and the inconsistent results reported in the participation literature. For parsimony, the study is restricted to situations where the supervisor's expertise is at least as great as the subordinate's expertise and the term "expertise" refers to the accumulated education, training, and experience which enables an individual to effectively use situation-specific knowledge in arriving at a decision. Based on the Vroom-Yetton leadership model as modified by Vroom and Jago (1988), it is hypothesized that a higher level of subordinate participation has a beneficial effect on attitudes and performance when subordinates perceive the difference in supervisor/subordinate task-specific expertise to be relatively low. A second hypothesis is that a higher participation level has a negative effect on attitudes and performance when subordinates perceive the difference in supervisor/ subordinate task-specific expertise to be relatively high. The remainder of this paper is organized as follows. First, the theoretical development is presented and the rationale for the expertise construct is developed. Next, study hypotheses are stated and the research methodology is explained. The final sections document study results and present a discussion of the findings.

THEORETICAL DEVELOPMENT

The causal link between participation and decision outcomes proposed by affective models of supervision is straightforward. Participation is thought to help fulfill subordinates' higher-order needs for self-expression, respect, independence, and equality (Miller and Monge 1986). As these higher-order needs are fulfilled via participation, subordinates perceive the decision process as more fair and become more satisfied and committed. In essence, subordinates tend to support what they help build (Vroom and Jago 1988, 136).

Participation is thought to improve performance by the following mechanism. Participation leads to increased subordinate trust, ego involvement, identification with the organization, and commitment to the decision (Locke et al. 1986, 69). These factors lead to increased motivation, which in turn should yield higher performance (Ajzen and Fishbein 1980). Support for this linkage comes from a number of studies which document a positive association between commitment and performance (Erez and Zidon 1984; Locke and Latham 1990; Lind et al. 1990; Hunton forthcoming).

The Vroom-Yetton Model and Predicted Participation Effects

Although relatively new to the accounting literature (for an early application see Pasewark and Welker 1990), the Vroom-Yetton model of leadership is well known in the management and psychology literatures.[3] The Vroom-Yetton leadership model, as revised by Vroom and Jago (1988), is a normative contingency model which uses knowledge of situational factors to suggest one of five levels of subordinate participation in decision making. Depending on 12 situational factors, including three related to subordinate commitment, the recommended level of participation can range from none (autocratic method) to completely participatory (group consensus method).

In situations where the supervisor wants to secure subordinate commitment to a decision, the level of participation recommended by the Vroom model depends on the likelihood that subordinates will accept a decision made solely by the supervisor. When it is believed that subordinates are not likely to accept a decision made solely by the supervisor, the Vroom model recommends a higher level of participation. This recommendation is based on an expectation that participation will generate increased support and cooperation from the subordinates (Vroom and Jago 1988, 136). Alternatively, when it is believed that subordinates are likely to accept a decision made solely by the supervisor, the Vroom model recommends a lower level of participation.

One factor which is thought to play a central role in determining subordinate acceptance of a supervisor's decision is subordinate perception of the relative task-specific expertise of the supervisor and subordinate.[4] Over 30 years ago, French and Raven (1959) suggested that one of the determinants of influence in social relationships is the perception of expertise or expert power. Vroom and Jago (1988, 139) argue that subordinate commitment to a supervisor's decision may be secured without participation when subordinates believe that the supervisor possesses superior expertise in the area of knowledge in which the decision is to be made.

Several other authors concur that perceptions of supervisor expertise are relevant to the participation decision. Kanter (1982) suggests that participation may be inappropriate when one individual clearly has greater expertise and those affected by the decision recognize and accept that expertise. Similarly, Locke and colleagues (1986) argue that participation may have adverse effects on satisfaction and productivity in circumstances where subordinates lack sufficient task-knowledge or expertise. In this situation, subordinate participation in decision making may engender feelings of inadequacy and discomfort. Hence, subordinates' attitudes may move from mere acceptance of an autocratic decision process to actual preference for an autocratic decision process when the difference in supervisor/subordinate task-specific expertise is relatively high.

Evidence from several sources provides support for the assertion that higher levels of participation are not always beneficial. A laboratory experiment by Calvin and colleagues (1957; cited in Heller 1991) found that participative leadership methods yielded improved performance for bright subjects but that authoritarian methods worked better for dull subjects. A field study by Heller (1971) involving large U.S. corporations disclosed that experienced managers tended to use higher (lower) levels of participation when small (large) differences in skill level were perceived to exist between themselves and their subordinates. Presumably, the work experiences of these senior managers had led them to conclude that this implementation strategy yielded the best overall results for the corporation.

Several studies also provide support for the assertion that higher levels of participation are not always desired by subordinates. In a study of Norwegian firms, Holter (1965; cited in Heller 1991) found that highly skilled employees were more interested in participative decision making than less skilled employees. A study of five large industrial Dutch firms by Hofstede (1968) found that subordinates preferred to participate in decision making only when they felt they could make a valid contribution. More recently, a study by Trafimow and Sniezek (1994) documented a positive association between self-perceptions of expertise and confidence in one's judgments. As applied in an organizational setting, it seems reasonable to expect that employees who perceive themselves as possessing low task-specific expertise will lack confidence in their own judgments and thus will be more willing to forego participation and accept a supervisor's decision when the manager is perceived to possess a high level of expertise.

HYPOTHESES

Hypothesis 1: When Participation Is Beneficial

Based on the preceding theoretical development, it seems reasonable to expect that where the difference in supervisor/subordinate task-specific expertise is perceived to be relatively low, subordinates will want to be consulted in decision making because such consultation will serve their needs for respect and recognition. Furthermore, in this circumstance, participation should not engender feelings of inadequacy or discomfort since the subordinate's expertise is perceived to be similar to that of the supervisor. In this situation, participation is expected to improve affective outcomes of the decision process and improve productivity. This line of reasoning leads to the first hypothesis:

Hypothesis 1.   When subordinates perceive the difference in supervisor/subordinate task-specific expertise to be relatively low, a higher level of participation provides more favorable attitudinal and performance outcomes than a lower level of participation.

Hypothesis 2: When Participation Is Not Beneficial

When subordinates perceive the difference in supervisor/subordinate task-specific expertise to be relatively high, a greater degree of participation may be undesirable. In this circumstance, participation may still serve subordinates' needs for respect and recognition, but these positive forces may be overwhelmed by feelings of inadequacy and cognitive discomfort which arise due to the subordinates' lack of expertise. Moreover, subordinates may believe that their participation will result in a lower quality decision since they lack the expertise to use situation-specific knowledge in arriving at a decision. As a result, participation may yield lower satisfaction and commitment by virtue of undermining subordinates' higher order needs and confidence in the final decision. This type of situation may result in subordinates favoring a more autocratic decision process and suggests Hypothesis 2:

Hypothesis 2.   When subordinates perceive the difference in supervisor/subordinate task-specific expertise to be relatively high, a higher level of participation provides less favorable attitudinal and performance outcomes than a lower level of participation.

Taken together, these hypotheses suggest an interaction between the level of participation and perceptions of relative supervisor/subordinate task-specific expertise in determining participation outcomes. The next section explains the procedures used to test for this hypothesized interaction.

METHODOLOGY

Subjects, Compensation, and Randomization Procedures

One hundred and twelve undergraduate auditing students participated in the experiment as partial fulfillment of a class requirement.[5] The average age of the subjects was 28 and classification of the subjects by gender indicated that 41 percent were male and 59 percent were female. At the time of the experiment, the semester was within two weeks of being completed. Hence, subjects had substantially completed their first auditing course.

Subjects were informed that, based on their performance, they would have a chance to earn state lottery tickets. Each lottery ticket provided a chance to win up to $10,000 as compensation. They were also told that their performance would not be compared to other subjects, but that a minimum level of performance was required to earn any lottery tickets. To encourage all subjects to perform at their highest level, the minimum performance level necessary to earn lottery tickets was not disclosed.

Subjects selected one of 12 experimental sessions subject to enrollment limitations. These 12 sessions were then randomized to one of four experimental cells. None of the experimental cells had sessions which were clustered by day or time. In each session, subjects worked individually in a separate cubicle containing a micro-computer. Each session averaged approximately nine subjects and required approximately 90 minutes to complete.

Experimental Design

The experimental design was a 2×2 fully factorial model. One factor consisted of subordinate participation on two levels: (1) low, and (2) high. The other factor consisted of perceived differences in supervisor/subordinate task-specific expertise on two levels: (1) a relatively low difference, and (2) a relatively high difference.

Experimental Procedures

To inhibit hypothesis-guessing, subjects were told that they were participating in an exercise to pilot test prototype software developed by a public accounting firm to be used in training new staff auditors in the selection of tolerable misstatement levels and budgeting audit hours in audits of accounts receivable. For purposes of the exercise, subjects were told they would assume the role of a recent accounting graduate hired as a new staff auditor and that the session facilitator (experimenter) would assume the role of an audit senior with the firm.

At the beginning of each session, subjects were seated in separate cubicles and given instructions which enabled them to initiate the program. Next, the experimenter introduced himself and described his background. As described later, these experimenter comments performed the manipulation of perceived expertise. Subjects were then provided with written instructions summarizing the purpose of the exercise and the procedures for the experimental task. At this point, the experimenter provided verbal information (discussed later) about the conduct of the experiment which began the participation manipulation. Once the instructions were explained and the manipulations were performed, subjects completed two practice cases after which the experimenter answered questions regarding procedures and operation of the software. When the practice cases were completed, subjects proceeded to work ten unrelated cases which comprised the body of the experiment.

Upon completion of the experimental task, subjects answered questions which inquired about their attitudes toward the session. Next, subjects answered a series of manipulation check questions followed by a series of demographic questions. Within each category of inquiry (attitudinal, manipulation check, and demographic), questions were presented in unique random order for each subject. Upon completion, subjects were debriefed and compensated.

Experimental Task

The experimental task was an adaptation of procedures developed by Brownell (1981) and required subjects to make two decisions in each of 10 unrelated cases. In each case, the experimenter and subject worked together to jointly determine the tolerable misstatement level used in the audit of an accounts receivable balance. Procedurally, each subject first reviewed the case facts and then entered into the computer his/her recommended tolerable misstatement level. After subjects had entered their recommendations, the recommendation of the experimenter was presented and the final tolerable misstatement level was determined via weighting procedures discussed below. As with the Brownell (1981) study, the combining of recommendations from each subject and the experimenter via use of differential weights served as the participation induction. Tolerable misstatement levels recommended by the experimenter were determined using a sliding scale function specified in the audit manual of KPMG Peat Marwick (1992).

At the second stage of each case, subjects recommended a number of budget hours to audit accounts receivable based on three factors: (1) the dollar balance in accounts receivable, (2) the number of accounts comprising the balance, and (3) the final tolerable misstatement level determined in the first stage of the case.

Based on the same data, the software produced an estimate of the actual hours to audit the balance.[6] This estimate was reported to the subject on the computer screen along with an error measure which was calculated as the difference in the budgeted hours recommended by the subject and the actual audit hours estimated by the software.

Manipulations

To set up the participation manipulation, as operational aspects of the software were explained, subjects were told that the following instructions had been prepared by the public accounting firm that developed the software.

> In practice, the senior and staff accountant would discuss the characteristics of the account to be audited, and after considering the recommendation of the staff accountant, the senior would decide on the tolerable misstatement level used. In the firm's classroom training environment, this is not practical due to the number of new staff present and the time constraints imposed on the educational exercise. To simulate this interaction between the senior and staff auditor, the training coordinator will select a recommended tolerable misstatement level and each new staff member will select a recommended tolerable misstatement level. These recommendations will be combined using weightings selected by the training coordinator which he/she deems appropriate.

In the low participation group, upon reading these instructions to the subjects, the experimenter announced that he had decided to give his recommendation an 80 percent weight and each subject's recommendation a 20 percent weight. In the high participation group, these weightings were reversed with each subject's recommendation being given an 80 percent weight and the experimenter's recommendation receiving a 20 percent weight. Thus, participation was operationalized as the amount of influence subjects had in determining the tolerable misstatement level.

The expertise manipulation was achieved by varying the content of the experimenter's introductory comments. In the relatively low difference expertise condition, the experimenter introduced himself as a Ph.D. student specializing in cost/managerial accounting. His work experience was described as three years in industry as a cost accountant and one year in public accounting setting up cost systems for clients. Also, the experimenter indicated that his last direct exposure to auditing had been in an undergraduate course he completed 15 years ago. In the relatively high difference expertise condition, the experimenter introduced himself as a Ph.D. student specializing in auditing. His work experience was described as four years on the audit staff of a Big 6 firm, with the last two years spent as an audit senior running audits of manufacturing and utility clients.

Response Measures

Measures of fairness, satisfaction, task commitment, and performance are commonly used in participation studies (see Locke and Schweiger 1979; Brownell

1981; Brownell and McInnes 1986; Earley and Lind 1987; Wagner and Gooding 1987; Lind et al. 1990; Shields and Young 1993; Scully et al. 1995). Since the purpose of this study was to investigate whether perceptions of task-specific expertise moderate participation outcomes, measurements on each of these commonly used constructs were taken.[7]

When all 10 cases had been completed, the software presented each subject with a series of questions designed to measure: (1) perceptions of fairness regarding the decision making process, (2) satisfaction with the decision process used to select tolerable misstatement levels, and (3) commitment to the task of recommending an appropriate tolerable misstatement level and time budget. For each of these three response measures, two questions were asked using a nine-point scale. Low numerical responses indicated low levels of perceived fairness, satisfaction, and task commitment. Performance in the budgeting task was measured as the sum, over the 10 cases, of the absolute values of the differences between the subject's recommended budget hours and the actual budget hours calculated by the software. Hence, higher performance scores represented poorer performance.

Data Analysis

Analysis of variance procedures were used to analyze the data since these procedures provide a test for interaction without requiring specification of the precise form of the interaction. The ability to test for all possible forms of interaction was an important factor in selecting a method of analysis since study hypotheses predicted an unspecified interaction between participation level and perceptions of supervisor/subordinate task-specific expertise. Because study hypotheses predicted differences between specific cells in the study design, ANOVA results were supplemented with cell-to-cell comparisons based on Duncan's Multiple-Range test.

RESULTS

Manipulation Checks and Reliability of Response Variables

To judge the success of the experimental manipulations, several manipulation check questions were administered.[8] For the participation manipulation, two separate questions asked subjects to indicate on a nine-point scale the degree of influence or weight they had in determining the tolerable misstatement level (1 = no influence and 9 = complete influence). These two questions yielded a Cronbach's Alpha of .81 and were combined and analyzed as a single index. Subjects in the high participation condition gave an average response of 6.8 (between moderate and complete influence) while subjects in the low participation condition gave an average response of 3.7 (between low and moderate influence). A two-way

ANOVA (participation × expertise difference) on this measure gave a statistically significant result on participation (p-value = .0001), but no significant results on expertise difference (p-value = .8714) or the interaction of participation and expertise difference (p-value = .3421). Based on these results, the participation manipulation appears to have been successful since subjects in the high participation condition perceived themselves to have had more influence than subjects in the low participation condition.

For the manipulation of perceived difference in expertise, two sets of questions were asked. The first set asked subjects to rate the experimenter's expertise in planning tolerable misstatement levels on a nine-point scale (1 = low expertise and 9 = high expertise). These questions yielded a Cronbach's Alpha of .94 and were combined into one index representing perceived experimenter expertise (EE). Subjects in the relatively low difference expertise condition gave an average response of EE = 6.4 while subjects in the relatively high difference expertise condition gave an average response of EE = 7.8. The second set of questions asked subjects to rate their own expertise in planning tolerable misstatement levels on a nine point scale (1 = low expertise and 9 = high expertise). These questions yielded a Cronbach's Alpha of .91 and were combined into one index representing perceived subject expertise (SE). As expected, due to the use of randomization procedures, subjects in both expertise conditions gave very similar responses (low condition mean SE = 4.4, high condition mean SE = 4.3).

To assess the outcome of the perceived difference in expertise manipulation, the difference of *EE–SE* was calculated for each subject followed by testing to determine if subjects in the high difference condition correctly perceived their expertise differences to be larger than subjects in the low difference condition. In the relatively low difference expertise condition, the perceived difference in experimenter expertise and subject expertise averaged 2.0. In the relatively high difference expertise condition, the perceived difference in experimenter expertise and subject expertise averaged 3.5. A two-way ANOVA (participation × expertise difference) on these differences gave a statistically significant result on perceived expertise difference (p-value = .0004) but no significant results on participation (p-value = .2094) or the interaction of perceived expertise difference and participation (p-value = .3922). For the relatively high difference expertise condition, these results are very good. The experimenter was perceived as possessing a degree of expertise on the upper end of the scale (EE = 7.8) and this measure was much higher than the perceived expertise of the subjects (SE = 4.3). For the relatively low difference expertise condition, the results are acceptable but not as strong. In this latter expertise difference condition, both the experimenter and the subjects were perceived as possessing a degree of expertise near the middle of the scale (a desirable outcome), but with the experimenter perceived as possessing a somewhat higher level of expertise (EE = 6.4 versus SE = 4.4). Based on these results, the perceived difference in expertise manipulation appears to have been successful since subjects in the high difference condition correctly perceived their difference in expertise to be larger than subjects in the low difference condition.

To judge the reliability of the three affective response measures (fairness, satisfaction, and task commitment), a Cronbach's Alpha was calculated for each set of questions. The resulting Cronbach's Alphas were .89, .91, and .95, respectively. Based on these results, the two individual questions for each response measure were combined resulting in one index for each affective response measure.

Tests for Predicted Interaction of Perceived Difference in Expertise and Participation

Figure 1 presents a plot of the relationships between perceived differences in relative expertise and participation for each of the four response variables. Panels A and B of Figure 1 show that rank-reversal interactions were present for the perceived fairness and satisfaction response variables. In each of these plots, a higher level of participation improved the response variable where the difference in supervisor/subordinate expertise was perceived to be relatively low. Also, in each plot a higher level of participation yielded a less favorable response variable where the difference in supervisor/subordinate task-specific expertise was perceived to be relatively high.

Panel C of Figure 1 presents a plot of the relationship between perceived differences in relative expertise and participation for the task commitment variable. In this plot, the sample means exhibit a different form of interaction. Although no rank-reversal interaction is apparent, participation does appear to increase task commitment for the low difference expertise condition while decreasing task commitment for the high difference expertise condition.

Finally, Panel D of Figure 1 presents a plot of the relationship between perceived differences in relative expertise and participation for the performance variable. Bear in mind that the performance measure used is an inverse performance measure—higher scores mean greater error in budgeting audit hours and thus poorer performance. In this plot, performance declines (i.e., there is poorer performance) in both expertise difference conditions as participation increases. For the condition where the difference in expertise was relatively high, these results are consistent with study hypotheses. In the condition where the difference in expertise was relatively low, increased participation appears to have diminished performance, which is not consistent with the study hypotheses.

To determine if the relationships observed in Figure 1 were statistically significant, a two-way ANOVA (expertise difference × participation) was run for each response variable (fairness, satisfaction, task commitment, and performance). Table 1 presents the results of each ANOVA and discloses that the interaction effect of expertise difference and participation was significant for both the fairness and satisfaction response variables, with *p*-values of .0001 each. For the task com-

Panel A: Perceived Fairness of Decision Making Process

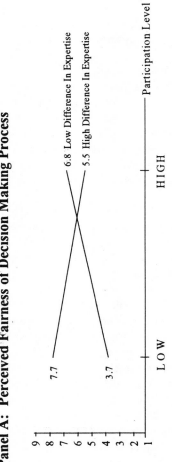

Panel B: Satisfaction with Decision Making Process

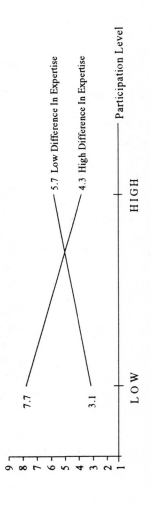

Panel C: Task Commitment

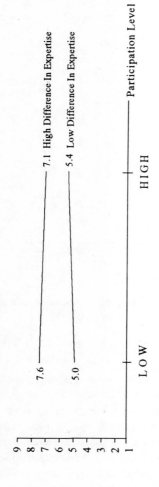

9
8
7 ———————— 7.6 ————————— 7.1 High Difference In Expertise
6
5 ———————— 5.0 ————————— 5.4 Low Difference In Expertise
4
3
2
1 ———————————————————————— Participation Level
    L O W   H I G H

Panel D: Performance[1]

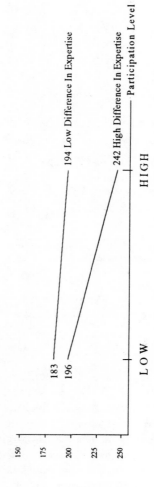

150
175
200
225
250

183 ———————————————————— 194 Low Difference In Expertise
196 ———————————————————— 242 High Difference In Expertise
———————————————————————— Participation Level
    L O W   H I G H

Note: [1]Performance variable is an inverse measure; thus, higher values represent lower performance.

Figure 1. Interactions of Perceived Difference in Supervisor/Subordinate Task-specific Expertise and Participation

97

Table 1.   ANOVA Results On Response Measures

Model Source	Statistic	Fairness	Satisfaction	Task Commitment	Performance
Perceived Difference In Expertise (D)	DF	1	1	1	1
	Mean square	51.20	73.40	130.60	25,785
	F-value	19.90	48.30	78.30	3.10
	p-value	.0001	.0001	.0001	.0817
	ω^2	.09	.15	.40	.02
Participation Level (L)	DF	1	1	1	1
	Mean square	3.90	4.40	<.1	22,365
	F-value	1.50	2.90	<.1	2.70
	p-value	.2197	.0902	.9541	.1046
	ω^2	*	.01	*	*
Interaction DxL	DF	1	1	1	1
	Mean square	191.90	245.10	5.60	7,989
	F-value	74.70	161.30	3.30	0.90
	p-value	.0001	.0001	.0702	.3302
	ω^2	.36	.50	.01	*

Note: *Since the related F-value is not statistically significant, the estimated ω^2 is not considered significantly different from zero.

mitment variable, the interaction *p*-value was .0702. For the performance variable, the interaction effect was not significant, with a *p*-value of .3302.

Test of Hypothesis 1

Hypothesis 1 predicted that increased participation would improve subordinates' attitudes and performance when the difference in supervisor/subordinate expertise was perceived to be relatively low. Panel A of Table 2 presents mean values for each response variable and results of testing these values for agreement with Hypothesis 1 using Duncan's Multiple-Range test. Data presented in Panel A of Table 2 show that, as predicted by Hypothesis 1, increased participation led to increases in each affective response variable, and that these increases were statistically significant for the fairness and satisfaction variables. Estimated effect sizes were +1.9, +2.1, and +.3 for fairness, satisfaction, and task commitment, respectively. Based on Cohen's (1988, 26) proposal that location shifts in excess of .8 standard deviations be classified as large, the estimated effect sizes for fairness and satisfaction appear to be quite large. For the task commitment response vari-

Table 2. Mean Values of Response Measures And
Test Results For Study Hypotheses

Panel A: Test of Hypothesis 1 that increased participation improves subordinates' attitudes and performance when perceived differences in supervisor/ subordinate task-specific expertise are low.

	Mean Value of Response Variable			
Participation Level	Fairness	Satisfaction	Task Commitment	Performance[1]
High	6.8[a]	5.7[a]	5.4[a]	194[a]
Low	3.7[b]	3.1[b]	5.0[a]	183[a]
Difference in means	+3.1	+2.6	+.4	+11
Estimated effect size[2]	+1.9	+2.1	+.3	+.1
Expected sign of effect size	+	+	+	-

Panel B: Test of Hypothesis 2 that increased participation degrades subordinates' attitudes and performance when perceived differences in supervisor/ subordinate task-specific expertise are high.

	Mean Value of Response Variable			
Participation Level	Fairness	Satisfaction	Task Commitment	Performance[1]
High	5.5[c]	4.3[c]	7.1[b]	242[a1]
Low	7.7[d]	7.7[d]	7.6[b]	196[a]
Difference in means	-2.2	-3.4	-.5	+46
Estimated effect size[2]	-1.4	-2.7	-.4	+.5
Expected sign of effect size	-	-	-	+

Notes: [1]Performance variable is an inverse measure; thus, higher values represent lower
performance.
[2]See Cohen (1988, 276) for computational details.
[A,A1,B,C,D]Within the analysis for each response variable across panels A and B,
means with different letter superscripts are significantly different with
an alpha level of .05 or less. In the analysis of performance, means with
the letter superscripts[a] and [a1] are significantly different, with an alpha
level of .10. These results are based on Duncan's Multiple-Range Test.

able, although the sample means moved in the predicted direction yielding a small
estimated effect size of +.3, the differences were not statistically significant.

The performance response variable did not move in the manner predicted by
Hypothesis 1. Since the performance measure used was an inverse measure,
Hypothesis 1 predicted that subjects' performance measures should decrease as

participation increased. However, sample means presented in Panel A of Table 2 do not exhibit this pattern. Statistical testing disclosed that these sample means were not significantly different, thus suggesting that increased participation had no discernible effect on performance.

Test of Hypothesis 2

Hypothesis 2 predicted that increased participation would degrade subordinates' attitudes and performance when the difference in supervisor/subordinate task-specific expertise was perceived to be relatively high. Panel B of Table 2 presents mean values for each response variable and results of testing these values for agreement with Hypothesis 2 using Duncan's Multiple-Range test. Data presented in Panel B of Table 2 show that each affective response variable decreased as participation increased, and that these differences were significant at the .05 level for fairness and satisfaction. Estimated effect sizes were −1.4, −2.7, and −.4 for the fairness, satisfaction, and task commitment variables, respectively. For the fairness and satisfaction variables, these estimated effect sizes are quite large and supportive of Hypothesis 2. For the task commitment response variable, although the sample means moved in the predicted direction, the differences were not statistically significant and the estimated effect size was small at −.4.

Unlike the results of testing Hypothesis 1, the performance response variable did move in the manner predicted by Hypothesis 2. Since the performance measure used was an inverse measure, Hypothesis 2 predicted that subjects' performance measures should increase as participation increased. Sample means presented in Panel B of Table 2 do exhibit this pattern, moving from 196 to 242 as participation increased, with a moderate estimated effect size of +.5. Results of applying Duncan's Multiple-Range test disclosed these means were statistically different at the .1 alpha level.

DISCUSSION OF RESULTS

Despite research efforts spanning 30 years, participation researchers have found it difficult to identify the conditions under which participation consistently produces positive consequences. Several authors have suggested the need to devote more effort to identifying and testing antecedent factors which may moderate the effects of participation (Shields and Young 1993; Greenberg et al. 1994). This research tested a conjecture that antecedent subordinate perceptions of supervisor/subordinate task-specific expertise moderate participation outcomes. Specifically, it was hypothesized that participation produces positive results when the perceived difference in supervisor/subordinate task-specific expertise is not too great, but that the benefits of participation diminish and eventually become negative as the perceived difference in supervisor/subordinate task-specific expertise widens in favor of the supervisor.

For the three attitudinal measures examined, all six cell-to-cell comparisons disclosed changes in sample means consistent with expectations. The four comparisons involving perceived fairness and satisfaction were statistically significant with large estimated effect sizes. While the test for interaction was moderately significant for the task commitment measure, cell-to-cell comparisons found no statistically significant differences in sample means. Results for the performance variable were mixed.[9] Contrary to expectations, when the perceived difference in supervisor/subordinate task-specific expertise was low, participation produced no performance benefits. However, when the perceived difference in supervisor/subordinate task-specific expertise widened, participation produced the expected negative performance consequences at a moderate level of statistical significance.

Based on these results, it appears that fairness and satisfaction perceptions are moderated by subordinate perceptions of relative supervisor/subordinate task-specific expertise. As the perceived difference in supervisor/subordinate task-specific expertise widens in favor of the supervisor, the likelihood that participation will yield positive consequences on these dimensions appears to decline. Results for the task commitment and performance measures are less clearcut. Although sample means generally moved as expected, the magnitudes of change were small. Given the known linkages between the four response variables studied (see Brownell and McInnes 1986; Locke et al. 1986; Earley and Lind 1987; Lind et al. 1990; Murray 1990; Lind et al. 1993), future research may yield more clearcut evidence that subordinate perceptions of supervisor expertise do moderate participation effects on task commitment and performance.

These findings have implications for the management of accounting personnel. In situations where a manager's level of expertise is similar to that of his or her subordinates, such as a junior partner in a public accounting firm working with an experienced manager, a high level of subordinate participation appears to be appropriate. A high participation level might also be appropriate where an experienced partner supervises a subordinate who possesses a high degree of technical expertise in EDP auditing, statistical sampling, or accounting/auditing practices of a specialized industry. In other situations, such as an experienced controller working with a new college graduate, a lower level of subordinate participation might be in order. If organizational constraints are such that variations in the level of participation are not feasible, it may be possible to manage the mix of personnel to fit the degree of participation permitted. As suggested by Locke and colleagues (1986), participation is a managerial technique that is appropriate in certain situations and inappropriate in other situations. Effective managers must learn to distinguish the two situations and respond accordingly.

Study findings also have implications for the methodology of participation experiments. It appears that a participation manipulation might produce positive, negative, or null results depending on the expertise perceptions of the subjects. To strengthen external validity, future participation researchers should consider the need to control or anchor subjects' perceptions regarding supervisor/subordinate task-specific expertise since this construct appears to interact with the participation construct (regarding problems which arise when selection and treatment interact see Cook and Campbell 1979, 73). Furthermore, it is important to recognize that randomization of subjects provides no protection against this interaction effect.

To illustrate this point, consider the results from this study where subjects were induced to hold heterogeneous perceptions of expertise. If observations across the factor representing perceived differences in expertise were pooled yielding a one-way design with participation as the treatment factor, test results would show that participation had no effect on outcomes (see test results on participation in Table 1). Yet, when subjects' perceptions were included in the analysis, very strong evidence of participation effects for the fairness and satisfaction measures were found. Alternatively, if subjects' relative expertise perceptions are homogeneous, experimental comparisons may be misleading. In the case of this study, if all subjects had perceived the difference in supervisor/subordinate expertise to be relatively low, conclusions would likely have been that participation improves outcomes (see Panel A of Table 2). Conversely, if all subjects had perceived that the difference in supervisor/subordinate expertise was relatively high, conclusions would likely have been that participation degrades outcomes (see Panel B of Table 2). Thus, study conclusions about the effects of participation would have been contingent upon the unknown perceptions of the subjects.

Finally, study results support the suggestions of several authors that progress in the participation literature may require greater consideration of antecedents which moderate the effects of participation (Murray 1990; Shields and Young 1993; Greenberg et al. 1994). Future research should consider other factors which may help explain when subordinates will (and will not) accept decisions made solely by a supervisor. These factors might include subordinate perceptions of supervisor knowledge, motivation, truthfulness, management style, and likeability. Organizational factors may also play a role in subordinate acceptance of supervisor decisions. For example, in traditional organizations such as public accounting firms, supervisors usually possess higher levels of knowledge and expertise than subordinates. However, with the increasing use of flat organizations, it seems likely that employees often will possess task-specific knowledge and expertise that equals or exceeds that of their supervisors. Hence, further study regarding the moderating effects of asymmetries in knowledge and expertise on participation outcomes seems warranted.

ACKNOWLEDGMENT

The authors thank the associate editor and two anonymous referees for their comments on earlier versions of this manuscript.

NOTES

1. Merchant (1981) suggested employing more experimental designs using contingency frameworks to examine moderators of participation-outcome relations taken a few at a time. Almost all studies appearing in the participative budgeting literature in the past 20 years have used a contingency approach, but only six of 33 published studies used experimental designs. Because field studies have been the most common form of investigation, causal inferences regarding the effects of participation must be limited since these studies rarely use a control group and other influences may be present to confound effects (Locke et al. 1986).

2. Expertise is a subconstruct of a more general construct known as "source credibility." Source credibility is a multidimensional construct which includes perceptions of expertise, trustworthiness, character, social status, and motivations (Arnold 1988; Beaulieu 1994; Chaiken and Maheswaran 1994; Grewal et al. 1994).

3. The Vroom model has been the subject of over 60 books and articles. Tjosvold and colleagues (1986, 125) describe the Vroom model as "perhaps the most widely known and empirically developed contingency perspective on organizational decision-making." In a meta-study focusing on the agreement of participative research results between laboratory and field, the Vroom model was said to be "the best example of systematic research focusing on situational predictors of PDM (participative decision making)" (Schweiger and Leana 1986, 155). Moreover, the results of studies examining the validity of the Vroom model have been relatively consistent across both lab and field settings (Schweiger and Leana 1986).

4. The expertise construct investigated in this study is different than the knowledge construct investigated in studies by Shields and Young (1993) and Scully and colleagues (1995). Task-specific expertise refers to the accumulated education, training, and experience which enables an individual to effectively use situation-specific knowledge in arriving at a decision. On the other hand, situation-specific knowledge refers to the particular cue/information set known to the decision maker and used in arriving at a decision. As with the expertise construct, it seems reasonable to expect that subordinate knowledge of information asymmetries between the subordinate and supervisor could affect subordinate motivation to accept a decision. If subordinates possess better or more complete information than the supervisor, it seems reasonable to expect that they will desire involvement in the decision process. Alternatively, if subordinates possess inferior information, they might be expected to prefer a lower level of participation.

5. The use of a laboratory study to investigate participation effects may be criticized due to concerns about external validity (e.g., a highly simplified environment, the relatively short duration of the interaction, and the use of students as surrogates for employees). While these concerns are appropriate, it should be recognized that in many cases the purpose of a laboratory experiment is to isolate a phenomena of interest to show that certain effects can occur (Dipboye 1990; Scully et al. 1995). Once an effect has been demonstrated in the laboratory, field studies may be employed as an important next step in validating laboratory results. With respect to the use of university students as subjects, research on this issue suggests that students are acceptable surrogates when investigating general leadership process issues or information processing/judgment issues and the direction of the treatment effect (not the exact magnitude) is the primary concern (Dipboye 1990; Ashton and Kramer 1980). Consistent with these findings, a recent meta-analytic examination of methodological moderators in participative budgeting research by Greenberg and colleagues (1994) compared results for studies that used students versus professionals and concluded that students and professionals could not be statistically distinguished. Because the current study investigates a general psychological behavior pattern in the leadership process domain, use of students as surrogates seems reasonable.

6. The functional relationship between actual audit hours and the three input factors was:

$$HRS = 20 + .000005 \ AB + .002 \ NA - .0002 \ TE$$

where: HRS = actual audit hours,
        AB   = account balance to be audited,
        NA   = number of accounts comprising the balance, and
        TE   = tolerable misstatement level determined in the first stage of the case.

The above function was developed with two goals in mind. First, a linear model was selected to minimize the complexity of the relationships. Second, the coefficient values were selected to provide reasonable estimates of the actual audit hours for the range of input values used in the experimental cases.

7.   Theory and research in the participation and procedural justice literatures suggest the presence of linkages between the response variables used in this study (see, e.g., Brownell and McInnes 1986; Locke et al. 1986; Earley and Lind 1987; Lind et al. 1990; Murray 1990; Lind et al. 1993). Depending on the circumstances, increased participation is thought to drive increased perceptions of control, fairness, and satisfaction. In turn, improved perceptions of control, fairness, and satisfaction are thought to lead to increased task commitment, motivation, and task performance. While investigating these linkages and how they are moderated is an important avenue of research, this study was limited to investigating whether such factors are moderated by perceptions of relative supervisor/subordinate task-specific expertise.

8.   Since subjects were told that their compensation would be based on their performance, there was some concern that undesired efficacy and/or expectancy perceptions might affect study results. In particular, the efficacy and expectancy concerns were that subjects in the low participation condition may have felt that their ability to accurately budget audit hours and earn compensation were constrained by the low weight given to their recommended tolerable misstatement levels. To investigate this issue, all subjects were asked a series of questions which probed for efficacy and expectancy effects. Statistical analysis of subjects' responses disclosed no significant evidence of efficacy or expectancy effects.

9.   Miller and Monge (1986) report that studies which have examined the relationship between participation and satisfaction versus participation and productivity found a stronger relationship between participation and satisfaction than between participation and productivity. Also, a review by Locke and Schweiger (1979) concluded that participation does not always lead to higher productivity. More recently, Murray (1990) noted that the impact of participation on performance remains unclear due to varied empirical findings. In light of these results reported in the literature, our findings of strong effects for several of the attitudinal variables and much weaker effects for the performance variable are not surprising. Given the short duration of the experiment, the subjects may have had insufficient time to master the budgeting task, or the functional form of the relationship between audit hours and the other factors may have been too complex, thus introducing a high level of noise in the data. Alternatively, participation may in fact have no performance effect. Resolution of this issue will require further study.

REFERENCES

Ajzen, I., and M. Fishbein. 1980. *Understanding Attitudes and Predicting Social Behavior.* Englewood Cliffs, NJ: Prentice Hall.

Argyris, C. 1952. *The Impact of Budgets on People.* New York: Controllership Foundation.

Arnold, V.D. 1988. Source credibility in persuasive oral communication. *Journal of Education for Business* (October): 43-45.

Ashton, R., and S. Kramer. 1980. Students as surrogates in behavioral accounting research: Some evidence. *Journal of Accounting Research* 18(1): 1-15.

Beaulieu, P.R. 1994. Commercial lenders' use of accounting information in interaction with source credibility. *Contemporary Accounting Research* 10(2, Spring): 557-585.

Becker, S., and D. Green. 1962. Budgeting and employee behavior. *Journal of Business* (January): 392-402.

Brownell, P. 1981. Participation in budgeting, locus of control and organizational effectiveness. *The Accounting Review* (October): 844-860.

Brownell, P., and M. McInnes. 1986. Budgetary participation, motivation, and managerial performance. *The Accounting Review* (October): 587-600.

Calvin, A.D., F.K. Hoffmann, and E.E. Hardin. 1957. The effect of intelligence and social atmosphere on groups' problem solving behavior. *Journal of Social Psychology* 45: 61-74.

Chaiken, S., and D. Maheswaran.1994. Heuristic processing can bias systematic processing: Effects of source credibility, argument ambiguity, and task importance on attitude judgment. *Journal of Personality and Social Psychology* 66(3): 460-473.

Chalos, P., and S. Haka. 1989. Participative budgeting and managerial performance. *Decision Sciences* 20: 334-347.

Cohen, J. 1988. *Statistical Power Analysis for the Behavioral Sciences.* Hillsdale, NJ: Lawrence Erlbaum Associates.

Cook, T.D., and D.T. Campbell. 1979. *Quasi-Experimentation: Design & Analysis Issues for Field Settings.* Chicago: Rand McNally.

Dipboye, R.L. 1990. Laboratory vs. field research in industrial and organizational psychology. In *International Review of Industrial and Organizational Psychology*, Vol. 5, eds. C.L. Cooper and I.T. Robertson, 1-34. New York: John Wiley & Sons.

Earley, P.C., and A.E. Lind. 1987. Procedural justice and participation in task selection: The role of control in mediating justice judgments. *Journal of Personality and Social Psychology* 52(6): 1148-1160.

Erez, M., and I. Zidon. 1984. Effects of goal acceptance on the relationship of goal difficulty to performance. *Journal of Applied Psychology* 69: 69-78.

French, J.R., and B. Raven. 1959. The bases of social power. In *Studies in Social Power*, ed. D. Cartwright, 150-167. Ann Arbor, MI: Institute for Social Research.

Greenberg, P.S., R.H. Greenberg, and H.N. Nouri. 1994. Participative budgeting: A meta-analytic examination of methodological moderators. *Journal of Accounting Literature* 13: 117-141.

Grewal, D., J. Gotlieb, and H. Marmorstein. 1994. The moderating effects of message framing and source credibility on the price-perceived risk relationship. *Journal of Consumer Research* 21(June): 145-153.

Heller, F. 1971. *Managerial Decision-making.* London: Tavistock.

Heller, F. 1991. Participation and competence: A necessary relationship. In *International Handbook of Participation In Organizations*, Vol. II, eds. R. Russell and V. Rus. London: Oxford University Press.

Hofstede, G. 1968. *The Game of Budget Control.* London: Van Gorcum.

Holter, H. 1965. Attitudes towards employee participation in company decision-making processes: A study of non-supervisory employees in some Norwegian firms. *Human Relations* 18: 297-321.

Hunton, J.E. Forthcoming. Procedural justice and user involvement in developing accounting software: The effects of instrumental voice, choice, noninstrumental voice, and involvement expectations. *The Journal of Information Systems.*

Kanter, R.M. 1982. Dilemmas of managing participation. *Organizational Dynamics* 11(1, Summer): 5-27.

KPMG Peat Marwick. 1992. *Client Service Manual: Audit Practice,* Vol. 1. April (internal document).

Lind, E.A., R. Kanfer, and P.C. Earley. 1990. Voice, control and procedural justice: Instrumental and noninstrumental concerns in fairness judgments. *Journal of Personality and Social Psychology* 59(5, November): 952-959.

Lind, E., C. Kulik, M. Ambrose, and M. de Vera Park. 1993. Individual and corporate dispute resolution: Using procedural fairness as a decision heuristic. *Administrative Science Quarterly* 38: 224-251.

Locke, E.A., and G.P. Latham. 1990. *A Theory of Goal Setting and Performance.* Englewood Cliffs, NJ: Prentice Hall.

Locke, E.A., and D.M. Schweiger. 1979. Participation in decision-making: One more look. In *Research in Organizational Behavior*, Vol. 1, ed. B.M. Staw, 265-339. Greenwich, CT: JAI Press.

Locke, E.A., D.M. Schweiger, and G.P. Latham. 1986. Participation in decision making: When should it be used?" *Organizational Dynamics* (March): 65-79.

Merchant, K.A. 1981. The design of the corporate budgeting system: Influences on managerial behavior and performance. *The Accounting Review* (October): 813-829.

Miller, K.I., and P.R. Monge. 1986. Participation, satisfaction, and productivity: A meta-analytic review. *Academy of Management Journal* 29(4): 727-753.

Murray, D. 1990. The performance effects of participative budgeting: An integration of intervening and moderating variables. *Behavioral Research In Accounting* 2: 104-123.

Pasewark, W.R., and R.B. Welker. 1990. A Vroom-Yetton evaluation of subordinate participation in budgetary decision making. *The Journal of Management Accounting Research* (Fall): 113-126.

Schweiger, D.M., and C.R. Leana. 1986. Participation in decision making. In *Generalizing From Laboratory to Field Settings: Research Findings from Industrial-Organizational Psychology, Organizational Behavior and Human Resource Management*, ed. E. Locke, 147-166. Lexington, MA: Lexington Books.

Scully, J.A., S.A. Kirkpatrick, and E.A. Locke. 1995. Locus of knowledge as a determinant of the effects of participation on performance, affect, and perceptions. *Organizational Behavior and Human Decision Processes* 61(3, March): 276-288.

Shields, M.D., and S.M. Young. 1993. Antecedents and consequences of participative budgeting: Evidence on the effects of asymmetrical information. *The Journal of Management Accounting Research* (Fall): 265-280.

Tjosvold, D., W.C. Wedley, and R.H.G. Field. 1986. Constructive controversy, the Vroom-Yetton model, and managerial decision-making. *Journal of Occupational Behavior* (July): 125-138.

Trafimow, D., and J. Sniezek. 1994. Perceived expertise and its effect on confidence. *Organizational Behavior and Human Decision Processes* 57: 290-302.

Vroom, V.H., and A.G. Jago. 1988. *The New Leadership: Managing Participation in Organizations.* Englewood Cliffs, NJ: Prentice-Hall.

Wagner, J.A., III, and R.Z. Gooding. 1987. Shared influence and organizational behavior: A meta-analysis of situational variables expected to moderate participation-outcome relationships. *Academy of Management Journal* (March): 524-541.

A COMPREHENSIVE ANALYSIS OF THE ADOPTION OF SFAS 96: ACCOUNTING FOR INCOME TAXES

Cynthia Firey Eakin

ABSTRACT

This study provides evidence regarding the incentives that may have motivated the early adoption, the timing of early adoption, and the method of adoption of SFAS 96. The incentives examined in prior early adoption literature suggest that early adoption of mandatory accounting standards is undertaken primarily for opportunistic reasons. This study provides evidence about efficient contracting incentives. Firms that adopted SFAS 96 in the first three years and reported favorable financial statement effects had fewer investment opportunities than firms that postponed adoption until after the first three years. This suggests SFAS 96 may have been adopted earlier than required because it was efficient to do so. Opportunistic incentives also are associated with SFAS 96 adoption. Adopting firms that reported favorable effects from SFAS 96 tended to be smaller and more highly leveraged, and to have lower earnings growth than similar firms that did not adopt within three years. In addition, firms that adopted in the first year possible had lower earnings growth than firms that adopted in the second and third years. When the effects of adoption were unfavorable, adopt-

Advances in Accounting, Volume 14, pages 107-133.

ing firms tended to be larger and less highly leveraged than postponing firms. Opportunistic incentives may have motivated the choice between the retroactive and prospective methods of adoption. Firms that used the method of adoption that minimized earnings tended to be larger and to have earnings that were either extremely high or extremely low relative to firms that maximized earnings. Overall, this study suggests that although contracting efficiency may have played a role in SFAS 96 adoption, the traditional opportunistic incentives also continue to be associated with early adoption.

SYNOPSIS AND INTRODUCTION

This study examines firms that adopted Statement of Financial Accounting Standards No. 96, "Accounting for Income Taxes" (SFAS 96), to provide evidence regarding the incentives that may have motivated the early adoption, the timing of early adoption, and the method of adoption of SFAS 96. SFAS 96 represents an extreme example of the Financial Accounting Standards Board's (FASB) current multiyear adoption policy. The FASB intended to allow a two-year adoption period, but the complex and controversial nature of the statement caused several postponements of the mandatory adoption date. In addition to the extended adoption period, firms were allowed to choose between the prospective and retroactive methods of disclosing the financial statement effects of adoption. Because the effects of adoption were expected to be large, and to occur primarily in the year of adoption, SFAS 96 adoption offered many firms a one-time opportunity to manage the financial reporting process, with little residual effect on future years' financial reports.[1]

Auditors promoted full use of this opportunity by encouraging managers to "determine which year of adoption and application is the most advantageous" (Coopers and Lybrand 1988, 19), and to consider such factors as reporting "good" news, and deemphasizing "bad" news (Price Waterhouse 1988, 120). Managers also were advised to consider the effects of SFAS 96 on "working capital and equity, and ratios and debt covenants" (Price Waterhouse 1988, 120), and on the "desire to enhance comparability between the company's current and previous years results" (Coopers and Lybrand 1988, 19).

The incentives examined in prior early adoption literature (Ayres 1986; Trombley 1989; Scott 1991; Sami and Welsh 1992; Langer and Lev 1993) reflect many of the factors emphasized by auditors and suggest that early adoption of mandatory accounting standards is undertaken primarily for opportunistic reasons. Recent evidence (Skinner 1993) suggests that accounting choice may also be associated with contracting efficiency (Holthausen 1990; Watts and Zimmerman 1990). To date there is little, if any, evidence regarding the role of contracting efficiency in early adoption, and as tests of opportunistic behavior, prior studies provide limited evidence regarding incentives that may motivate managers to use early adoption to decrease earnings.

This study contributes to the early adoption literature in several ways. First, this study provides evidence about the role of efficient contracting in the early adoption decision. Firms that adopted the standard in the first three years and reported favorable financial statement effects had fewer investment opportunities than firms that postponed adoption until after the first three years. This suggests SFAS 96 may have been adopted earlier than required because it was efficient to do so.

Second, this study provides evidence about the relationship between opportunistic incentives and early adoption. Firms that adopted in the first three years and reported retained earnings increases tended to be smaller, more highly leveraged, and to have lower earnings growth than similar firms that did not adopt within three years. More importantly, these incentives have explanatory power even in the presence of controls for efficient contracting. Opportunistic incentives also are associated with the choice between prospective and retroactive methods of SFAS 96 adoption. Firms that used the method of adoption that minimized earnings tended to be larger and to have earnings that were either extremely high or extremely low relative to firms that maximized earnings.

Finally, this study provides evidence on incentives that may motivate early adoption when adoption results in a retained earnings decrease. Adopters that reported decreases to retained earnings tended to be larger and less highly leveraged than similar firms that postponed adoption. Neither earnings growth nor investment opportunities were associated with SFAS 96 adoption when adoption resulted in a decrease to retained earnings.

The following sections of this paper present an overview of SFAS 96, review prior early adoption studies, and develop the hypotheses examined. Additional sections describe the sample selection process and the statistical methods used. The final sections present the relevant descriptive statistics, summarize the empirical results, and present concluding remarks.

OVERVIEW OF SFAS 96

The FASB released SFAS 96 in December of 1987. Initially, adoption of the Statement was required in the first quarter of fiscal years beginning after December 15, 1988. The FASB encouraged earlier adoption, and calendar-year-end firms were permitted to apply the Statement's provisions as early as 1987. However, concerns about the degree of complexity involved in implementing SFAS 96 as well as concerns about the restrictions placed on recognition of deferred tax assets resulted in three postponements of the mandatory adoption date. In December 1991, the FASB replaced SFAS 96 with SFAS 109. The multiple postponements and the replacement resulted in a six-year adoption window.

Deferred taxes under SFAS 96 were measured using the tax laws and rates enacted for the future periods when deferred amounts would become taxable or deductible. Thus, the reduction of corporate tax rates from 46 percent to 34 percent enacted in the Tax Reform Act of 1986 (TRA 86) added an interesting twist to SFAS 96 adoption. For the majority of firms with existing deferred tax credits, the largest effect from SFAS 96 adoption was expected to be the reduction of previously recorded deferred tax credits to reflect the lower tax rates enacted in TRA 86 (Knutson 1988).

Whether the reduction in deferred tax credits increased net income in the adoption year depended on whether the adopting firm chose prospective or retroactive adoption. As a simple example, consider a firm that had one temporary difference equal to $100 that originated in 1985 and was expected to reverse and become taxable in 1988. Prior to SFAS 96, if the firm's marginal tax rate in 1985 was 46 percent, the firm would have recorded a deferred tax credit for 1985 of $46. This $46 deferred tax credit would have remained on the books until it reversed in 1988. If the firm adopted SFAS 96 in 1987, the $46 deferred tax credit would be reduced to $34. This is because under TRA 86, the tax rate expected to be in effect in 1988 was 34 percent.[2] If the firm used the prospective method of adoption, the $12 reduction in deferred taxes would be added to 1987 net income as a cumulative effect adjustment. However, if the firm used the retroactive method to restate prior financial results, the $12 reduction would be added to net income for 1986. In this example, retroactive adoption would not affect net income for 1987. This is because TRA 86 was enacted in 1986, and SFAS 96 required deferred tax amounts to be revised to reflect new tax rates in the year the new rates were enacted.

Firms could also report unfavorable effects from SFAS 96 adoption. Firms with previously recorded deferred tax debits may have reported decreases to retained earnings upon adoption because SFAS 96 made recognition of deferred tax assets more difficult (Martin et al. 1989). A reduction in existing deferred tax debits would result in a decrease to retained earnings. Also, firms with prior period business combinations were required to establish deferred tax liabilities for any differences in book and tax bases of the acquired assets and liabilities, which also would decrease retained earnings.[3]

PRIOR LITERATURE

Prior studies examined the early adoption of SFAS 52 (Ayres 1986), SFAS 86 (Trombley 1989), and SFAS 87 (Scott 1991; Sami and Welsh 1992; Langer and Lev 1993). These studies typically used the management compensation, political costs, and contracting costs theories suggested by positive theory (Watts and Zimmerman 1986, 1990) to identify financial statement characteristics that might affect the early adoption decision. Overall, these studies suggest that when early adoption results in an earnings increase, firms that choose early adoption tend to be smaller and more highly leveraged and to have lower earnings growth than later adopters.

The evidence regarding firms that report earnings decreases from early adoption is limited. Langer and Lev (1993) found that of firms that reported decreases from SFAS 87 adoption, those with more loans outstanding tended to adopt late.[4] Also, Sweeney (1994) suggests that managers of firms facing technical violation of debt covenants tended to delay adoption of earnings-decreasing mandatory accounting changes.

Watts and Zimmerman (1990) contend that the association between accounting method choice and firm size, leverage, and earnings growth also may be explained by the link between firms' investment opportunities and their accounting policies. Skinner (1993) examined this contention and provides empirical evidence that firms' investment opportunities are correlated with their accounting choices. For depreciation and goodwill accounting choices, Skinner found that firms with fewer investment opportunities were more likely to choose income-increasing procedures. However, Skinner also found that opportunistic explanations of accounting choice were important even after controlling for the effects of investment opportunities.

Finally, Gujarathi and Hoskin (1992) examined whether managers' choice of method of adoption of SFAS 96 was motivated by earnings management incentives. They found that firms with favorable income effects tended to choose prospective adoption, and firms with unfavorable effects tended to choose retroactive adoption. They provide descriptive evidence that some firms that reported earnings increases from SFAS 96 would have had negative earnings growth if SFAS 96 had not been adopted. In addition, they found that some firms that reported earnings decreases from SFAS 96 adoption had preadoption earnings growth that was either extremely high or extremely low. They did not compare characteristics of early adopters with those of later adopters. Indeed, they suggest that this is an area for future research.

HYPOTHESIS DEVELOPMENT

Incentives Motivating SFAS 96 Adoption and the Timing of Adoption

Earnings Growth

Langer and Lev (1993) suggest that managers' desire to increase earnings appears to motivate early adoption decisions. This finding is typically explained in terms of management compensation incentives. Because management compensation is often based on some measure of profitability, managers are motivated to increase earnings. Ayres (1986, 147) characterizes management as "striving to attain a level of earnings which is some increasing function of prior years earnings." Trombley (1989) points out that, even in the absence of formal employment agreements, managers are rewarded for high levels of reported earnings and can be expected to be concerned with possible termination resulting from extremely poor reported performance.

Healy (1985) suggests that managers can use income-increasing procedures to increase compensation only when the firm's earnings are within a specified target range. If earnings are below or above the range, increases in income will not produce increases in compensation. This suggests that if a manager is faced with reporting an earnings decrease, the manager would prefer to report the decrease in a period when earnings are either above or below the specified target range so that the decrease will not effect compensation. Based on the above discussion, earnings growth is expected to affect SFAS 96 adoption as follows:

Hypothesis 1. When SFAS 96 adoption results in an increase to net income, firms with lower levels of earnings growth are more likely to adopt the standard, and to adopt in the first year possible, but when SFAS 96 adoption results in a decrease to net income, firms with extreme levels of earnings growth are more likely to adopt the standard, and to adopt in the first year possible.

Firm Size

The size hypothesis (Watts and Zimmerman 1986, 235) describes a relationship between political visibility, for which firm size is a proxy, and the likelihood of adopting accounting procedures that affect reported earnings. Specifically, managers of smaller firms are less likely to be concerned with the costs associated with the increased political visibility that may result from reporting high profit levels and are more likely to choose accounting methods that increase earnings. Managers of larger, more visible firms are more likely to be concerned with the costs associated with increased political visibility. To avoid additional political costs, these managers are more likely to postpone opportunities to increase income.

Langer and Lev (1993) suggest that firm size affects early adoption in a different way. They contend that larger firms have better accounting systems and are able to adopt complex accounting standards earlier than smaller firms. Their evidence on SFAS 87 adoption is consistent with this prediction. However, the transition provisions of SFAS 87 allowed smaller firms to have a longer transition period than larger firms. This may explain, in part, why early adopters of SFAS 87 were larger than later adopters. Also, with respect to SFAS 96, it is possible that larger firms might have more complex income tax accounting provisions and, therefore, find early adoption more difficult than smaller, less complex firms. Consistent with the political costs hypothesis, firm size is expected to affect early adoption as follows:

Hypothesis 2. When SFAS 96 adoption results in an increase to net income, smaller firms are more likely to adopt the standard, and to adopt it in the first year possible, but when SFAS 96 adoption results in a decrease to net income, larger firms are more likely to adopt the standard, and to adopt it in the first year possible.

Leverage

The debt/equity hypothesis (Watts and Zimmerman 1986, 216) suggests that managers of firms that have higher leverage ratios are closer to violating the accounting based constraints found in debt covenants, and are more likely to choose accounting alternatives that increase retained earnings and decrease the leverage ratio. If adoption decreases retained earnings, Langer and Lev (1993) suggest that firms that are closer to violation of debt covenants will postpone adoption to allow more time to renegotiate debt covenants. Also, Sweeney's (1994) results suggest that firms facing technical default of debt covenants are more likely to delay adoption of income-decreasing mandatory accounting methods such as SFAS 96. The third hypothesis is:

Hypothesis 3. When SFAS 96 adoption results in an increase to retained earnings, firms that have higher leverage are more likely to adopt the standard, and to adopt it in the first year possible, but when SFAS 96 adoption results in an decrease to retained earnings, firms that have higher leverage are less likely to adopt the standard, and less likely to adopt it in the first year possible.

Investment Opportunities

The hypotheses related to earnings growth, firm size, and debt contracting costs focus on managerial opportunism. An alternative explanation is that managers choose accounting methods from predetermined "accepted sets" of methods that minimize agency costs and maximize firm value. This is the efficient contracting hypothesis (Holthausen 1990; Watts and Zimmerman 1990). In determining which accounting methods will be included in the accepted set, firms face a dilemma. On the one hand, if firms do not restrict managers' choices of accounting methods, managers might choose less efficient methods that maximize their own wealth at the expense of other stakeholders. On the other hand, managers are likely to have the best information about which accounting methods maximize the value of the firm (Skinner 1993). If the restrictions placed on accounting choices are too limiting, then the firm cannot benefit from information possessed by managers.

Skinner (1993) contends that the relative costs and benefits of restricting managerial choice vary across firms as a function of their investment opportunities. From this perspective, the market value of the firm can be characterized as a combination of the present value of assets in place and the present value of future investment opportunities (Myers 1977). This characterization is important to accounting method choice because the ultimate value of a firm's investment opportunities depends on managers' future discretionary investments. However, managers' investment choices are difficult to monitor because the set of future investment opportunities is difficult to observe. Thus, managers of firms that have more investment opportunities have more opportunity to act opportunistically. This, in turn, suggests that these managers are more likely to have restrictions placed on their ability to choose income-increasing accounting methods. In the context of SFAS 96 adoption, if firms with more investment opportunities are more likely to be precluded from using income-increasing accounting methods, it is also likely that they would be precluded from opportunistically timing the income increases associated with SFAS 96 adoption.

Investment opportunities may also affect accounting policy indirectly through the contracting process. Skinner (1993) provides evidence that firms with more assets in place are more likely to base managers' compensation on accounting earnings, presumably because accounting earnings are better performance measures in these firms. If firms with more assets in place and fewer investment opportunities are more likely to base compensation on earnings, then these firms have additional incentives to increase earnings via SFAS 96 adoption. Likewise, when adoption decreases earnings, these firms have incentives to postpone adoption as as way to postpone decreases to compensation. Based on the above discussion, investment opportunities are expected to have the following effects on SFAS 96 adoption:

Hypothesis 4.   When SFAS 96 adoption results in an increase to net income, firms with fewer investment opportunities are more likely to adopt the standard, and to adopt it in the first year possible, but when SFAS 96 adoption results in a decrease to net income, firms with fewer investment opportunities are less likely to adopt the standard, and less likely to adopt it in the first year possible.

Incentives for Choosing the Method of Adoption

Firm Size

The choice between the prospective or retroactive methods of adoption offers managers some interesting ways to manage the reporting process. For example, managers of large, highly leveraged firms for which adoption results in an increase to retained earnings have incentives to decrease leverage through adoption of SFAS 96. However, for these managers, the increase to earnings resulting from prospective adoption may not be appealing from the standpoint of political visibility. Managers of such firms have incentives to adopt SFAS 96 retroactively as a way to decrease the leverage ratio, yet avoid reporting the associated increase to net income.

In some instances, prospective adoption results in an earnings decrease. Consider the case in which the cumulative effect of adoption is negative, but the effect on income before extraordinary items (IBE) in the adoption year is positive. If the cumulative effect is larger than the IBE effect, prospective adoption results in lower net income because the negative cumulative effect is included in the adoption-year net income. Retroactive adoption results in higher net income because the negative cumulative effect is applied to prior years' results. Large firms facing this combination of effects have incentives to use the prospective method to minimize net income. This suggests the following hypothesis:

Hypothesis 5.   Larger firms are more likely to use the method of adoption that minimizes net income.

Earnings Growth

Healy's (1985) bonus maximization hypothesis can be extended to explain the choice of method of adoption. If firms are more likely to increase earnings when earnings are within "normal" levels, then they also should be more likely to use the method of adoption that maximizes earnings when preadoption earnings are normal, and to use the method that minimizes earnings when preadoption earnings are either extremely high or extremely low. This suggests the following hypothesis:

Hypothesis 6.   Firms with extreme earnings growth are more likely to use the method of adoption that minimizes net income.

METHODOLOGY

Definition of Variables

The data required to measure the independent variables were collected from the Compustat database. Table 1 summarizes the dependent and independent variables used in this study. Discussion of the choices regarding the independent variables is presented below.

ROA (Hypothesis 1).   This variable is measured as the percentage change in return on assets (net income/total ending assets) from the prior year. As such, ROA measures earnings growth over a short horizon. Although Skinner (1993) uses a 10-year average return on assets, he points out that it may not be a good proxy for short periods of poor performance that could cause managers to change accounting procedures. This is a particularly important factor in this study because, in general SFAS 96 adoption allows managers a one-time opportunity to manage net income. It is not unreasonable to suggest that managers might use this one-time opportunity to improve results during a short period of poor performance.

Table 1. Definition of Dependent and Independent Variables

Variable	*Description*
Adopters versus Postponers:	*Models 1, 2, 3, and 4.*
Dependent Variable:	Coded 1 if the firm adopted SFAS 96, 0 otherwise.
Independent Variables:	Independent variables are measured in the year in which the adopting member of the matched pair adopted SFAS 96. For adopting firms, variables are measured without SFAS 96 adoption effects.
ROA	Models 1 and 2. The percentage change in return on assets (net income / total assets) from the prior year.
EXT	Models 3 and 4. The absolute value of ROA as defined above.
SIZE	The natural log of total ending assets.
LEV	The ratio of debt to equity, where debt does not include deferred taxes.
IOS	The ratio of total assets to the sum of the ending market value of common equity plus the book value of debt.
Early vs. Late Adopters:	*Models 5 and 7.*
Dependent variable:	Coded 1 if the firm adopted SFAS 96 in the first year possible, 0 otherwise.
Independent variables:	Measured in the year of adoption and without SFAS 96 adoption effects for early adopters, and in the first year adoption was possible for later adopters.
ROA	Model 5 only. As above.
EXT	Model 7 only. As above.
SIZE	As above.
LEV	As above.
IOS	As above.
Early vs. Late Adopters, Industry Adjusted:[a]	*Models 6 and 8.*
Dependent variable:	Coded 1 if the firm adopted SFAS 96 in the first year possible, 0 otherwise.
Independent variables:	Measured in the year of adoption and without SFAS 96 adoption effects for early adopters, and in the first year adoption was possible for later adopters.
ROA	Model 6 only. The percentage difference between firm specific ROA and industry average ROA.
EXT	Model 8 only. The natural log of the absolute value of industry-adjusted ROA.
SIZE	The percentage difference between firm-specific SIZE and industry-average SIZE.

(continued)

Table 1.   (Continued)

Variable	Description
LEV	The percentage difference between firm-specific LEV and industry-average LEV.
IOS	The percentage difference between firm-specific IOS and industry-average IOS.
Income Minimizers versus Income Maximizers:	*Model 9.*
Dependent variable:	Coded 1 if the firm used the method of adoption that minimized net income, 0 otherwise.
Independent variables:	Measured in the year of adoption and without SFAS 96 adoption effects.
EXT	The absolute value of the percentage change in return on assets (net income/total assets) from the prior year.
SIZE	The natural log of total ending assets.

Note: [a]Industry is based on two-digit SIC codes.

EXT (Hypotheses 1 and 6).   This variable is measured as the absolute value of ROA as described above. As such, larger values of this variable represent either extremely high or extremely low earnings growth. Smaller values represent "normal" earnings growth.

SIZE (Hypotheses 2 and 5).   Firm size is measured as total ending assets.

LEV (Hypothesis 3).   This variable is defined as the ratio of the book value of long-term debt to the book value of common equity. This is the most commonly used proxy for closeness to debt covenants. Duke and Hunt (1990) suggest that, across a variety of measures, the leverage ratio is positively correlated with the existence and tightness of retained earnings restrictions, working capital restrictions, and net tangible asset restrictions.

IOS (Hypothesis 4).   Following Smith and Watts (1992), this variable is defined as the ratio of total ending assets to the sum of ending market value of common equity plus the book value of total debt, where total debt is defined as total assets minus total stockholders equity. This form of investment opportunities proxy is likely to be a reasonable measure of growth opportunities across a variety of industries.

Identification of SFAS 96 Adopters

Early adopters of SFAS 96 were identified by searching the 1989 Compustat files for firms that made income tax accounting changes in 1987, 1988, or 1989. The financial statements of these firms were examined to ensure that the change was adoption of SFAS 96 and to determine the income effects of adoption.[5] The

118 CYNTHIA FIREY EAKIN

search identified 610 adopting firms representing 61 two-digit and 238 four-digit Standard Industrial Classification (SIC) codes. A large number (286) of these firms were in the manufacturing industries (SIC codes 2000 to 4000). Eighty firms were in the finance and insurance industries (SIC codes 6000 to 7000), and 70 firms were in the service industries (SIC codes 7000 to 9000). Sixty firms were in the wholesale and retail industries (SIC codes 5000 to 6000). The remaining 40 firms were divided among the agriculture, mining, and construction industries (SIC codes 100 to 2000).

Of the 610 adopting firms, 386 reported increases to retained earnings as a result of adoption and 98 reported decreases to retained earnings. The Compustat data base contained the required financial statement information for 339 of the 386 adopting firms that reported increases to retained earnings, and for 82 of the 98 firms that reported decreases.[6] For 83 firms, the only effect of adoption was to change the way net operating loss carryovers (NOLs) were reported. Prior to SFAS 96, NOLs were reported as extraordinary gains. Under SFAS 96, NOLs were used to reduce income tax expense. Thus, for these 83 firms, SFAS 96 adoption did not affect retained earnings or net income but did increase income before extraordinary items (IBE). Because of the absence of retained earnings effects, these firms are excluded from the final sample. In addition, 43 firms reported adoption of SFAS 96 but did not disclose the effects of adoption on the financial statements. These firms are also excluded from the final sample.

Identification of Firms Postponing SFAS 96 Adoption

To examine incentives that may have motivated adoption of SFAS 96 in the first three years of the adoption period, the 339 firms that reported increases and the 82 firms that reported decreases to retained earnings were pair-matched with control samples that did not adopt in 1987, 1988, or 1989. To control for general economic effects, firms were matched on year. To control for the direction of SFAS 96 adoption effects (increase or decrease to retained earnings), firms were matched on the proportion of deferred taxes to total assets. Firms adopting in 1987 were also matched on fiscal year end.[7] This sample selection criteria resulted in a control sample of 339 firms that probably would have reported increases to retained earnings had they adopted SFAS 96, and 82 firms that probably would have reported decreases. To control for possible industry effects, a second control sample matched firms on year, direction of adoption effects, and two-digit SIC codes. The second sample consists of 319 control firms that probably would have reported increases to retained earnings had SFAS 96 been adopted, and 82 firms that probably would have reported decreases.

The purpose of matching on the level of deferred taxes as a proportion of total assets (DTA) is to choose control firms that probably would report retained earnings effects similar to the pair-matched sample firm. Selecting a control sample with appropriately high levels of DTA increases the likelihood that the control

firms would have reported an increase to retained earnings had the firm adopted
SFAS 96. Likewise, selecting a control sample with low DTA increases the likelihood that the control firms would have reported a decrease to retained earnings
had SFAS 96 been adopted. This assumption is supported by noting that adopting
firms that reported increases to retained earnings had preadoption DTA ratios that
were, on average, 35 percent *above* the industry average DTA ratios.[8] Adopting
firms that reported decreases to retained earnings had preadoption DTA ratios that
were 66.3 percent *below* the industry average. The difference between the two
means is significant ($p < .001$).[9]

Identification of Early and Late Adopters

To examine the choice of year of SFAS 96 adoption, adopting firms are categorized as either early adopters or late adopters. Early adopters are those firms that
adopted in the first year possible. Thus, early adopters are defined as all calendar
year-end firms that adopted in 1987 and all fiscal year-end firms that adopted in
1988. Late adopters are defined as all calendar year-end firms that adopted in
1988, and all fiscal year-end 1989 adopters. All adopting firms with available
financial statement data for the first year that adoption was possible are included in
the sample. Of the firms that reported increases to retained earnings from SFAS 96
adoption, 183 adopted early and 154 adopted late. Of firms that reported decreases
to retained earnings, 30 adopted early and 51 adopted late.

Identification of Income-Minimizing Firms and Income-Maximizing Firms

To examine managers' use of the prospective and retroactive adoption methods,
adopting firms are categorized as either *income minimizers* or *income maximizers*
based upon the effect on income of the chosen method of SFAS 96 adoption.
Income maximizers are firms that reported increases to retained earnings as a
result of adoption and chose to include the adoption effect in net income via prospective adoption (n=345).[10] Firms that reported decreases to retained earnings
and chose to exclude the effect from net income via retroactive adoption are also
income maximizers (n=61). Income minimizers are firms that reported an increase
to retained earnings and chose retroactive adoption ($n = 41$). Prospective adopters
that reported decreases to retained earnings as a result of adoption are also classified as income minimizers ($n = 37$). Overall, 397 firms used the method of adoption to maximize income, and 74 firms used the method of adoption to minimize
income.[11]

Statistical Method

Nine multivariate logit models are used to examine the six hypotheses.[12] Models 1, 2, 3, and 4 provide evidence about the first four hypotheses by comparing

firms that adopted the standard in the first three years (adopters) with pair-matched control firms that did not adopt in the first three years (postponers).[13] Adopters in Models 1 and 2 reported increases to retained earnings. Adopters in Models 3 and 4 reported decreases to retained earnings. Control firms in Models 1 and 3 are matched on year and on direction of the retained earnings effect had SFAS 96 been adopted. In addition to year and direction of retained earnings effects, control firms in Models 2 and 4 are also matched on industry as defined by two-digit SIC codes.

Models 5, 6, 7, and 8 examine the first four hypotheses over a shorter adoption horizon by comparing firms that adopted SFAS 96 in the first year possible (early adopters) with firms that adopted in the second and third years (late adopters). Models 5 and 6 examine firms that reported increases to retained earnings from SFAS 96 adoption, and Models 7 and 8 examine firms that reported decreases. Models 6 and 8 control for industry by adjusting all variables for industry effects as described in Table 1. Model 9 examines the fifth and sixth hypotheses by comparing firms that used the method of adoption that minimized net income with firms that used the method that maximized net income.

The performance of all models is evaluated by the likelihood ratio index (LRI) as a measure of "goodness of fit" (Judge et al. 1988, 794). The likelihood ratio test (chi-square) is employed as a measure of the significance of the model (Judge et al. 1988, 794). The chi-square statistic measures the significance of the parameter estimates for the independent variables.

EMPIRICAL RESULTS

Descriptive Statistics

Of the 484 adopters that reported retained earnings effects from SFAS 96 adoption, 372 reported increases to net income, 42 reported decreases to net income, and 70 reported no effects to net income. Table 2 summarizes the income effects of adoption as a proportion of adoption year net income, and the retained earnings effect as a proportion of total assets. The average income effect of adoption ranged from −42.7 percent for early adopters that reported income decreases to 63 percent for early adopters that reported increases. Although the income effects for later adopters were smaller, the differences were not significant. The retained earnings effects ranged from −1.4 percent for early adopters reporting decreases to 1.5 percent for late adopters reporting increases. Again the difference between early and late adopters was not significant.

Univariate results of all eight models are presented in Table 3. The results for ROA are as predicted in Models 1, 5, and 6. This suggests that when SFAS 96 results in a retained earnings increase, firms with lower earnings growth are more likely to adopt the standard (Model 1) and to adopt it in the first year possible

Table 2. Financial Statement Effects of SFAS 96 Adoption
Descriptive Statistics by Timing of Adoption

	NIEFF/NI		
	Early Adopters	Late Adopters	t (One-tailed p-value)
Firms reporting increases to Net Income	n = 192	n = 180	
Mean	.630	.476	.630
(Median)	(.166)	(.166)	(.260)
S.D.	3.111	1.258	
Firms reporting decreases to Net Income	n = 17	n = 25	
Mean	−.427	−.323	.480
(Median)	(−.131)	(−.112)	(.320)
S.D.	.661	.734	

	REEF/TA		
	Early Adopters	Late Adopters	t (One-tailed p-value)
Firms reporting increases to Retained Earnings	n = 201	n = 185	
Mean	.014	.016	−1.12
(Median)	(.010)	(.009)	(.130)
S.D.	.013	.023	
Firms reporting decreases to Retained Earnings	n = 62	n = 36	
Mean	−.014	−.016	.368
(Median)	(−.009)	(−.007)	(.350)
S.D.	.024	.021	

Where:

NIEFF/NI = The net income effect of SFAS 96 adoption deflated by net income for the year of adoption.

REEF/TA = The retained earnings effect of SFAS 96 adoption deflated by total assets for the year of adoption.

EARLY ADOPTERS = Calendar-year-end 1987 adopters and fiscal year-end 1988 adopters.

LATE ADOPTERS = Calendar-year-end 1988 adopters and all 1989 adopters.

Table 3. Univariate Analysis of Independent Variables

		Models							
		Adopters vs. Postponers				Early vs. Late Adopters			
		1	*2*	*3*	*4*	*5*	*6*	*7*	*8*
Variable	*Firms*	*Mean (S.D.)*	*Mean (S.D.)*	*Mean (S.D.)*	*Mean (S.D.)*	*Mean (S.D.)*	*Mean (S.D.)*	*Mean (S.D.)*	*Mean (S.D.)*
ROA	Sample	-.210 (6.338)	-.627 (6.431)	NA	NA	-1.004 (6.580)	-1.653 (5.757)	NA	NA
	Control	1.655 (7.333)	.028 (4.211)			.434 (3.077)	-.444 (3.566)		
	p-value	.0059	.5953			.0215	.0277		
EXT	Sample			1.484 (2.280)	1.484 (2.280)			1.292 (1.731)	1.620 (1.264)
	Control	NA	NA	1.527 (2.104)	2.263 (5.190)	NA	NA	2.221 (3.746)	2.388 (2.660)
	p-value			.9023	.8499			.2384	.1566
SIZE ($MIL)	Sample	1511 (7120)	1595 (7347)	5081 (12421)	5081 (12421)	869.3 (3392)	.162 (.244)	4162 (11982)	.237 (2.261)
	Control	3535 (11253)	1182 (5349)	1359 (4715)	3364 (10550)	2105 (9114)	.243 (7.427)	5009 (11417)	.078 (1.431)
	p-value	.0001	.0002	.0004	.0005	.1452	.8988	.4496	.6959

LEV	Sample	1.205	.814	1.053	1.053	1.274	.552	.974	.813
		(3.405)	(3.060)	(1.255)	(1.255)	(3.618)	(4.314)	(1.290)	(3.193)
	Control	.988	.731	1.457	1.422	.793	-.027	.870	-.175
		(3.104)	(2.567)	(4.091)	(2.856)	(1.350)	(1.051)	(1.075)	(.791)
	p-value	.4351	.1614	.4008	.8739	.1639	.1608	.6919	.0797
IOS	Sample	.854	.843	.858	.858	.868	.056	.833	-.038
		(.274)	(.269)	(.248)	(.248)	(.273)	(.357)	(.217)	(.264)
	Control	.786	.810	.809	.934	.884	.041	.940	.082
		(.263)	(.256)	(.292)	(.355)	(.288)	(.311)	(.292)	(.321)
	p-value	.0012	.2181	.2381	.1459	.5962	.6868	.0940	.0947

Where: Adopters in Models 1, 2, 5, and 6 reported increases to retained earnings from SFAS 96 adoption.
Adopters in Models 3, 4, 7, and 8 reported decreases to retained earnings from SFAS 96 adoption.
Models 1 and 3: Adopters versus postponers matched on calendar year.
Models 2 and 4: Adopters versus postponers matched on calendar year and on two-digit SIC codes.
Independent variables are defined in Table 1.
Sample Firms = Adopters for Models 1, 2, 3, and 4, and early adopters for Models 5, 6, 7, and 8.
Control Firms = Postponers for Models 1, 2, 3, and 4, and late adopters for Models 5, 6, 7, and 8.
The p-value for Models 1, 2, 3, and 4 is based on a univariate logit analysis of the differenced variables as described in Bowen et al. (1981).
The p-value for Models 5, 6, 7, and 8 is based on a univariate logit analysis.

(Models 5 and 6). The coefficient of SIZE is significant and in the predicted direction in Models 1, 2, 3 and 4. This suggests that when adoption increased retained earnings, smaller firms tended to adopt the standard (Models 1 and 2). Alternatively, when adoption decreased retained earnings, larger firms tended to adopt (Models 3 and 4). The only other variable that is significant is IOS in Model 1. This suggests that when adoption increased retained earnings, firms with fewer investment opportunities tended to adopt the standard.

Models 1-4:   Incentives Motivating Adoption of SFAS 96
Over a Longer Adoption Horizon

The univariate significance, or lack thereof, does not account for the interrelationships among the independent variables. The multivariate results for the first four models are summarized in Table 4. Model 1 suggests that for firms that reported retained earnings increases from SFAS 96, ROA, SIZE, LEV, and IOS are all significantly associated with the adoption decision. Adopters tended to be smaller and more highly leveraged, and tended to have lower earnings growth and fewer investment opportunities. The significance of IOS is particularly interesting because it suggests that firms may have adopted SFAS 96 because it was efficient to do so. However, it is important to note that the opportunistic variables represented by ROA, SIZE, and LEV continue to have explanatory power, even in the presence of controls for efficient contracting incentives (IOS).

When control firms are matched on industry (Model 2), only firm size and leverage are significant. When considered together, the results of Models 1 and 2 suggest ROA and IOS are significantly associated with early adoption across but not within industries. The lack of significance of ROA in Model 2 suggests that the "lure" of reporting improved earnings growth may not be as powerful as suggested by prior studies. The lack of significance of IOS in Model 2 supports Skinner's (1993) contention that investment opportunities vary more across industries than within industries and that the investment opportunity set may explain why firms within the same industry tend to use similar accounting methods.

Models 3 and 4 examine firms that reported decreases from SFAS 96. The only variable that is significant in both models is SIZE. When SFAS 96 adoption decreased retained earnings, larger firms tended to adopt in the first three years. LEV is also significant and in the predicted direction in Model 3. This suggests that across industries, firms with higher leverage tended to postpone adoption of SFAS 96 when adoption would have resulted in a decrease to retained earnings. EXT is not significantly associated with adoption in either model. One explanation for this result is that the majority of firms in this sample used the retroactive method of adoption to remove the negative adoption effects from income. Of the 82 firms in this model, only 32 reported earnings decreases from SFAS 96. Of the remaining 50 firms, 15 reported earnings increases and 35 reported no earnings effects. Thus, a finding of no significant difference in earnings growth is reason-

Table 4. Results of Logit Models: Adopters versus Postponers

Variable	Firms Reporting Increases to Retained Earnings		Firms Reporting Decreases to Retained Earnings	
	Model 1 (n = 339 pairs) Coefficient (p-value) (Predicted Sign)	Model 2 (n = 319 pairs) (Industry-Matched) Coefficient (p-value) (Predicted Sign)	Model 3 (n = 82 pairs) Coefficient (p-value) (Predicted Sign)	Model 4 (n = 82 pairs) (Industry-Matched) Coefficient (p-value) (Predicted Sign)
ROA	-.0433 (.0113) (-)	.0039 (.8527) (-)	NA	NA
EXT	NA	NA	.0467 (.5817) (+)	-.0464 (.3435) (+)
SIZE	-.3094 (.0001) (-)	-.2208 (.0001) (-)	.4121 (.0002) (+)	.4513 (.0004) (+)
LEV	.0703 (.0187) (+)	.1843 (.0387) (+)	-.1830 (.0341) (-)	-.0944 (.3615) (-)
IOS	.8380 (.0136) (+)	.1527 (.6625) (+)	.1040 (.8893) (-)	-.8886 (.1450) (-)
Chi-square	77.886	20.312	22.462	20.914
(p-value)	(.0001)	(.0004)	(.0002)	(.0003)
LRI	.1657	.0477	.1975	.1839

Notes: Models 1 and 3: Adopters versus postponers matched on calendar year.
Models 2 and 4: Adopters versus postponers matched on calendar year and on two-digit SIC codes.

All Models:
Dependent variables: Coded 1 if firm adopted SFAS 96 within the first three years, 0 otherwise.
Independent variables: Defined in Table 1.

LRI: The likelihood ratio index as defined in Judge et al. (1988, 794).

able. Finally, IOS is not significant in either model. This suggests that when SFAS 96 decreased retained earnings, efficient contracting may not have been a strong adoption incentive.

Overall, the results of all four models with respect to SIZE are consistent with the political costs hypothesis. However, it is possible that there are other explanations for this result. Prior research (Brown and Feroz 1992) provides evidence that the FASB may be influenced more by larger firms than by smaller firms. In Models 1 and 2, it is possible that larger firms had more influence on the FASB's decision-making process, and may have been better able to assess the likelihood that SFAS 96 would undergo significant revisions before implementation was required.

An alternative explanation for the results of SIZE in Models 3 and 4 relates to the accounting for purchase-type acquisitions under SFAS 96. For acquisitions made prior to SFAS 96 adoption, the transition to SFAS 96 may have been troublesome and may have resulted in unfavorable adoption effects. However, for acquisitions entered into in the adoption year and in subsequent years, the method of recording acquisitions under SFAS 96 was less complex than the prior method.[14] To the extent that larger firms were more likely to make purchase-type acquisitions both before and after SFAS 96 adoption, they may have adopted early as a way to minimize the bookkeeping costs of future acquisitions, even though adoption resulted in decreased retained earnings.

Models 5-8:   Incentives Motivating SFAS 96 Adoption Over a Shorter Adoption Horizon

The results of the multivariate logit analysis for Models 5, 6, 7, and 8 are presented in Table 5. Models 5 and 6 compare early and late adopters that reported increases from SFAS 96. The only variable that is statistically significant in either model is ROA. Across and within industries, firms with lower earnings growth tended to adopt in the first year possible. An analysis of year-to-year changes in earnings growth suggests that for later adopters, the mean earnings growth in the first year adoption was possible was 105 percent. Whereas, the mean earnings growth in the year of adoption was −107 percent. This is significantly lower ($p <$ .023) than earnings growth in the first year adoption was possible, and supports the conclusion that the opportunity to improve otherwise poor earnings growth may have motivated the timing of early adoption.

When considered together, the results of Models 1, 2, 5, and 6 suggest a scenario in which managers of smaller and more highly leveraged firms tended to adopt SFAS 96 within the first three years, but within that three-year period tended to adopt in a year in which earnings growth was low. By delaying adoption, late adopters also delayed recognition of the benefits associated with the incentives related to SIZE and LEV. This suggests that reporting improved earnings growth may have been a more powerful incentive than those represented by firm size or leverage.

Table 5. Results of Logit Models: Early versus Late Adopters

| | Firms Reporting Increases to Retained Earnings | | Firms Reporting Decreases to Retained Earnings | |
| | Model 5 (n = 183 Early and 154 Late Adopters) | Model 6 (n = 183 Early and 154 Late Adopters) (Industry-Adjusted) | Model 7 (n = 30 Early and 51 Late Adopters) | Model 8 (n = 30 Early and 51 Late Adopters) (Industry-Adjusted) |
Variable	Coefficient (p-value) (Predicted Sign)	Coefficient (p-value) (Predicted Sign)	Coefficient (p-value) (Predicted Sign)	Coefficient (p-value) (Predicted Sign)
Intercept	.8031 (.0885)	.1116 (.3274)	1.4069 (.1706)	−.1913 (.5926)
ROA	−.0603 (.0218) (−)	−.0599 (.0183) (−)	NA	NA
EXT	NA	NA	−.1578 (.1965) (+)	−.1950 (.1853) (+)
SIZE	−.0944 (.0997) (−)	−.0013 (.9452) (−)	−.0726 (.5197) (+)	.0665 (.6162) (+)
LEV	.1003 (.1306) (+)	.0778 (.1752) (+)	.1832 (.3740) (−)	.4476 (.0441) (−)
IOS	−.3141 (.4336) (+)	.0326, (.9223) (+)	−1.5694 (.0868) (−)	−1.6208 (.0673) (−)

(continued)

127

Table 5. (Continued)

Variable	Firms Reporting Increases to Retained Earnings		Firms Reporting Decreases to Retained Earnings	
	Model 5 (n = 183 Early and 154 Late Adopters)	Model 6 (n = 183 Early and 154 Late Adopters) (Industry-Adjusted)	Model 7 (n = 30 Early and 51 Late Adopters)	Model 8 (n = 30 Early and 51 Late Adopters) (Industry-Adjusted)
	Coefficient (p-value) (Predicted Sign)	Coefficient (p-value) (Predicted Sign)	Coefficient (p-value) (Predicted Sign)	Coefficient (p-value) (Predicted Sign)
Chi square	12.793	9.532	6.265	11.867
(p value)	(.0123)	(.0491)	(.1802)	(.0184)
LRI	.0275	.0205	.0586	.1111

Notes: All Models:

Dependent variables: Coded 1 if firm adopted in the first year possible, 0 otherwise.

Independent Variables: As defined in Table 1.

LRI: The likelihood ratio index as defined in Judge et al. (1988, 794).

Models 7 and 8 compare early and late adopters that reported decreases to retained earnings from SFAS 96 adoption. Model 7 is not significant at conventional levels ($p < .1802$) and does little to explain the timing of adoption across industries. In Model 8, the sign of the coefficient of IOS is in the predicted direction and is marginally significant ($p < .0673$). This suggests that, within industries, firms with more investment opportunities tended to adopt in the first year possible. LEV is also significant in Model 8, but the sign of the coefficient is opposite to predictions. Firms with higher leverage tended to adopt in the first year possible. One explanation for this result is that LEV is correlated with an omitted variable. Prior research (Press and Weintrop 1990) suggests that leverage may be a proxy for firms' investment opportunity sets. However, in this study, LEV has explanatory power even when controlling for the investment opportunity set. A second explanation is that these firms took advantage of an opportunity to "clean up" the balance sheet in an effort to report improved leverage in subsequent periods.

Model 9:   Method of Adoption

The results of Model 9 are summarized in Table 6. Model 9 suggests that, as predicted, SIZE and EXT are significantly associated with the choice of method of adoption. Larger firms and firms with extreme earnings growth tended to use the method of adoption that minimized net income. This result extends the results of Gujarathi and Hoskin (1992). They did not consider the effects of firm size on the method of adoption decision. Yet, when modeled as a choice between maximizing and minimizing net income, firm size is a highly significant factor ($p < .0078$). In addition, the results with respect to EXT provide statistical support for their observations regarding the relationship between extreme earnings levels and the choice of method of SFAS 96 adoption.

Although the results with respect to EXT are consistent with the general hypothesis proposed by Healy (1985), there are important differences in interpretation. In a general sense, Healy suggests that in periods when income is extremely high or extremely low, managers tend to postpone recognition of additional income. Thus, Healy suggests that income is shifted between periods to maximize bonus compensation. However, minimizing income via the method of SFAS 96 adoption does not mean that managers can shift unrecognized earnings to subsequent periods. Rather, the benefit derived from using the method of adoption to minimize income is in the year-to-year comparisons of net income. Minimizing adoption-year earnings results in lower earnings growth in the adoption year and in a lower benchmark for subsequent years' earnings. This suggests that firms with extremely high earnings growth in the adoption year that minimize adoption-year income may be concerned with reporting a smoother earnings stream. Firms with extremely low earnings growth that minimize income may be concerned with reporting improved results in periods subsequent to the adoption year. This is consistent with the "big bath" phenomenon and suggests that enhancing year-to-year

130 CYNTHIA FIREY EAKIN

Table 6. Results of Logit Model 9—Method of Adoption: Income
Maximizers ($n = 397$) versus Income Minimizers ($n = 74$)

Variable (predicted sign)	Intercept	SIZE (+)	EXT (+)
Coefficient	−2.4566	.1556	.2363
(p-value)	(.0001)	(.0078)	(.0016)
Chi-square	14.878		
(p-value)	(.0006)	LRI	.0364

Notes: Dependent variable: Coded "1" if method of adoption minimized net income, coded "0" if method of adoption maximized net income.

Independent Variables are defined in Table 1.

LRI: The likelihood ratio index as defined in Judge et al. (1988, 794).

comparability of earnings may be a more important objective than maximizing earnings.

CONCLUSION

This study has examined financial statement characteristics of firms that adopted SFAS 96 in the first three years of the extended adoption period. Characteristics of adopting firms were compared with a matched sample of firms that did not adopt within the first three years, and characteristics of first-year adopters were compared with those of second- and third-year adopters. In addition, characteristics of firms that used the method of adoption that maximized earnings were compared with characteristics of firms that used the adoption method that minimized earnings. There are three principal results of this study.

First, the results suggest that firms' investment opportunities may be directly associated with the early adoption decision for firms that reported retained earnings increases from SFAS 96 adoption. As predicted, of firms that reported retained earnings increases, those that had fewer investment opportunities tended to adopt SFAS 96 in the first three years adoption was possible. This result is consistent with Skinner's (1993) results. The results also provide limited evidence that investment opportunities are associated with the timing of early adoption for firms that reported retained earnings decreases from SFAS 96 adoption. Of firms that reported decreases, those that had more investment opportunities tended to adopt in the first year possible. The association between investment opportunities and early adoption suggests that these choices may have been made for efficiency reasons.

Second, the results suggest that opportunistic incentives may play an important role in the early adoption decision, even in the presence of controls for firms' investment opportunities. Of firms that adopted in the first three years and reported increases to retained earnings, results were as predicted. Across industries, adopters were smaller, more highly leveraged, and had lower earnings growth than similar firms that did not adopt in the first three years. In addition, first-year adopters had lower earnings growth than second- and third-year adopters. These results are consistent with the results of prior early adoption studies and suggest that the traditional opportunistic incentives are robust to inclusion of investment opportunities in the model.

For firms that reported decreases to retained earnings, the results for the opportunistic incentives were not always as predicted. Over the longer adoption horizon, larger firms and firms with lower leverage tended to adopt SFAS 96. However, over the shorter horizon, the association between opportunistic incentives and early adoption was weak. Although leverage was associated with adoption timing, the results were opposite to predictions. Of firms reporting unfavorable adoption effects, firms with higher leverage tended to adopt in the first year possible. This suggests that these firms may have used SFAS 96 adoption to "cleanse" the balance sheet as a way to report improved results in subsequent years. Results with respect to earnings growth were not significant. One caveat to these results is that the sample of adopters that reported decreases to retained earnings is relatively small and may not be representative of such adopters in general. Clearly, more research on the incentives that motivate firms to use early adoption to report unfavorable effects is warranted.

Third, the results suggest that opportunistic incentives related to firm size and earnings growth may have motivated the choice between the prospective and retroactive methods of adoption. Specifically, larger firms and firms with extreme earnings growth tended to use the method of adoption that minimized net income. In this context, this result suggests that managers were concerned with managing year-to-year comparisons of earnings growth.

Overall, this study contributes to the literature by analyzing the incentives associated with the early adoption and the method of early adoption of one of the most complex and controversial accounting standards issued by the FASB. Although examination of this standard is interesting in its own right, the results also add to a larger body of knowledge regarding early adoption and accounting method choice. As Skinner (1993) points out, there has been speculation about the effect of investment opportunities on accounting choices. This study provides evidence regarding the direct role that investment opportunities may play in early adoption and in the timing of early adoption of SFAS 96. Just as important, however, this study suggests that opportunistic incentives play an important role even when controlling for investment opportunities. As Watts and Zimmerman (1990, 146) suggest, "Accounting changes likely are due to both efficiency reasons and managerial opportunism."

ACKNOWLEDGMENT

This paper is based on the author's dissertation. I appreciate the interest and help of my committee chairman, Thomas Schaefer of the Florida State University. I also thank my committee members, James Hasselback, Gary Benesh, and Susan Pourciau; my colleagues at the University of Hawai'i (Mānoa), John Wendell, Jeff Gramlich, and Terry Gregson; and two anonymous reviewers and the associate editor.

NOTES

1. If corporate tax rates increased during the transition period, early adopters faced the risk that their financial reports would be penalized relative to those of non-adopters.
2. This analysis ignores graduated tax rates and the phase-in provisions of TRA 86.
3. Clarke (1990) and Martin et al. (1989) provide detailed numerical analyses of the application of SFAS 96.
4. Langer and Lev (1993) found that when the variable representing the number of loans was omitted from the model, firm size was significantly associated with early adoption.
5. Examination of financial statements was limited to those available in Q-data Corporation's microfiche file of annual reports.
6. Of the 63 firms with missing data, 55 were missing the data necessary to calculate ending market value of equity. The other eight firms were missing the data necessary to calculate earnings growth.
7. This is necessary because only firms with December 31 year ends were able to adopt SFAS 96 in fiscal 1987.
8. Control firms matched to experimental firms reporting decreases to retained earnings had DTA ratios at least 66.3 percent below the average industry ratio. Control firms matched to firms reporting increases had DTA ratios at least 21 percent greater than the industry average. This represents the lower bound of a 95 percent confidence interval around the mean deviation of DTA ratios from the industry average. Using the 21 percent boundary was necessary to increase the number of available matches.
9. This method of control sample selection is not without error. It is possible that some firms selected for each control sample would have reported effects different than those suggested by the DTA ratio had SFAS 96 been adopted. This increases the chance of making a Type II error. An alternative control sample selection method would be to choose only those non-adopting firms that disclosed what the effects of SFAS 96 adoption would have been had the standard been adopted. However, little is known about firms that make preadoption disclosures. It is possible that larger firms are more likely to make pre-adoption disclosures than smaller firms, and the control sample would be biased.
10. Four retroactive adopters among the firms that reported increases to retained earnings, were included as income maximizers because the positive current-year effect was greater than the negative cumulative effect.
11. Nine income maximizers and four income minimizers were dropped from the final sample because the required information was not available in the Compustat data base.
12. Stone and Rasp (1991) suggest that logit is the preferable model for accounting choice studies.
13. Models 1, 2, 3, and 4 are matched-pairs models that employ the method described in Bowen et. al (1981).
14. In a survey of controllers of firms that adopted SFAS 96, Cassidy et al. (1992) note that one reason adoption was undertaken was because of the increased ease of reporting purchase acquisitions under SFAS 96.

REFERENCES

Ayres, F.L. 1986. Characteristics of firms electing early adoption of SFAS 52. *Journal of Accounting and Economics* (8): 143-158.
Bowen, R.M., E.W. Noreen, and J.M. Lacey. 1981. Determinants of the corporate decision to capitalize interest. *Journal of Accounting and Economics* (3): 151-179.

Brown, L.D., and E.H. Feroz. 1992. Does the FASB listen to corporations? *Journal of Business Finance and Accounting* (September): 715-731.

Cassidy, J., F.R. Urbancic, J. Sylvestre, and F. Ralston. 1992. Accounting for income taxes: A study of early vs. postponed adoption decisions for controversial accounting standards. *Journal of Applied Business Research* 9(3): 52-57.

Clarke, M.W. 1990. Assessing the potential impact on earnings of the transition to SFAS No. 96. *The Ohio CPA Journal* (Summer): 18-26.

Coopers and Lybrand. 1988. *Accounting for Income Taxes: Focusing in on FASB Statement 96.* Coopers and Lybrand.

Duke, J.C., and H.G. Hunt, III. 1990. An empirical examination of debt covenant restrictions and accounting-related debt proxies. *Journal of Accounting and Economics* (January): 45-63.

Gujarathi, M.R., and R.E. Hoskin. 1992. Evidence of earnings management by the early adopters of SFAS 96. *Accounting Horizons* (December): 18-31.

Healy, P.M. 1985. The effect of bonus schemes on accounting decisions. *Journal of Accounting and Economics* (7): 85-107.

Holthausen, R.W. 1990. Accounting method choice: Opportunistic behavior, efficient contracting, and informational perspectives. *Journal of Accounting and Economics* (12): 207-218.

Judge, G.G., R.C. Hill, W.E. Griffiths, H. Lütkepohl, and T. Lee. 1988. *Introduction to the Theory and Practice of Econometrics.* New York: John Wiley and Sons.

Knutson, P.H. 1988. FAS 96—Implications for analysts. *Financial Analysts Journal* (November/December): 117-118.

Langer, R., and B. Lev. 1993. The FASB's policy of extended adoption for new standards: An examination of FAS No. 87. *The Accounting Review* (July): 515-533.

Martin, D.R., H.I. Wolk, and D. Beets. 1989. Accounting for income taxes: Illustrations and critique. *Ohio CPA Journal* (Autumn): 24-31.

Myers, S. 1977. Determinants of corporate borrowing. *Journal of Financial Economics* (4): 147-176.

Press, E.G., and J.B. Weintrop. 1990. Accounting-based constraints in public and private debt agreements. *Journal of Accounting and Economics* (12): 65-95.

Price Waterhouse. 1988. *The New Accounting for Income Taxes: Implementing FAS 96.* Price Waterhouse.

Sami, H., and M.J. Welsh. 1992. Characteristics of early and late adopters of pension accounting standard SFAS No. 87. *Contemporary Accounting Research* (Fall): 212-236.

Scott, T.W. 1991. Pension disclosures under SFAS No. 87: Theory and evidence. *Contemporary Accounting Research* (Fall): 62-81.

Skinner, D.J. 1993. The investment opportunity set and accounting procedure choice. *Journal of Accounting and Economics* (16): 407-445.

Smith, C.W., and R.L. Watts. 1992. The investment opportunity set and corporate financing, dividend, and compensation policies. *Journal of Financial Economics* (32): 263-292.

Stone, M., and J. Rasp. 1991. Tradeoffs in the choice between logit and OLS for accounting choice studies. *The Accounting Review* (January): 170-187.

Sweeney, A.P. 1994. Debt-covenant violations and managers' accounting responses. *Journal of Accounting and Economics* (17): 281-308.

Trombley, M.A. 1989. Firms electing early adoption of SFAS No. 86. *The Accounting Review* (July): 529-538.

Watts, R.L., and J.L. Zimmerman. 1986. *Positive Accounting Theory.* Englewood Cliffs, NJ: Prentice-Hall.

———. 1990. Positive Accounting Theory: A Ten Year Perspective. *The Accounting Review* (January): 131-156.

A THEORETICAL AND EXPERIMENTAL EXAMINATION OF STRATEGIC AUDITOR-CLIENT INTERACTION

Joseph Fisher, Jeffrey W. Schatzberg, and
Brian P. Shapiro

ABSTRACT

Strategic behavior between an auditor and a client can significantly increase both audit cost and achieved audit risk. This paper tests the widely cited Fellingham and Newman (1985) analytic model of strategic auditor-client interaction in a series of controlled experiments. The Fellingham and Newman model is tested in both single-period and multiperiod settings, with parameter values chosen to yield either a pure or a mixed Nash equilibrium strategy that is Pareto dominated by a strategy of mutual auditor-client cooperation. The Fellingham and Newman model is best supported by auditor behavior in both the single- and multiperiod experiments of the mixed strategy Nash equilibrium setting. Generally, the Fellingham and Newman

Advances in Accounting, Volume 14, pages 135-160.
ISBN: 0-7623-0161-9.

model fails to predict a significant proportion of observed auditor and client behavior. Much of the observed non-Nash behavior involves the socially beneficial strategy of mutual cooperation. Client and auditor behavior is also found to be sensitive to both the time horizon and the asymmetric nature of the auditor and client payoffs. Limitations of the Fellingham and Newman model and implications for future modeling of strategic auditor-client behavior in multiperiod settings are discussed.

INTRODUCTION

An efficient and effective audit requires the auditor to assess the risks that a client's unaudited financial statements are materially misstated, develop an audit plan to appropriately address those risks, and then issue an appropriate opinion as to whether the client's financial statements are fairly stated. If the auditor and client cooperate, the client designs an effective accounting and internal control system which allows the auditor to achieve a reasonably low level of audit risk at reasonable cost. However, strategic behavior between an auditor and a client can reduce auditor-client cooperation and, thereby, increase both audit cost and achieved audit risk. Fellingham and Newman (1985) developed a stylized game-theoretic model of the relationship between audit planning and risk that explicitly considers auditor-client strategic interaction in an audit environment. The Fellingham and Newman model is widely acclaimed as having significantly advanced the existing audit literature beyond the decision theoretic approach (e.g., Kinney 1975a, 1975b), which did not address the impact of one party's behavior on another party's decisions. Specifically, Fellingham and Newman analytically demonstrated with game-theoretic concepts how auditor-client strategic interaction affects both auditor and client behavior, with the predicted behavior depending on the specific values of the model parameters. For many parameter values, the Fellingham and Newman model predicts that auditors and clients will adopt a Nash equilibrium strategy, even though a cooperative strategy exists that would make both auditors and clients better off.

The competing Fellingham and Newman Nash equilibrium and cooperation strategies yield an interesting setting for an experimental investigation of the Fellingham and Newman model. Such an investigation can test the robustness of the theory, affect our degree of confidence as to the model's generalizability to the extant auditing environment (cf. Smith et al. 1987), and provide useful insights for developing alternative theoretical models. This paper contributes to the accounting literature by investigating the Fellingham and Newman model in a series of controlled experiments. It tests the robustness of the predicted Nash equilibrium derived by the Fellingham and Newman model in four principal ways. First, it examines whether auditor and client behavior are influenced by structural characteristics of the Fellingham and Newman model that are predicted to influence auditor and client behavior (e.g., various parameter values). Second, it examines whether auditor and client behavior are also influenced by structural characteristics that the Fellingham and Newman model does not address (e.g., the single-period versus multiperiod time horizon and asymmetry in the payoffs faced by auditors and clients). Third, it examines auditor and client behavior in two different settings. The Fellingham and Newman model predicts a pure Nash equilibrium in one setting and a mixed Nash equilibrium in the other.[1] Fourth, it considers how the Fellingham and Newman model reduces to a payoff matrix similar to a prisoners' dilemma game. Previous research has demonstrated that human behavior in a prisoners' dilemma game often diverges from the predicted Nash equilibrium strategy, whereby subjects engage in cooperative behavior (e.g., Rapoport and Chammah 1965; Selten and Stoecker 1986; Friedman and Rosenthal 1987; Kadane and Larkey 1982; Fisher and Schatzberg 1991). Auditor-client cooperation is worth investigating, for it can yield an effective audit at lower audit cost.

Overall, the experimental results reveal that the Fellingham and Newman Nash equilibrium predictions fail to describe a significant proportion of auditor and client behavior. Additionally, the correspondence between predicted and observed behavior is found to be sensitive to both the time horizon as well as the asymmetric nature of auditor and client payoffs. It is encouraging that much of the observed non-Nash behavior involves the socially beneficial strategy of mutual auditor-client cooperation. Mutual cooperation was evident in the single-period experiments but was most pronounced in the multiperiod experiments. However, consistent with prior empirical work in the prisoners' dilemma, the frequency of cooperation decreased over time in the multiperiod setting.

This paper is organized in four sections. The first section provides theoretical observations of the Fellingham and Newman model, reviews empirical regularities from the prisoners' dilemma literature, and develops testable hypotheses. The second and third sections describe the experimental method and results, respectively. The fourth section summarizes our conclusions, considers their implications for audit practice, and explores some opportunities for future auditing research.

THEORY DEVELOPMENT AND HYPOTHESES

In this section, we first briefly summarize the Fellingham and Newman model in terms of client and auditor decisions, costs, strategies, and similarities to a prisoners' dilemma game. We then develop hypotheses about how auditor and client behavior will be influenced by the time horizon (e.g., single-period versus multiperiod settings) and asymmetry in auditor versus client payoffs.

Client and Auditor Decisions

In the single-period Fellingham and Newman model, a client and an auditor each make private action choices. The client chooses between one of two actions, either high effort (E_1) or low effort (E_2). E_1 is assumed to reduce the probability of a material financial statement misstatement, such that if p is the conditional probability of a material misstatement given E_1 and if q is the conditional probability of a material misstatement given E_2, then $p < q$.[2]

The auditor makes two decisions. First, at the same time that the client chooses an effort level, the auditor selects either a high (A_1) or low (A_2) level of audit procedures. A_1 is analogous to extending substantive audit procedures in order to reduce detection risk below the level associated with A_2. Second, the auditor subsequently selects a report, either qualified (Q) or not qualified (NQ). It is assumed that prior to the auditor's reporting decision, A_1 perfectly reveals whether the client chose E_1 or E_2. $(A_1$ does not, however, reveal whether there is in fact a material misstatement.) In contrast, A_2 provides no information about the client's effort level and, therefore, the auditor must make a reporting decision without this information.

Client and Auditor Costs

Because E_1 is more costly than E_2, the client is assumed to prefer E_2 to E_1, ceteris paribus. Similarly, because A_1 is more costly than A_2, the auditor is assumed to prefer A_2 to A_1, ceteris paribus. In more detail, the three costs incurred by the auditor are as follows: C_1 = the auditor's expected cost of qualifying given no material misstatement (e.g., loss of client and reputation); C_2 = the auditor's expected cost of not qualifying given a material misstatement (e.g., loss of reputation, future litigation costs, and potential loss of client); and C_A = the auditor's incremental cost of A_1 over A_2, with A_2 normalized to zero. The four costs incurred by the client are as follows: C_H = the client's incremental cost of E_1 over E_2, with E_2 normalized to zero; C_Q = the client's expected cost of a qualified opinion (e.g., adverse stock market reaction and various sanctions); CE_Q = the client's expected cost of a material misstatement when the opinion is qualified; and CE_{NQ} = the client's expected cost of a material misstatement when the opinion is not qualified. It is assumed that $CE_Q > CE_{NQ}$. Note that whereas the *realized* cost of a discovered material misstatement may be the same for both CE_Q and CE_{NQ}, the *expected* cost of the former is higher because the misstatement has a higher probability of detection.[3]

Client and Auditor Strategies

The client chooses only one of two strategies $(E_1$ or $E_2)$. Fellingham and Newman analytically demonstrated that the auditor will adopt one of the following three strategies: (1) a pure A_1,NQ,Q strategy which involves always selecting A_1 and then reporting NQ when the client selects E_1 and reporting Q when the client selects E_2; (2) a pure A_2,Q strategy which involves always selecting A_2 and always reporting Q; or (3) a pure A_2,NQ strategy which involves always selecting A_2 and

Table 1. Auditor-Client Game in Strategic Form (Cell Contents Are Auditor and Client Costs, Respectively)

	Client Strategies	
Nondominated Auditor Strategies	E_1	E_2
A_1,NQ,Q	(C_A+pC_2, C_H+pCE_{NQ})	$(C_A+(1-q)C_1, C_Q+qCE_Q)$
A_2,Q	$((1-p)C_1, C_H+C_Q+pCE_Q)$	$((1-q)C_1, C_Q+qCE_Q)$
A_2,NQ	(pC_2, C_H+pCE_{NQ})	(qC_2, qCE_{NQ})

always reporting NQ. Table 1 presents these three nondominated auditor strategies and the two client strategies in a 3×2 matrix. The cell contents represent the expected costs borne by the auditor and client, respectively.

Furthermore, the following observations can be demonstrated (proofs available from the authors). First, regardless of the values of p and q, the auditor would never select the above A_1,NQ,Q strategy as a pure strategy (specifically, the auditor would not always select A_1). Second, A_2 is a possible pure auditor strategy, such that the auditor might always select either A_2,NQ or A_2,Q. Of these two latter strategies, $A_2,Q:E_2$ is Pareto dominated by the mutually cooperative $A_2,NQ:E_1$ strategy. Third, the Fellingham and Newman assumptions that $p < q$ and $CE_Q > CE_{NQ}$ imply that *multiple* Nash equilibria are not possible (i.e., the derived Nash equilibrium is unique). Fourth, a mixed Nash equilibrium strategy of A_1,NQ,Q with A_2,Q is not possible. Finally, the two mixed Nash equilibrium strategies (i.e., A_1,NQ,Q with A_2,NQ, or A_2,Q with A_2,NQ) are both Pareto dominated by the pure $A_2,NQ:E_1$ strategy of mutual cooperation.

The upshot of the above observations is that only three types of Nash equilibrium strategies are possible: (1) a unique pure strategy Nash equilibrium ($A_2,Q:E_1$ or $A_2,Q:E_2$ or $A_2,NQ:E_1$ or $A_2,NQ:E_2$); (2) the unique pure strategy Nash equilibrium $A_2,Q:E_2$ that is Pareto dominated by $A_2,NQ:E_1$; and (3) a unique mixed strategy Nash equilibrium (with the auditor mixing A_1,NQ,Q with A_2,NQ or mixing A_2,Q with A_2,NQ, and the client mixing E_1 and E_2) that is always Pareto dominated by $A_2,NQ:E_1$. Note that if a Nash equilibrium is Pareto dominated, the dominating strategy is always the mutually cooperative $A_2,NQ:E_1$. The specific cost and probability values determine which of these three strategies is possible. For the parameter values we selected in two different matrices (see below), the Fellingham and Newman model predicts a pure Nash equilibrium strategy ($A_2,Q:E_2$) in one matrix and a mixed Nash equilibrium strategy in the other (wherein the auditor selects A_2,Q some of the time and A_2,NQ the remainder of the time, while the client selects E_1 some of the time and E2 the remainder of the time). These pure and mixed strategies pertain to Matrix 1 and Matrix 2 of Table 2, respectively.

Table 2.   Experimental Matrices (Cell Contents are Auditor and Client
Payoffs, Respectively)

	Matrix 1 (Pure Strategy)	
	E_1	E_2
A_1,NQ,Q	370,500	250,400
A_2,Q	330,150	380,400
A_2,NQ	550,500	200,800
	Matrix 2 (Mixed Strategy)	
	E_1	E_2
A_1,NQ,Q	250,630	157, 25
A_2,Q	310,295	350, 25
A_2,NQ	443,630	217,900

Notes: Row headings denote auditor strategies and column headings denote client strategies. For Matrix
1, the predicted pure Nash equilibrium strategy is $A_2,Q{:}E_2$. For Matrix 2, the predicted mixed
strategy involves the auditor selecting A_2,Q 50 percent of the time and A_2,NQ 50 percent of the
time, and the client selecting E_1 50 percent of the time and E_2 50 percent of the time. In both matrices, the mutually cooperative strategy is $A_2,NQ{:}E_1$.

In both matrices, the predicted Nash equilibrium strategy is Pareto-dominated by
$A_2,NQ{:}E_1$.

Similarities to a Prisoners' Dilemma Game

It can be shown that matrices 1 and 2 each collapse from a 3×2 matrix to a 2×2 matrix (with the A_1,NQ,Q row removed), with some similarities to the traditional prisoners' dilemma game. For example, similarly to a prisoners' dilemma matrix, matrices 1 and 2 each have a Pareto-dominated Nash equilibrium. However, the traditional prisoners' dilemma involves some additional constraints on the payoffs that may or may not hold in matrices 1 and 2. In the traditional prisoners' dilemma game, the payoffs are symmetric and both players have incentives to defect from cooperation. In contrast, the relative payoffs in our matrices might yield differential incentives for auditors versus clients to cooperate. For example, although $A_2,NQ{:}E_1$ in Matrix 1 is similar to the cooperative point of the traditional prisoners' dilemma inasmuch as the client has an incentive to defect (i.e., select E_2) when he or she believes that the auditor selects A_2,NQ, the auditor has no incentive to defect (i.e., the auditor will always select A_2,NQ, so long as he or she believes that the client selects E_1). Likewise, the relative payoff rankings of Matrix 2 are such that the payoffs for the client but not for the auditor are consistent with a prisoners' dilemma game. If one defines the Pareto-dominating strategy of $A_2,NQ{:}E_1$ *in Matrix 2 as cooperation and the mixed Nash equilibrium as noncooperation,* then the ordering of client and auditor payoffs in Matrix 2 parallels the payoff ordering in Matrix 1.

Selecting Parameter Values for Matrices 1 and 2

To provide a stronger test of the Fellingham and Newman predictions, we selected values for costs and probabilities that yield an alternative strategy (cooperation) that competes with the predicted Nash equilibrium of the Fellingham and Newman model. In particular, our selection of parameter values was guided by the prisoners' dilemma literature which has demonstrated that under certain conditions subjects will engage in cooperative (non-Nash) behavior (Rapoport and Chammah 1965; Selten and Stoecker 1986; Friedman and Rosenthal 1987; Kadane and Larkey 1982; Fisher and Schatzberg 1991). The possibility of auditor-client mutual cooperation is worth investigating, because such cooperation can yield more cost-efficient and socially beneficial outcomes in the current auditing environment. In both Matrix 1 and Matrix 2, $p = .05$ and $q = .25$. These probabilities describe a setting in which the effectiveness of the client's internal control structure (ICS) depends significantly on the client's effort (here, E_1 or E_2). This is an intuitively appealing setting, because it captures the idea that key factors in an effective ICS are the control environment (e.g., management's philosophy and commitment to building, maintaining, and adhering to a sound system of controls) and the competence and integrity of client personnel. These probabilities (and the respective costs and budgets we selected) yield the associated expected payoffs in Table 2. The expected payoffs of Matrix 1 yield a predicted pure Nash equilibrium strategy of $A_2,Q:E_2$. Similarly, the expected payoffs of Matrix 2 yield a mixed Nash equilibrium strategy (the auditor selects A_2,Q 50 percent and A_2,NQ 50 percent, while the client selects E_1 50 percent and E_2 50 percent). From these matrices, specific hypotheses can now be developed.

Hypotheses About the Time Horizon

The first issue relates to the time horizon (either single-period or multiperiod) of the model and corresponding laboratory experiments. For a single-period time horizon, the Fellingham and Newman model predicts a noncooperative Nash equilibrium. However, based on the prior prisoners' dilemma research cited above and the similarities between our matrices and the prisoners' dilemma, there is reason to expect that at least some players will engage in cooperative behavior. Accordingly, the following hypothesis will be tested:

Hypothesis 1. In Matrix 1 (Matrix 2), the auditor and client will play a pure (mixed) Nash equilibrium strategy in a single-period game.

Hypotheses 2-4 relate to a multiperiod time horizon and its relation to the single-period horizon. In auditing context, it is important to examine the multiperiod time horizon for at least two reasons. First, most audits are of a repeated nature. While the Fellingham and Newman model is for a single period only, it can be demonstrated with backward induction that the Nash equilibrium strategy should be played in every period of a finitely repeated game with complete information. On the other hand, experimental studies of prisoners' dilemma games have also shown that the number of periods played can affect behavior. Specifically, iterative games of longer length (i.e., more than three periods) tend to exhibit more cooperation (Lave 1965). Second, in some cases, the last period of a multiperiod audit setting is known with certainty (e.g., with mandatory rotation of auditors for governmental engagements). Rapoport and Chammah (1965) and Selten and Stoecker (1986) reported the *end game effect* in finitely repeated games, whereby less cooperation occurs in the final periods relative to earlier periods (see also Feinberg and Husted 1993). Thus, whereas the Fellingham and Newman model predicts that no cooperative behavior will be observed, the multiperiod effect predicts that some cooperative behavior will be observed. Moreover, the end game effect predicts that less cooperation will be observed in later versus early periods. Accordingly, we also conducted multiperiod experiments wherein subjects knew that they would consist of five periods each. The following hypotheses test these concepts:

Hypothesis 2.   In Matrix 1 (Matrix 2), the auditor and client will play a pure (mixed) Nash equilibrium strategy in a multiperiod setting.

Hypothesis 3.   In Matrix 1 (Matrix 2), the percentage of pure (mixed) Nash equilibrium strategies will not vary with the time horizon (i.e., single-period versus multiperiod setting).

Hypothesis 4.   In Matrix 1 (Matrix 2), the auditor and client will play the same percentage of the pure (mixed) Nash equilibrium strategies for each period of a multiperiod setting.

Hypothesis About the Auditor and Client Payoffs

The Fellingham and Newman model and Nash equilibrium theory predict that if relative payoff rankings are retained, variations in the magnitude of payoffs (i.e., payoff asymmetry across auditors and clients) should have no effect on the predicted Nash equilibrium behavior. Nevertheless, Fisher and Schatzberg (1991) report experimental evidence that variation in the magnitude of payoffs does influence the extent to which cooperation is observed. Their results suggest that the asymmetric payoffs in our matrices will yield some auditor cooperation. Specifically, in Table 2, the bottom two rows of matrices 1 and 2 exhibit asymmetric payoffs for the auditor and client and give only the client a prisoners' dilemma incentive to defect. For example, in Matrix 1, the auditor has no incentive to defect from cooperation (A_2, NQ) even when the auditor expects the client to defect (E_2), but the client has an incentive to defect when he or she expects the auditor to select A_2, NQ. Similar observations pertain to Matrix 2, but the predicted mixed strategy makes it more difficult to isolate the effect of payoff asymmetry in an experimental setting. Thus, the following null hypothesis is tested for Matrix 1 only:

Hypothesis 5. In Matrix 1, the auditor will play the Nash equilibrium strategy as often as the client.

EXPERIMENTAL DESIGN

A series of noncomputerized (paper-and-pencil) laboratory experiments were conducted to test the Fellingham and Newman model. In total, four experiments with Matrix 1 and three experiments with Matrix 2 are presented below.[4] Six subjects participated in each experiment. Each subject participated in two experiments, one for Matrix 1 and one for Matrix 2. In a given experiment, each subject played as an auditor and a client (whereby the role designation randomly varied over time) and was randomly re-paired with different subjects over time.

Each experiment consisted of multiple repeated playing years, with subjects making decisions over repeated periods within each playing year. The single-period (multiperiod) experiments consisted of one (five) periods within each playing year. In each experiment, subjects were randomly paired for 15 single-period years and for 5 five-period years. To control for order effects, the order of the experimental treatments (Matrix 1 and Matrix 2, and the 5 five period and 15 single-period playing years) was counterbalanced within subjects. For each period in a given playing year, a subject retained his or her role designation and subject pairing. Each auditor-client subject pair simultaneously selected a row-column from the relevant matrix. Next, each subject was informed of the selection made by his or her paired subject and then calculated his or her payoffs for the period. At the end of each playing year, subjects were randomly reassigned to be either an auditor or a client, and were randomly re-paired with another subject for the next playing year.[5]

Subjects were volunteer undergraduate students at the University of Arizona. In accordance with the theory of induced value (Smith 1976) and in order to minimize role playing, the experiments use generic terms such as player 1, player 2, and TYPES instead of auditor, client, and strategies (e.g., A_2, NQ or E_2), respectively. Subjects were told that the matrix payoffs were in francs, where 1 franc = 1/25 cent (see Appendix for the instructions). The experiments lasted approximately three hours and subjects earned an average of $17.

RESULTS

The results are presented first for the pure Nash equilibrium of Matrix 1 and then for the mixed strategy Nash equilibrium of Matrix 2. Most results are aggregated across experiments. The results of each individual experiment are generally consistent with these aggregates. The statistical tests involve chi-square tests of proportions that compare the predicted versus actual frequencies of auditor and client

Table 3. Outcome Percentages for Matrix 1
(Predicted Pure Strategy), by Time Horizon and Strategy

	Single-Period Experiments		
	E_1	E_2	Total
A_1,NQ,Q	.01	.01	.02
A_2,Q	.11	.51	.62
A_2,NQ	.08	.28	.36
Total	.20	.80	1.00

	Five-Period Experiments		
	E_1	E_2	Total
A_1,NQ,Q	.02	.02	.04
A_2,Q	.11	.50	.61
A_2,NQ	.21	.14	.35
Total	.34	.66	1.00

Notes: Row headings denote auditor strategies and column headings denote client strategies. The predicted pure Nash equilibrium strategy is $A_2,Q:E_2$. The cooperative strategy is $A_2,NQ:E_1$.

behavior. For brevity, we report only whether the chi-square tests are statistically significant, with significance set at the conventional .05 level.

Matrix 1 (Pure Strategy): Single-Period Aggregate Results

Table 3 reports the single-period results from Matrix 1. As predicted, the auditor almost never selects A_1,NQ,Q (2 percent of the time). With respect to Hypothesis 1, auditors (clients) selected the predicted Nash response 62 percent (80 percent) of the time, with the noncooperative Nash outcome of $A_2,Q:E_2$ attained 51 percent of the time. A test of proportions comparing the actual versus predicted Nash equilibrium strategy reveals that Hypothesis 1 can be rejected. There is also some evidence of cooperation: auditors (clients) attempted cooperation 36 percent (20 percent) of the time, and mutual cooperation ($A_2,NQ:E_1$) occurred 8 percent of the time. Thus, the Fellingham and Newman Nash equilibrium fails to describe a substantial proportion of auditor-client strategic behavior.

Matrix 1 (Pure Strategy): Multiperiod Aggregate Results

Table 3 shows the percentage of subjects who selected each strategy in the five-period experiments. As in the single-period experiments, auditors rarely selected A_1,NQ,Q (only 4 percent of the time). The auditors (clients) played the Nash response 61 percent (66 percent) of the time, and the Nash outcome was attained

50 percent of the time. There is more evidence of mutual cooperation in the five-period experiments (21 percent) than in the single-period experiments (8 percent). Most of this difference is attributable to an increase in client cooperative behavior. Whereas auditors selected A_2,NQ 35 percent of the time (compared with 36 percent in the single-period experiments), clients selected E_1 34 percent of the time (compared with 20 percent in the single-period experiments).

More formally, a test of proportions rejects Hypothesis 2, which predicted that both auditors and clients would only select the Nash strategy in the five-period game. In addition, another test of proportions reveals that differences in strategies across the single- and five-period experiments is significant for clients but not for auditors. Therefore, Hypothesis 3 is rejected for clients but not for auditors. Like the single-period results of Matrix 1, these multiperiod results demonstrate that the Fellingham and Newman Nash equilibrium fails to predict a significant proportion of auditor-client behavior.

Further Analysis of Cooperation in Multiperiod Experiments of Matrix 1 (Pure Strategy)

Hypothesis 4 predicted that the auditor and client play the same Nash strategy in every period of the multiperiod experiment. Figure 1 shows the percentage of auditors (clients) who selected the cooperative A_2,NQ (E_1) strategy for each of the five periods. Auditor (client) cooperation declined from 58 percent (45 percent) in the first period to 14 percent (20 percent) in the fifth period. A test of proportions reveals that this decline in cooperative behavior is significant. Thus, Hypothesis 4 can be rejected.

Further analysis reveals that the decline in auditor cooperation is most evident over periods 1-2 and 4-5 and that the decline in client cooperation is most pronounced over periods 1-2. The approximately equal percentage of auditors and clients who cooperated in periods 2-4 indicates that the experiments had already achieved stable strategies of mutual cooperation or noncooperation during those periods. There is, however, some evidence of the end period effect in the fifth period, wherein the least amount of mutual cooperation was observed. Thus, again contrary to the prediction of Hypothesis 4 that auditor-client behavior will remain constant over time, the percentages of cooperative and noncooperative strategies differ significantly across time periods. The results suggest that the person who selects noncooperation in the first period "leads" the experiments toward mutual noncooperation in subsequent periods, such that eventually the cooperation rates of auditors and clients become roughly equivalent after the first period. This is interesting because it relates to issues of history and reputation, both of which arguably exist in present-day audit markets.

Next, recall that Hypothesis 5 predicted that the auditor will play the Nash strategy as often as the client. Tests for differences in proportions in auditor versus client cooperation reveal that auditors cooperated significantly more often than

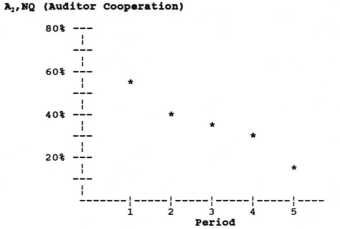

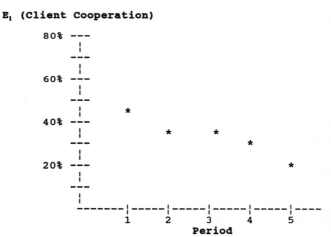

Figure 1. Matrix 1 Percentage of Strategies Played
in the Five-Period Experiments, by Period

clients in the single-period experiments (36 percent versus 20 percent, respectively), but not in the five-period experiments (35 percent versus 34 percent, respectively). Thus, Hypothesis 5 is rejected for the single-period experiments only. In the five-period experiments, however, the first-period cooperation percentage is somewhat higher for the auditor than for the client. The direction of this pattern of differences between auditors and clients is consistent with the argument presented above that the payoff ranking for the auditor and the client induces the auditor to engage in cooperative behavior more often than the client. Overall, the results indicate that the magnitude of the payoffs (even holding constant the relative ranking of these amounts) can significantly affect the strategy played. As such, the predicted Nash equilibrium strategy does not capture how the asymmetric and relative ranking of the matrix payoffs derived from the Fellingham and Newman model may, in fact, differentially affect the tendencies of auditors and clients to engage in cooperative behavior.

Period-by-Period Analysis of the Five-Period Experiments of Matrix 1 (Pure Strategy)

To further examine strategic choice in the multiperiod context, we conducted a period-by-period analysis of the five-period experiments of Matrix 1. The analysis reveals four basic strategies. First, 6 percent of the experiments displayed mutual cooperation in all five periods. Second, for 24 percent of the experiments, mutual cooperation occurred in the initial period with defection occurring in the fourth or fifth period. Third, for 38 percent of the experiments, one player defected in the initial period and all players followed mutual noncooperation thereafter. Consistent with prior discussions that auditors have stronger incentives to cooperate, in 71 percent of the first periods of these experiments, the auditors cooperated when the clients defected, while in the other 29 percent of the first periods, the auditor defected and the client cooperated. Fourth, for 18 percent of the experiments, mutual noncooperation was obtained in all five periods. Overall, these results and the results reported above are consistent with subjects attempting to cooperate, with the level of cooperation attained depending significantly on the history of behavior between auditors and clients.

As further evidence of the effect of prior behavior on subsequent decisions, Table 4 shows the outcomes of period N and the strategies selected in period $N+1$. Following the notation used in earlier prisoner dilemma work (Rapoport and Chammah 1965; Selten and Stoecker 1986), let the outcomes for period N be denoted as follows: x = mutual cooperation; y = the auditor cooperates while the client defects; z = the auditor defects while the client cooperates; and w = mutual noncooperation. Given these outcomes, in period $N+1$ a player can select either cooperation (c) or noncooperation (d). Table 4 shows that the most frequent outcomes are x paired with c, and w paired with d. In addition, x decreases across periods, while w increases. Finally, the (w,d) sequence of mutual noncooperation followed by (w,d) increases across time periods. Overall, these percentages reveal that cooperative players tended to defect and continued to defect after an unsuccessful (i.e., unilateral) attempt to cooperate.

In summary, the above results for Matrix 1 (particularly those pertaining to Hypotheses 3 and 5) show that the first period in a multiperiod time horizon can be an important determinant of subsequent period behavior. Specifically, when a player defects in the first period, it is highly likely that mutual noncooperation will be observed in subsequent periods. This "history" effect should be considered in

Table 4.   Matrix 1 Percentage of Strategy Selection Subsequent to
Previous Outcome

	Period 1-2								
	x		*y*		*z*		*w*		
	c	*d*	*c*	*d*	*c*	*d*	*c*	*d*	*Total*
Auditor	27	4	6	23	6	9	0	25	100%
Client	28	3	6	9	1	28	3	22	100%

	Period 2-3								
	x		*y*		*z*		*w*		
	c	*d*	*c*	*d*	*c*	*d*	*c*	*d*	*Total*
Auditor	29	1	0	9	0	7	4	50	100%
Client	28	3	0	7	1	7	9	45	100%

	Period 3-4								
	x		*y*		*z*		*w*		
	c	*d*	*c*	*d*	*c*	*d*	*c*	*d*	*Total*
Auditor	25	1	0	9	4	9	1	51	100%
Client	25	1	1	12	3	6	0	52	100%

	Period 4-5								
	x		*y*		*z*		*w*		
	c	*d*	*c*	*d*	*c*	*d*	*c*	*d*	*Total*
Auditor	13	10	1	9	0	6	0	61	100%
Client	18	4	1	4	1	9	0	63	100%

Explanation of Strategies: The period N strategies are x = mutual cooperation; y = the auditor cooperates while the client defects; z = the auditor defects while the client cooper-
ates; and w = mutual noncooperation. The period N+1 strategies are
cooperation (c) or noncooperation (d).

models of auditor-client interaction in multiperiod contexts, particularly in models
that investigate issues related to auditor and client reputation.

Matrix 2 Results

Table 5 presents the percentage of outcomes selected by players for the three
experiments of Matrix 2, separately for the single- and five-period experiments.
Figures 2-4 present time-series for the average percentage of cooperation by auditors (A_2, NQ) and clients (E_1). Recall that the predicted mixed Nash equilibrium

Table 5. Outcome Percentages for Matrix 2
(Mixed Strategy), by Time Horizon and Strategy

	Single-Period Experiments		
	E_1	E_2	*Total*
A_1,NQ,Q	.00	.00	.00
A_2,Q	.34	.15	.49
A_2,NQ	.39	.12	.51
Total	.73	.27	1.00

	Five-Period Experiments		
	E_1	E_2	*Total*
A_1,NQ,Q	.01	.00	.01
A_2,Q	.38	.07	.45
A_2,NQ	.44	.10	.54
Total	.83	.17	1.00

Notes: Row headings denote auditor strategies and column headings denote client strategies. The predicted pure Nash equilibrium strategy involves the auditor selecting A_2,Q 50 percent of the time and A_2, NQ 50 percent of the time, and the client selecting E_1 50 percent of the time and E_2 50 percent of the time. The mutually cooperative strategy is $A_2,NQ:E_1$.

strategy of Matrix 2 has the auditor select A_2,NQ 50 percent of the time and A_2,Q the other 50 percent of the time, and has the client select E_1 50 percent of the time and E_2 the other 50 percent of the time.

As shown in the totals column of Table 5 for the single-period experiments, auditors selected A_2,Q 49 percent and A_2,NQ 51 percent of the time, very close to the 50 percent/50 percent prediction. As predicted, auditors did not select strategy A_1,NQ,Q. Clients selected E_1 73 percent of the time and E_2 27 percent of the time. A test of proportions comparing the actual percentages with the 50 percent/50 percent predictions was significant for clients but not for auditors. Thus, the Hypothesis 1 prediction that both auditors and clients would play the Nash mixed strategy is rejected for clients but not for auditors.

In the five-period experiments, auditors selected A_2,Q 45 percent of the time and A_2,NQ 54 percent of the time, while clients selected E_1 84 percent of the time and E_2 16 percent of the time (see the bottom panel of Table 5). Again, consistent with our predictions, the auditors hardly ever selected A_1,NQ,Q (frequency of only 1 percent). As in the single-period experiments, a test of proportions comparing the actual percentages with the 50 percent/50 percent predictions was significant for the client but not for the auditor. Thus, the Hypothesis 2 prediction that auditors and clients would play only the Nash mixed strategy in the five-period experiments is rejected for the clients but not for the auditors. It is interesting to note that

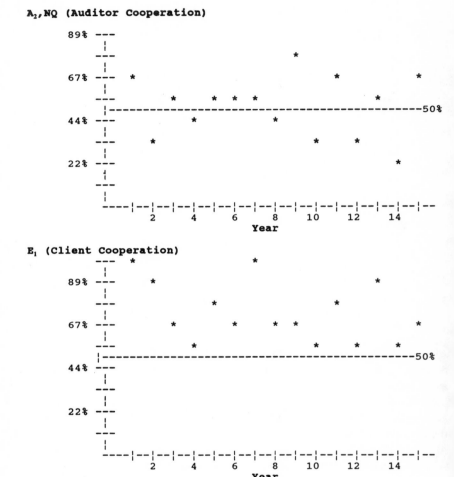

Figure 2. Matrix 2 Percentage of Strategies Played
in Single-Period Experiments, by Year

subjects achieved mutual cooperation $(A_2,NQ:E_1)$ more often in the five-period
experiments than in the single-period experiments (44 percent versus 39 percent)

The time-series frequency of cooperation (Figures 2-4) supports the conclusion
that auditors played the Nash mixed strategy while clients more often selected
cooperation (E_1). Figures 2-3 show that the frequency of cooperation tended to
alternate between increasing and decreasing across adjacent periods. Figure 4
shows a decline in cooperation across periods within a year, with the decline in
cooperation frequency most pronounced in periods 4 and 5. A test for differences

A₂,NQ (Auditor Cooperation)

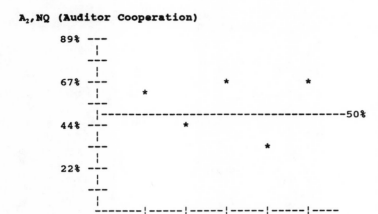

E₁ (Client Cooperation)

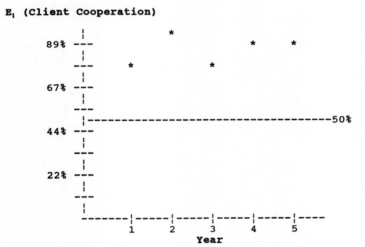

Figure 3. Matrix 2 Percentage of Strategies Played
in Five-Period Experiments, by Year

in proportions across periods is significantly different for both auditors and clients. Thus, the Hypothesis 4 prediction that auditors and clients will play the same Nash strategy in each period of the multiperiod experiments is rejected.

Hypothesis 3 predicted that percentage of mixed Nash equilibrium strategies played by the auditors and clients would not vary across the single-period and five-period experiments. A test of proportions rejects Hypothesis 3 for clients but not for auditors. The insignificant result for auditors reflects the results reported above that auditors generally selected the same strategy in both the single-period and

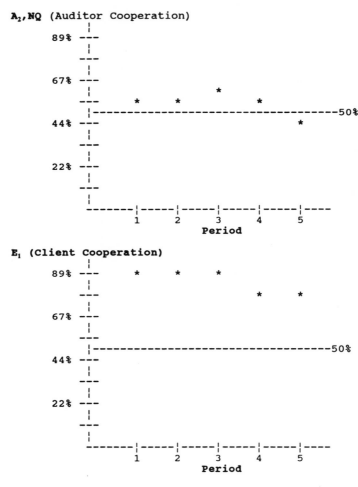

Figure 4. Matrix 2 Percentage of Strategies Played
in Five-Period Experiments, by Period

five-period experiments, whereas clients selected cooperation (E_1) more often in
the five-period than in the single-period experiments (83 percent versus 73 percent). Thus, the auditor and client behavior in Matrix 2 is consistent with that
exhibited in Matrix 1: auditors tended to play the same strategy in both the single-
period and five-period experiments, while clients appeared to increase their level
of cooperation in the five-period experiments relative to the single-period experiments. Overall, these results demonstrate a multiperiod effect in both the pure and

Table 6. Matrix 2 (Mixed Strategy) Data Disaggregated by Subject, Time Horizon, and Role

	A2, NQ Percentage		E1 Percentage	
	Single-Period	*Five-Period*	*Single-Period*	*Five-Period*
Experiment 1				
Subject 1	63	93	57	90
Subject 2	88	80	43	80
Subject 3	63	53	71	90
Subject 4	0	0	100	100
Subject 5	71	60	50	70
Subject 6	0	0	100	93
Experiment 2				
Subject 1	13	53	86	90
Subject 2	63	80	29	80
Subject 3	75	60	71	80
Subject 4	29	0	88	100
Subject 5	71	20	50	90
Subject 6	14	40	88	67
Experiment 3				
Subject 1	100	87	100	100
Subject 2	0	70	71	67
Subject 3	100	73	100	100
Subject 4	14	50	100	67
Subject 5	57	40	13	60
Subject 6	86	90	88	87
Average	51	54	73	83

Notes: The predicted mixed Nash equilibrium strategy involves the auditor selecting A_2,Q 50 percent of the time and A_2,NQ 50 percent of the time, and the client selecting E_1 50 percent of the time and E_2 50 percent of the time. The mutually cooperative strategy is $A_2,NQ:E_1$.

mixed strategy Nash equilibrium experiments. The multiperiod effect thus appears to be an important factor in modeling auditor-client strategies.[6]

Matrix 2 Data, Disaggregated by Experiments and Subjects

Table 6 presents disaggregated data for Matrix 2 of the average percentage of cooperation (i.e., the auditor selects A_2,NQ or a client selects E_1), for each subject in each experiment. In both the single-period and five-period experiments, some subjects did not play a mixed strategy. For example, in the single-period experiments, five of 18 subjects played the pure strategy of cooperation (A_2,NQ when playing as auditors, or E_1 when playing as clients). Of these five subjects, two played cooperation when both an auditor and client, and three played cooperation when a client. For the five-period experiments, four of 18 subjects played a pure strategy when playing as clients. Of these four subjects, three also played a pure strategy when playing as clients in the single-period experiments, and two played cooperation when playing as auditors in the single-period experiments. Evidence for these cooperative pure strategies is interesting, because it reveals that some subjects will play a cooperative strategy regardless of role (auditor versus client) and time horizon (single-period versus multiperiod).

It should also be noted that subjects in the single-period experiments were not necessarily penalized for playing a pure strategy. This is because subject pairings and identifications were changed after each period, making it more difficult for a subject to infer the strategies of other players. However, subjects were punished if they played a pure strategy other than cooperation in the five-period experiments. For example, in the five-period experiments, three of 18 subjects who always selected the pure strategy A_2,Q when playing as auditors were always punished (their paired clients made them worse off by selecting E_1 instead of E_2).

Additionally, there is evidence that some individual pairs of subjects mutually cooperated in the five-period experiments. Specifically, three out of 45 possible yearly pairings (7 percent) attained A_2,NQ:E_1 for all five periods with a year; nine of 45 (20 percent) attained A_2,NQ:E_1 for the first four periods; and 13 of 45 yearly pairings (29 percent) attained A_2,NQ:E_1 in the first three periods of the five-period experiments. A crude benchmark for comparing these results can be constructed by assuming that each period in a year is independent and then using the percentages of A_2,NQ and E_1 selected in the single-period experiments (i.e., 51 percent and 73 percent, respectively). This benchmark yields the following probabilities of the above sequences for the five-period experiments: $[(.51)(.73)]5 = .007$, $[(.51)(.73)]4 = .02$, and $[(.51)(.73)]3 = .05$, respectively. This crude benchmark suggests that auditor-client pairs attained mutual cooperation more often in the five-period experiments than in the single-period experiments. This result is encouraging; it suggests that the multiperiod characteristic of the extant audit environment can help promote attainment of the socially beneficial outcome of cooperation.

CONCLUSIONS

As game-theoretic models of auditing become increasingly complex, predicted and actual behavior are more likely to diverge, and experimental investigation becomes more necessary to test their descriptive validity. This paper conducted an examination of Fellingham and Newman's model of strategic interaction in auditing. Game-theoretical observations were presented concerning the characteristics of the matrices and the corresponding Nash equilibrium. A unique pure strategy Nash equilibrium matrix and a mixed strategy Nash equilibrium matrix were identified, each of which is Pareto dominated by a strategy of mutual cooperation. Additionally, it was shown that these matrices exhibit some of the characteristics found in the traditional prisoners' dilemma game. Below, we summarize the results and discuss their implications for audit practice and theory.

Effect of Time Horizon and Asymmetric Payoffs on Auditor-Client Strategic Behavior

The experimental results reveal that the predicted Fellingham and Newman Nash equilibrium strategy is not completely descriptive of actual behavior. Specifically, the correspondence between predicted and observed behavior was sensitive to the time horizon as well as the asymmetric nature of the payoff matrices. With respect to time horizon, it should be noted that whereas the Fellingham and Newman model is a single-period model, its predictions can be extended to the multiperiod setting by backward induction. Overall, the experimental evidence reveals that the Fellingham and Newman predictions are less descriptive of the multiperiod context than of the single-period context, but the single-period experiments also reveal that the Fellingham and Newman Nash equilibrium fails to describe a significant portion of behavior. The Fellingham and Newman predictions were best supported by auditor behavior in both the single- and multiperiod experiments, particularly in the mixed-strategy Nash equilibrium setting. On an optimistic note, much of the non-Nash behavior involved the strategy of cooperation. Cooperation was even more pronounced in the multiperiod experiments, but decreased over time (as in prior empirical work in prisoners' dilemmas). This is an interesting result in an audit setting because it suggests that a socially preferred outcome may be obtained. Specifically, when clients exert more effort, auditors can simultaneously reduce both audit cost and audit risk.

With respect to the asymmetry in payoffs between auditors and clients, results for the pure strategy Nash equilibrium of Matrix 1 support the prediction that asymmetric subject payoffs impact behavior in prisoners' dilemma environments. Specifically, in the single-period experiments, auditors engaged in cooperative behavior more often than clients. In the multiperiod experiments, asymmetric payoffs appeared to affect cooperative behavior mainly in the first period; in subsequent periods, the history effect tended to dominate the behavior. For example, auditors were more cooperative than clients in the first period, but those cooperative auditors very frequently defected when their initial cooperative behavior was met by a client's noncooperative behavior. These results are consistent with the general expectation that when a client expends low effort, auditors will need to expend more effort and will report a qualified opinion if the financial statements are considered to be materially misstated.

In summary, the Fellingham and Newman model fails to predict all auditor and client behavior in both single-period and multiperiod settings, as well as pure and mixed Nash equilibrium settings. In addition, the duration, sequence, and history in a multiperiod environment appear to affect behavior. Finally, asymmetry in the payoffs faced by auditors versus clients also seems to significantly influence strategic behavior. These results are relevant for future modelling and empirical testing, particularly because the extant auditing environment is generally of a multiperiod nature and generally exhibits asymmetry in auditor and client payoffs. Below, we consider some extensions of the Fellingham and Newman model that could yield auditor-client cooperation and coordination in multiperiod settings.

Conditions for Auditor-Client Cooperation in Multiperiod Settings

Future research could develop and examine an explicit multiperiod model that incorporates the results reported in this paper, in several ways. First, recent behavioral theories of prisoners' dilemma strategies, such as "tit for tat" (Axelrod 1980) and "trigger" theory (Friedman 1986), may provide additional insights into auditor-client strategic behavior, particularly with respect to the possibility of the socially beneficial outcome of sustained mutual cooperation in multiperiod settings. Second, future research could further address the behavioral effects of asymmetry in the payoffs faced by auditors and clients, particularly where the normative Nash solution predicts no effect on behavior. Third, further exploration of how the end period effect can undermine cooperation in multiperiod settings may offer some important insights into the relative costs and benefits of mandatory auditor rotation. Finally, research could examine the potentially beneficial roles played by third parties, such as active audit committees and boards of directors which the Advisory Panel on Auditor Independence (1994) argued could help strengthen audit quality.

Conditions for Auditor-Client Coordination

One criticism of the Fellingham and Newman model is that it does not explicitly incorporate sampling risk and related evidence gathering concepts. Explicit incorporation of richer evidence gathering concepts could help the model's predictions to conform more closely to what is generally observed in the extant audit environment, especially in multiperiod settings. For example, consider how the Fellingham and Newman model predicts that when auditors choose low audit effort, they will sometimes have incentives to issue qualified opinions even though they detect no errors. A more ecologically valid interpretation of audit evidence gathering and reporting decisions would be as follows. When auditors choose small sample sizes (low audit effort) for testing details of account balances, the estimated upper bound of total population misstatements will generally be higher than for larger sample sizes (higher audit effort). Thus, consistent with the Fellingham and Newman model, low audit effort will more often lead the auditor to conclude that the client's financial statements are materially misstated. However, unlike in the Fellingham and Newman model, real world auditors are not constrained to issuing qualified opinions in these circumstances. Auditors may instead extend their sample sizes in an attempt to achieve more precision in their estimates of total population misstatements, or request that the client adjust the account balances in question. In either case, the eventual outcome may appropriately be an unqualified opinion. Additionally, auditors may include in their management letters some recommendations as to how management may improve its accounting and internal control systems. Such improvements would simultaneously reduce both the likelihood of material misstatements in the client's unaudited financial statements and future audit costs. Moreover, if the client does make such improvements, in subsequent periods the auditor would be more likely to test key client controls (another source of evidence about client effort that is absent in the Fellingham and Newman model) in order to justify a reduction in more costly substantive tests. In the long run, auditor-client coordination and cooperation in multiperiod settings can yield lower levels of audit risk at lower audit cost.

In conclusion, we believe that it is worthwhile to develop and experimentally test models of strategic auditor-client interaction, even if the models (at least initially) are highly stylized and abstract away from some of the important and interesting features in the extant audit environment. Inconsistencies between the models' predictions and actual behavior in the laboratory or field can help us to more fully understand the functional roles of various features of the extant audit environment.

APPENDIX

Matrix 1 Single-Period Experimental Instructions

Note: [] and [[ ]] refer to the five-period experiments and Matrix 2 instructions, respectively.

Instructions

This is an experiment in decision making. The instructions are simple and if you follow them carefully and make good decisions, you can earn a considerable amount of money, which will be paid to you in cash at the end of the experiment.

In this experiment, there are two kinds of players, PLAYER 1 and PLAYER 2, with each player having their own TYPE. Specifically, PLAYER 1 can be one of three TYPES, TYPE 1, TYPE 2, or TYPE 3. PLAYER 2 can be one of two TYPES, TYPE A or TYPE B.

The experiment consists of a PLAYER 1 and PLAYER 2 being paired together over a series of playing years, with each year consisting of ONE [FIVE] periods.

At the beginning of each year, you are told which PLAYER you are for the year and paired with a player of the other kind. You remain paired together for all periods of the playing year. After the end of the final period of a playing year, you will be randomly reassigned as a PLAYER 1 or PLAYER 2 and paired with a new player of the other kind. Then, a new independent playing year begins.

Each period of a playing year consists of a paired PLAYER 1 and PLAYER 2 simultaneously selecting their own TYPE. Specifically, PLAYER 1 selects either TYPE 1, 2, or 3. PLAYER 2 selects either TYPE A or B. NOTE THAT AT THE TIME OF THEIR SELECTION, EACH PLAYER DOES NOT KNOW THE OTHER PLAYER's SELECTION. After both players independently make their selection, each player is informed of the other paired player's selection, and each player receives a payoff that depends on the TYPE selected by both paired players. Specifically, the payoffs each receives is presented in the table below IN FRANCS (a Franc is worth 1/25th of a CENT), where the payoff for PLAYER 1 and PLAYER 2 are displayed in each cell (PLAYER 1 payoff, PLAYER 2 payoff) of the table:

	Player 2's Type	
Player 1's Type	A	B
1	(370,500)	(250,400)
2	(330,150)	(380,400)
3	(550,500)	(200,800)

For example, if PLAYER 1 selects TYPE 2 and PLAYER 2 selects TYPE A, then PLAYER 1 receives 330 Francs and PLAYER 2 receives 150 Francs.

[[	Player 2's Type	
Player 1's Type	A	B
1	(250,630)	(157, 25)
2	(310,295)	(350, 25)
3	(443,630)	(217,900)

For example, if PLAYER 1 selects TYPE 2 and PLAYER 2 selects TYPE A, then PLAYER 1 receives 310 Francs and PLAYER 2 receives 295 Francs.]]

You will note that there is a summary sheet in your file, on which you should record and accumulate the payoffs you are receiving over the course of the experiment. Additionally, you should also record the prior selections that were made by you and your paired player within a playing year.

In summary, the sequence of events in a period is as follows:

1. PLAYER 1 selects his or her TYPE, either 1, 2, or 3, and PLAYER 2 simultaneously selects his or her TYPE, either A or B.

2. Each player is informed of the other paired player's selection, and payoffs are distributed to each player based on the table above.

You will be paid in cash the sum total of Francs received over the periods played, where a Franc is worth 1/25th of a cent. You are free to make as much money as you can.

ACKNOWLEDGMENT

This paper has benefitted from the comments of Doug DeJong, Bill Felix, Rick Young, participants at the American Accounting Association (AAA) national meetings, AAA western regional meetings, the Economic Science Association national meetings, the associate editor, and two anonymous reviewers.

NOTES

1. In the setting we investigate, a pure auditor strategy involves the selection by the auditor of only one effort level/reporting combination, whereas a mixed strategy involves randomization among two such effort level/reporting combinations. Similarly, a pure client strategy involves selection by the client of only one effort level, whereas a mixed strategy involves randomization among two effort levels.

2. The values of p and q can be interpreted in terms of the interaction between the client's internal control structure (ICS) and the client's effort, as follows: (1) If both p and q are low, the ICS is very effective regardless of the client's effort; (2) if both p and q are high, the ICS is weak regardless of the client's effort; and (3) if p is low while q is high, the effectiveness of the ICS is highly dependent on the client's effort.

3. For simplicity, Fellingham and Newman further assume that: (1) the auditor knows the values of p and q before selecting A_1 or A_2 (this is analogous the substantive testing phase of the audit, where the implications of the client's ICS conditional on the client's effort are already known); (2) both the auditor and client know the preferences and payoffs of the opponent; (3) the auditor and client agree on all other model parameters; and (4) the auditor and client view each other as rational. Relaxing these simplifying assumptions does not significantly alter the basic conclusions of the Fellingham and Newman model.

4. A fourth mixed strategy experiment with a matrix that reduced the risk associated with player action choices was conducted in order to examine the effect of risk preferences. The results are qualitatively similar to the three mixed strategy replications reported below.

5. Subjects were all in the same room but did not know with whom they were paired at any time. Thus, the auditor-client pairings were done anonymously. However, because subjects could infer that there was a 1 in 5 chance of being repaired with a particular person in a playing year, the assumption of strict independence between playing years (for both the single-period and multiperiod experiments) may not completely hold.

6. Auditors tended to select the Nash equilibrium strategy in both the single-period and five-period experiments, but the clients selected the cooperative solution (E_1) more often than predicted by the Nash strategy. The Fellingham and Newman model's Nash prediction of 50 percent assumes risk-neutrality. However, if subjects are risk-averse and believe other subjects play each strategy 50 percent of the time, the auditor prefers A_2, Q rather than A_2, NQ, and the client prefers E_1 over E_2, because the variance of these respective gambles is lower. While we attribute the observed client behavior to cooperation per se, it may also be confounded with risk preferences, such that risk aversion might provide

clients with more incentive to cooperate and auditors with more incentive to defect. To test whether risk aversion might explain the observed pattern of auditor-client cooperation, we conducted additional experiments with a procedure to induce risk neutrality (Roth and Malouf 1979; Berg et al. 1986). These experiments exhibited substantially the same behavior as in the experiments presented above and, thereby, suggest that the observed behavior may not be attributable to uncontrolled risk preferences.

REFERENCES

Advisory Panel on Auditor Independence. 1994. Strengthening the Professionalism of the Independent Auditor. Report to the Public Oversight Board of the SEC Practice Section. Stamford, CT: AICPA.

Axelrod, R. 1984. The Evolution of Cooperation. New York: Basic Books.

Berg, J., L. Daley, J. Dickhaut, and J. O'Brien. 1986. Controlling Preferences for lotteries on units of experimental exchange. The Quarterly Journal of Economics (May): 281-306.

Feinberg, R.M., and T.A. Husted. 1993. An experimental test of discount-rate effects on collusive behavior in duopoly markets. Journal of Industrial Economics (June): 153-160.

Fellingham, J.C., and D.P. Newman. 1985. Strategic considerations in auditing. Accounting Review (October): 634-650.

Fisher, J., and J. Schatzberg. 1991. A theoretical and empirical examination of asymmetric prisoners' dilemma games. Working Paper, University of Arizona.

Friedman, J.W. 1986. Game Theory with Applications to Economics. New York: Oxford University Press.

Friedman, J.W., and R.W. Rosenthal. 1986. A positive approach to non-cooperative games. Journal of Economic Behavior and Organization 7: 236-251.

Kadane, J.B., and P.D. Larkey. 1982. Subjective probability and the theory of games. Management Science (February): 113-125. New York:

Kinney, W.R., Jr. 1975a. A decision theory approach to the sampling problem in auditing. Journal of Accounting Research (Spring): 117-132.

———. 1975b. Decision theory aspects of internal control system design/compliance and substantive tests. Journal of Accounting Research (Supplement): 14-29.

Kreps, D., P. Milgrom, J. Roberts, and R. Wilson. 1982. Rational cooperation in the finitely repeated prisoners' dilemma. Journal of Economic Theory 27: 245-252.

Lave, L.B. 1965. Factors affecting cooperation in the prisoners' dilemma. Behavioral Science 10(1): pp. 26-38.

Rapoport, A., and A.M. Chammah. 1965. Prisoners' Dilemma. Ann Arbor, MI.

Roth, A., and A. Malouf. 1979. Game theoretic models and the role of information in bargaining. Psychological Review 86(6): 575-594.

Selten, R. 1978. The chain store paradox. Theory and Decision 9(2): 127-159.

Selten, R., and R. Stoecker. 1986. End behavior in sequences of finite prisoners' dilemma supergames. Journal of Economic Behavior and Organization 7: 47-70.

Smith, V. 1976. Experimental economics: Induced value theory. American Economic Review (May): 274-279.

Smith, V., J. Schatzberg, and W. Waller. 1987. Experimental economics and auditing. Auditing: A Journal of Practice and Theory (Fall): 71-93.

ASSOCIATION BETWEEN ENVIRONMENTAL PERFORMANCE AND ENVIRONMENTAL DISCLOSURES:
AN ASSESSMENT

Martin Freedman and Bikki Jaggi

ABSTRACT

This paper focuses on the relationship between environmental performance and environmental disclosure of U.S. companies from two highly polluting industries. Although similar analyses were done previously and the results have been reported in the management and accounting literature, the earlier studies were concluded when the environmental movement in the United States was in its infancy and most companies had not yet adopted long-range plans to reduce pollution. The current study focuses on a period 10 to 15 years after the passage of the initial air and water pollution laws. The results of this study thus provide information to enable us to evaluate whether environmental performance required by environmental laws has influenced the environmental disclosures by firms.

Advances in Accounting, Volume 14, pages 161-178.
Copyright © 1996 by JAI Press Inc.
All rights of reproduction in any form reserved.
ISBN: 0-7623-0161-9.

The results of this study suggest that there is no association between environmental performance and environmental disclosures for electric utilities. The association between environmental performance and disclosures for pulp and paper firms is negative for the litigation category and for the total environmental disclosures. On the basis of these results, it can reasonably be concluded that environmental disclosures as they exist cannot be used as a proxy for pollution performance. The results provide support to the argument that mandated disclosure requirements are needed for truthful representation of environmental performance and that strict enforcement of the SEC's disclosure requirements would be desirable.

INTRODUCTION

At the World Environmental Congress held in Rio de Janeiro in 1992, United Nations members agreed to take major steps to protect the environment to ensure future planetary survival. The United States, at that time, did not sign the agreement. Then President Bush argued that the United States had done more to protect the environment than had other countries and, therefore, the United States was justified in pushing economic development even if it involved some environmental degradation (Begley and Larson 1992).

A question one may ask is whether President Bush was correct in his assertion of the relative effectiveness of the U.S. environmental policy. This paper addresses this issue on a micro level. Do firms own up to their environmental responsibilities and accurately report their environmental performance or do they misrepresent their relationship to the environment? One way to examine this issue is to look at firm environmental disclosures and see if they mirror their environmental performance.

Several studies have previously examined the association between environmental disclosures contained in financial statements and environmental performance by U.S. firms, but all of them have been based on data generated in 1970s, which could be described as the period of the first wave of environmental movement in the United States. Since that time, several pollution protection laws have been enacted, including CERCLA, SARA (Superfund), and the 1977 and 1990 Clean Air Act and Amendments. Furthermore, the need for environmental disclosures has been strengthened with the passage of SAB 92-1 EITF 90-8 and 93-5. These developments have heightened the public interest and concern for the environment and have sensitized U.S. firms to the need for better environmental performance. The Exxon Valdez disaster has further contributed to the society's renewed interest in the environmental performance of U.S. firms and also to the U.S. firms' awareness of society's concern for environmental impact of corporate activities. This renewed interest and concern creates demands for increased environmental disclosure by firms. Thus, the association between environmental disclosures and environmental performance needs to be reexamined on the basis of data generated after the new laws were enacted, so that investors, regulators and society can better evaluate the environmental performance of U.S. firms.

This paper examines whether environmental disclosures contained in financial statements and 10Ks during the 1978-1987 time period reflect actual environmental performance of U.S. firms. Though information on environmental performance is available to outsiders through several sources, such as financial statements, special reports filed with the regulatory agencies, press releases, and so forth, the most important free and public sources of such information are still the annual financial statements and 10Ks filed with the Securities and Exchange Commission. Therefore, this study focuses on environmental disclosures contained in these two sources.

The remaining paper is organized into five sections. The first section contains a brief review of the literature on the association between environmental performance and environmental disclosures. The second section evaluates the arguments supporting disclosure of environmental information and its association with environmental performance. In this section, we also develop the hypothesis for the study. The research design is explained in the third section. Results are discussed in the fourth section, and the last section presents the limitations and conclusion of the study.

LITERATURE REVIEW

Earlier important studies on the association between environmental disclosures and performance were based on data reported by the CEP pollution studies on pulp and paper (Ellen, Kaufman, and Underwood 1972), steel (Cannon 1974), and oil refining (Kerlin and Rabovsky 1975). Ingram and Frazier (1980) based their study on pollution data for electric utilities (CEP 1977a), whereas Freedman and Jaggi (1982) based their study on an expanded data base which included pollution data from four polluting industry groups—namely, pulp and paper, chemicals, steel, and utilities. They supplemented the CEP data with data obtained from 10Ks of the firms. Freedman and Wasley (1990) conducted a comparative analysis of updated CEP data (1977c) and data obtained from 10Ks and annual reports. Wiseman (1982) and Rockness (1985) also used data published by the CEP pollution studies.

Despite differences in the methodology used by different studies, they all came to the conclusion that there was no relationship between the extensiveness of pollution disclosures and pollution performance of the firms.

The studies examining the market reaction to environmental disclosures (see, e.g., Balkaoui 1977, Jaggi and Freedman 1982), however, concluded that environmental disclosures triggered a market reaction. This anomaly in results could either be explained by the fact that market did not look into the association between environmental disclosures and performance or that the market interpreted the environmental performance in terms of the long term effects.

The current study is based on the pollution data base which utilized data from 1978-1987, which is well after the initial clean air and clean water laws were put into effect. We expect that the analyses based on actual environmental data reported by firms after the environmental laws were promulgated, would show a more realistic association between environmental disclosures and performance compared to studies based on data before or in the earliest years these laws were put into force.

ENVIRONMENTAL DISCLOSURES AND HYPOTHESES

Before we empirically test the association between environmental disclosures and environmental performance, we will evaluate the theoretical justification for this association as presented in the literature. Although much of the theoretical justification presented here concerns disclosure of social disclosures in general (of which pollution disclosure is a subset), it can still be applied to pollution disclosures.

Guthrie and Parker (1990) have presented two arguments in support of disclosure of social information by firms. The first argument is based on the user utility concept (see also Arnold 1990), which suggests that social disclosures are influenced by corporate stakeholders' demand for information. If management perceives that stakeholders are demanding disclosure of certain type of social information, it would provide such information to meet the perceived needs. The second argument is based on the political economy concept, which considers social disclosures to be a social, political and economic tool for management. According to this argument, disclosure of environmental information would be influenced by the management's desire to advance the corporate political or ideological goals. Patten (1992) has combined both of these arguments into the legitimacy argument, which suggests that social disclosures are made to influence the development of public policy and to mitigate the effects of public pressures for mandated disclosure requirements. Following Ramanathan's (1975) arguments, Gray, Owen, and Maunders (1991) developed a normative perspective, which is based on the notion that there is a social contract between the corporation and society. Corporations, therefore, must be made accountable to society for their actions and must provide information on their activities, including environmental information. This argument can be interpreted to mean that environmental disclosures are essential and should include information on the a firm's environmental performance.

The arguments presented in the literature strongly support disclosure of social information including environmental information. However, the rationale of arguments supporting such disclosures differ and these differences in arguments have led to differences in the nature of such disclosures. On one hand, it has been argued that environmental disclosures should reflect environmental performance, and on the other, there appears to be a feeling that firms make environmental disclosures to improve the corporate image and that these disclosures can even be used to mitigate public pressures for more disclosures.

This study empirical tests the association between environmental disclosures and environmental performance using data from the 1978-1987 period to evaluate whether environmental disclosures reflect environmental performance. The following null hypothesis is developed to test this association:

Hypothesis O. There is no association between environmental disclosures contained in annual reports and 10K reports and corporate environmental performance of electric utilities and pulp and paper firms.

Rejection of the null hypothesis would support the argument that there is an association between environmental disclosures and environmental performance, and the sign of correlation will indicate whether the association is positive or negative.

RESEARCH DESIGN

Sample and Time Periods of the Study

This study is based on firms from two highly polluting industries—namely, pulp and paper firms and electric utilities. The study covers six different time periods, 1972, 1975, 1978, 1983, 1986, and 1987. These time periods have been selected because of the availability of environmental performance data. The pulp and paper firms' analysis relates to the following four periods: 1972, 1978, 1983, and 1986. Data on electric utilities are from the years 1975 and 1987. The 1972 data for pulp and paper firms used in this study is borrowed from the Freedman and Wasley (1990) study, and the 1975 data for electric utilities is borrowed from the Freedman and Wasley (1990) and White (1977) studies.

There have been minor changes in the sample size for pulp and paper firms over different time periods because of mergers and acquisitions; as a result of these changes, the sample size may differ between different years. The sample size for pulp and paper firms consisted of 13 firms in 1978. From 1978 to 1983, two more firms were included in the sample, which resulted in 15 sample firms for 1983. The sample for 1986 was reduced to 12 firms because three of the firms were acquired between 1984 and 1986.[1]

The sample for electric utilities consisted of 14 firms for 1987 and 1975. Table 1 lists the sample firms for different study years.

Pollution Performance Index

The Pollution Performance Index for pulp and paper firms for 1978, 1983, and 1986 was developed by Freedman and Jaggi (1988) as an update of the 1972 CEP

Table 1.   Sample Firms

Electric Utilities 1987 (14)	*Pulp and Paper 1978 (13)*
American Electric Power	Boise Cascade
Baltimore Gas & Electric	Champion International
Commonwealth Edison	Crown Zellerbach
Consolidated Edison	Georgia Pacific
Duke Power	Great Northern Nekoosa
Florida Power & Light	Hammermill
Northern States Power	International Paper
Pacific Gas & Electric	Mead
Pacific Power & Light (PACIFICORP)	Potlatch
Pennsylvania Power & Light	St. Regis
Southern California Edison	Scott Paper
Southern Company	Westvaco
Union Electric	Weyerhaeuser
Virginia Electric & Power	
(Dominion Resources)	*Pulp and Paper 1983 (15)*
	Same as 1978 plus:
	Kimberly Clark
	Union Camp
	Pulp and Paper 1986 (12)
	Same as 1983 minus:
	Crown Zellerbach
	Hammermill
	St. Regis

pollution data base. The 1975 Pollution Performance Index for electric utilitie was developed from the data generated by the White (1977) study, and the 198 index is based on the update developed by Freedman and Jaggi (1990).

The 1978, 1983, and 1986 pulp and paper updates are based on actual water pol lution emissions that plant managers reported to the EPA, whereas CEP's 197 and 1972 pulp and paper pollution datasets were based on researchers' observa tions of pollution performance by the firms (Ellen, Kaufman, and Underwoo 1972). The electric utilities 1987 update is based on reports submitted by plan managers of the utilities to the U.S. Department of Energy.

Both of these indices incorporate facets of environmental performance. Th pulp and paper index utilizes water pollution emissions as the key determinant o pollution performance. Water pollution is a major problem for pulp and pape plants. The electric utility index is based on air pollution emissions. These emis sions are not only the major pollution problem for fossil fuel burning electric plants but are the key components of the 1990 Clean Air Act.

It needs to be pointed out that the goals of the original Clean Air and Clean Water Acts focused on achievements that were to occur by the mid-1980s. Therefore, the pollution performance indices based on 1983, 1986, and 1987 data should reflect some long-run achievements.

The pollution performance indices for different study years are provided in Table 2. The lower the value of pollution performance index the better the pollution performance. Procedures for developing these indices are provided in Appendix A.

Pollution Disclosure Index

Disclosures on corporate pollution-related activities can be obtained from several sources, including newspaper articles, special corporate reports, court documents, reports of private organizations (e.g., CEP), and corporate pollution reports filed with government agencies. Although all of these sources are publicly available, acquiring and researching these sources can be costly. The most easily accessible and commonly used reports are probably the annual corporate reports provided to shareholders and the 10Ks filed by the firms with Securities and Exchange Commission (SEC). Previous research studies have used pollution disclosures either from annual reports, or 10Ks, or both.

The annual reports contain pollution information disclosed on both a mandatory and a voluntary basis, and most of the firms from highly polluting industries have been disclosing pollution information on a voluntary basis. All firms materially affected by pollution abatement expenditures, however, are required to disclose the amount of estimated expenditures for current pollution control activities and also estimated expenditures for such future activities in 10Ks. Moreover, information on any material litigation (including environmental fines and lawsuits) needs to be included in 10Ks. Firms may also, on a voluntary basis, describe the environmental improvements achieved and disclose information whether they are in compliance with the environmental regulations.

Since both annual reports and 10Ks provide relevant and important pollution data, both of these sources have been considered appropriate for this study to assess the firms' pollution disclosures. Rather than utilizing the Freedman-Wasley (1990) approach that considered both disclosures separately, this study combines disclosures from both sources to develop a combined disclosure index for firms. While developing the disclosure index, the study carefully avoids double counting from both sources. The method used for developing the disclosure index is a modified version of the method developed by Wiseman (1982). The Wiseman method, based on the quality of disclosures, can be considered superior to the method of merely counting disclosure lines. The modification of the Wiseman method includes extraction of data from both financial statements and 10Ks, and a proce-

Table 2. Pollution Performance Index by Company and Year From Best to Worst

Electric Utilities

Company	1987		1975	
	Score	Rank	Score	Rank
Pacific Gas & Electric	1.19	1	14.87	1
Southern California Edison	15.85	2	34.19	2
Con Edison	20.41	3	43.78	3
Florida Power & Light	23.33	4	45.34	4
Duke Power	58.88	5	90.87	7
Virigina Electric & Power	68.29	6	87.32	5
Pacific Power & Light	78.54	7	172.68	13
Pennsylvania Power & Light	80.08	8	109.20	8
Southern Company	89.20	9	168.78	11
Northern States Power	90.33	10	172.34	12
Baltimore Gas & Electric	94.54	11	89.05	6
American Electric Power	104.86	12	178.16	14
Tennessee Valley Authority	106.40	13	250.56	15
Commonwealth Edison	129.27	14	167.61	10
Union Electric	133.83	15	161.00	9

Pulp and Paper

Company	1986 Score	1986 Rank	1983 Score	1983 Rank	1978 Score	1978 Rank
Champion	4.86	1	8.25	1	33.38	4
St. Regis	14.68	2	21.41	3	40.48	5
Great N. Nekoosa	15.65	3	128.76	15	69.76	7
Westvaco	18.08	4	12.01	2	24.72	3
Potlatch	23.81	5	35.86	5	103.38	8
Union Camp	25.01	6	25.28	4		
Mead	25.46	7	38.58	6	12.92	1
Boise Cascade	29.71	8	55.30	10	57.44	6
Hammermill	33.59	9	44.73	7	17.60	2
Kimberly Clark	39.06	10	46.23	8		
Weyerhaeuser	49.90	11	47.16	9	121.27	10
Georgia Pacific	53.83	12	86.91	12	141.92	11
Scott	59.69	13	101.01	13	112.22	9
Int'l Paper	106.02	14	70.98	11	168.10	13
Crown Zellerbach	144.10	15	123.07	14	160.51	12

Table 3.   Disclosure Categories and Items of Information

I.   Cost Factors
      1. Past and Current Expenditures for Pollution Control Equipment and Facilities
      2. Past and Current Operating Costs of Pollution Control Equipment and Facilities
      3. Future Estimates of Expenditures for Pollution Control Equipment and Facilities
      4. Future Estimates and Operating Costs for Pollution Control Equipment and Facilities
      5. Financing for Pollution Control Equipment and Facilities

II.   Litigation
      6. Present Litigation
      7. Potential Litigation

III. Pollution Abatement
      8. Air Emission Information
      9. Water Discharge Information
      10. Solid Waste Disposal Information
      11. Control, Installations, Facilities, or Processes Described
      12. Compliance Status of Facilities

IV.   Other Environmentally Related Information
      13. Discussion of Regulations and Requirements
      14. Environmental Policies or Company Concern for the Environment
      15. Conservation of Natural Resources
      16. Awards for Environmental Protection
      17. Departments or Offices for Pollution Control

Source: Wiseman (1982, Appendix B).

dure to break down disclosures into four major categories, which are then subdivided into 17 individual items of disclosure. These items are described in Table 3.

In the second step, environmental disclosures obtained from both sources for the sample firms for the years covered in this study, were assessed by three independent judges to develop the disclosure index. The judges were graduate students in accounting who were trained by the authors.

Based on the quality of disclosures, the judges assigned a score ranging from 0 to 3 for each disclosure item. If the disclosure was made in monetary or quantitative terms, the highest score of 3 was assigned. The rationale for assigning the highest score was that the quantitative information in a monetary form is comparatively more objective and more useful to investors than a mere description of environmental information, which does not indicate whether the firm is doing anything for cleaning up the environment. If the disclosure was specific but nonquan-

Table 4.

Part A. Electric Utility Disclosures by Category

Company Name	Cost Factors 1975	Cost Factors 1987	Litigation 1975	Litigation 1987	Abatement 1975	Abatement 1987	Other 1975	Other 1987	Total 1975	Total 1987
American Elec Power	0	1	0	2	0	8	0	1	0	12
Baltimore G&E	6	6	0	0	7	13	1	1	14	20
Commonwealth Edison	6	0	1	2	0	5	0	1	7	8
Con Edison	0	6	2	3	5	2	1	1	8	12
Duke Power	3	3	0	0	3	4	1	1	7	8
Florida P&L	12	6	0	0	3	3	1	1	16	10
Northern States Power	6	6	0	0	4	2	1	1	11	9
Pacific G&E	6	6	3	0	5	8	2	1	16	15
Pacific P&L	3	6	0	0	5	4	3	1	11	11
Pa P&L	6	6	2	0	5	7	1	1	14	14
Southern Co.	0	6	0	0	0	1	0	1	0	8
So. Calif. Electric	6	6	0	0	11	10	1	1	18	17
Union Electric	0	0	0	0	0	1	0	0	0	1
Virginia Electric	6	3	0	0	8	6	1	0	15	9

(continued)

Table 4. (Continued)

Part B. Pulp and Paper Disclosures by Category

Co. Name	Cost Factors			Litigation			Abatement			Other			Total		
	1978	1983	1986	1978	1983	1986	1978	1983	1986	1978	1983	1986	1978	1983	1986
Boise Cascade	6	6	6	3	3	0	0	0	0	1	0	0	10	9	6
Champion Int'l	6	6	6	0	0	0	0	0	0	1	1	1	7	7	7
Crown Zellerbach	6	6		3	0		0	0		1	1		10	7	
Georgia Pacific	6	6	6	0	3	1	5	4	0	0	0	2	11	13	9
Great N. Nekoosa	6	6	0	2	1	0	0	0	0	0	0	0	8	7	0
Hammermill	6	6		3	0		0	0		1	1		10	7	
Int'l Paper	9	9	9	3	3	3	0	0	0	1	0	1	13	12	13
Kimberly Clark		6	6		0			0			1			7	6
Mead	6	6	6	0	0	0	0	0	0	1	1	1	7	7	6
Potlatch	0	0	0	0	0	0	0	0	0	1	1	1	1	1	1
St. Regis	9	9		2	2		0	3		1	1		12	15	
Scott	7	7	7	3	1	3	2	0	0	1	1	1	13	9	11
Union Camp		6	5		0	0		0	3		1	1		7	9
Westvaco	6	6	6	3	0	0	2	0	0	1	2	1	12	8	7
Weyerhaeuser	2	2	2	3	3	3	0	2	0	1	1	1	6	8	6

titative, a score of 2 was assigned. The environmental disclosure in a more general and descriptive form received the score of 1. If no environment disclosure was made by the firm, the score of 0 was assigned. This scoring system is consistent with the system used by earlier studies (including Freedman and Wasley 1990) and, therefore, makes it easier to compare the results with that previous study. A sample of different types of disclosures is contained in Appendix B.

Evaluations by independent judges were converted into an average score for each item, and the item scores were added to obtain the category score. Scores of all categories were added to obtain an overall disclosure index for each firm for the appropriate year. All categories were given equal weight. The disclosure scores for each disclosure category and the overall disclosure index for each firm are contained in Table 4. Spearman correlation tests were conducted for each disclosure category with the performance index for each study year; Table 5 presents the results.

TEST RESULTS

Results on Electric Utilities

The results for electric utilities indicate that there is a positive association between the total pollution disclosure index and pollution performance index both

Table 5. Spearman Rank-Correlations Between Pollution Performance and Pollution Disclosures

Year	N	Disclosure Categories				Total
		Cost Factors	Litigation	Abatement	Other	
Electric Utilities						
1975*	14	.53	.14	.08	.24	.34
1987	14	.46	−.38	.05	.07	.44
		(.10)				(.12)
Pulp And Paper Firms						
1972*	21	−.06	.10	.07	−.19	−.04
1978	13	−.11	−.46	−.39	−.51	−.23
			(.11)		(.08)	
1983	15	−.40	−.83	−.29	−.50	−.46
			(.01)		(.06)	(.08)
1986	12	−.26	−.47	−.39	−.34	−.59
			(.12)			(.05)

Note: Significance level shown in parentheses.
Source: *Freedman and Wasley (1990, 190).

for 1975 and 1987. A positive association indicates that better (worse) pollution performance correlates with more extensive (less) disclosure. Similarly, the association between individual pollution disclosure categories and pollution performance index for both years is positive. This positive association is, however, not statistically significant. In the absence of statistically significant correlations, the positive association between environmental performance and environmental disclosures does not provide any strong evidence that pollution disclosures reflect pollution performance.

A comparison of 1975 and 1987 results indicates that the results for both periods are similar and there has been no change in the association between the two variables from 1975 to 1987. These results can be interpreted to mean that despite renewed interests in environmental concerns, the association between environmental performance and environmental disclosures did not improve in 1987 compared to the association for 1975, which suggests that there has been no improvement in pollution disclosures to reflect environmental performance of electric utilities since the passage of the 1977 Clean Air Act.

On the basis of the above results, we cannot reject the null hypothesis for electric utilities that there is no association between environmental performance and environmental disclosures. These results, thus, do not support the general expectation that the renewed interest in environmental concerns would lead to environmental disclosure which better reflects environmental performance.

The absence of a statistically significant association between environmental disclosures and environmental performance of electric utilities could have been influenced by the regulatory nature of the industry. It would, therefore, be of interest to investors and the general public to know how environmental performance and disclosures are decided by these firms. In order to have a better understanding of the processes, an extensive research study in this direction would be useful.

Results on Pulp and Paper Firms

The results relating to pulp and paper firms, however, provide a different picture. The association between environmental performance and environmental disclosures for 1972, as reported by Freedman and Wasley (1990), was negative for the total disclosure category and also negative for some individual disclosure categories (cost factors, other categories), but positive for other individual categories (litigation and abatement categories). However, none of the correlations were statistically significant. These results are contained in Table 5.

The correlation results of our analyses for 1978, 1983, and 1986 indicate that correlations for all categories is negative. The correlation coefficient for the total disclosure category for 1986 is significant at the .05 level, and the litigation category for 1983 is also significant at the .01 level. On the basis of just two significant categories for two different time period, we cannot reject the null hypothesis for pulp and paper firms that there is no association between environmental perfornance and environmental disclosures. These results do not support the general expectation that pollution disclosures reflect pollution performance.

The statistically significant negative association for the 1983 litigation category is probably due to the fact that higher litigation was associated with worse pollution performance. This negative association for the litigation category suggests that the firms that pollute more may find themselves having to defend their actions in courts more often, and that results in more disclosures. In this case, it would appear that disclosure reflects performance. Most disclosures in this category are, however, mandated by the SEC. The results of this category thus may not be representative of other categories or overall disclosures.

The 1986 results for total disclosures may suggest that on an overall basis the poorer pollution performance for pulp and paper firms was associated with higher disclosures because poor performance firms engaged in more disclosures to look good. These firms probably engage in more disclosures as a smokescreen to hide their pollution performance. By disclosing more pollution information, the firms convey to outsiders that they are greatly concerned about the environment, while their performance does not support it. The negative association thus suggests that U.S. pulp and paper firms are paying more lip service to the environment than they are cleaning the environment.

The results of this study for pulp and paper firms differ from earlier studies. Earlier studies have been based on data prior to or in the early years of the environmental laws and SEC mandatory requirements. These earlier studies correlated initial pollution performance and ad hoc disclosure policies, which probably reflected short-run policies. The current study is based on data for the period after the passage of key environmental acts and after the SEC disclosure requirements were promulgated. Therefore, what is being captured in this study is possibly the long run pollution performance correlated with well formulated disclosure policies.

CONCLUSION AND LIMITATIONS

The results of this study do not provide support for the general expectation that meaningful environmental information is disclosed which would enable stakeholders to intelligently assess the corporation's pollution performance. These findings present a challenge to policy makers to examine other means and methods to encourage or require firms to disclose environmental information which would truly reflect their environmental performance. The inconsistency in disclosures and performance is probably being encouraged by the SEC's lack of meaningful environmental disclosure requirements and the SEC's weak enforcement of current disclosure requirements. The U.S. Steel case especially shows a weak enforcement policy. It was over seventeen years ago that the SEC admonished U.S. Steel for their lack of pollution disclosures. But despite this admonishment, there are still firms that are not meeting the SEC's disclosure requirements.

These findings also suggest that policymakers should carefully consider the nature of disclosure requirements and that these requirements should be meaning ful and realistic. If these requirements are not meaningful, environmental disclo sures will not serve any useful purpose. If we continue with the current practices firms will just pay lip service to their environmental responsibilities while they continue a policy of environmental degradation.

The findings of this study should, however, be interpreted with caution because of limitations of the study. Only two industries were examined and each industry group included 15 or fewer firms. As a result of this small sample size, the finding of this study need to be revalidated. Despite the size limitation, the sample firm included in the industry groups are among the largest in the industry and, there fore, the findings of this study can be expected to have validity for firms withit these groups. Another limitation of this study relates to generalization of these findings to other industry groups. The two industries examined may have peculiar characteristics (e.g., electric utilities are regulated), which may limit the validity of the conclusion to other industry groups.

Most sample firms in this study are large. In the absence of small firms, we could not conduct a comparative analysis of large versus small firms to evaluate the validity of the argument that large firms are likely to be more in the public eye and would tend to provide more extensive environmental information than small firms (Belkaoui and Karpik, 1987).

The analysis technique utilized in this study may also limit the validity of the findings. This method required subjective assessment of independent judges. Although the judges were in close agreement, their evaluation of pollution disclo sures was still subjective. This technique, however, was utilized in two other ear lier studies, which made it possible to compare the results of this study to the results of the earlier studies.

APPENDIX A

The Pollution Performance Index

In composing the index for pulp and paper firms, water pollution data for three measures of pollution for each company is first determined. The three measures of pollution: BOD, Total Suspended Solids, and pH are first treated independently with firms ranked relative to their performance in abating each pollution measure. The firm with the highest measure of a given pollutant in any of the three years (1978, 1983, or 1986) is given a score of 100 and all the other firms are scored rel ative to that. For example, in 1978 Crown Zellerbach had the highest measure of BOD per ton of production, which was 21.4, so it received a score of 100 for that measure in 1978. Georgia Pacific, with a BOD measure of 16.23 in 1978, received a score of 75.84 (i.e., [16.23/21.4] [100]). After each pollution measure for each company was scored, the scores for each company by year were summed to arrive at an overall pollution score for that year. What is presented in Table 2 is the total scores for each pulp and paper company for 1978, 1983, and 1986 and their ranking.

The process for creating the pollution performance index for electric utilities was similar to that of the pulp and paper firms. However, the index is of air pollution and it is based on the pollution emission for three pollutants: sulfur dioxide, nitrous oxides and particulates. Also, only two years of data are presented: 1975 and 1987.

APPENDIX B

Examples of Pollution Disclosures

An example of a cost factor that received a score of 3 is:

Capital expenditures for pollution control facilities in 1986 were approximately $19 million (Georgia Pacific 1986 10K, p. 5).

An example of an "other" factor that received a score of 2 is:

In 1986, waste paper totalling approximately 600,000 tons was recycled by the companies pulp and paper operation (Georgia Pacific 1986 10K, p. 5).

A an example of a litigation that received a score of 1 is:

The corporation has been notified that it is a potentially responsible party in actions by the U.S. Environmental Protection Agency and various state agencies with respect to a number of hazardous waste disposal sites which seek remedial action (Georgia Pacific 1986 10K, p. 6).

A piece of data that received a score of zero is:

Environmental control standards require, in many instances, balancing the need for additional quantities of energy in future years with then need to protect the environment. The company cannot now estimate the precise effect of existing and potential regulations and legislation upon its existing or proposed facilities and operations (Commonwealth Edison 1987 10K, p. 9).

NOTE

1. Between 1983 and 1986, three firms were acquired by other companies and were eliminated from the 1986 disclosure sample: Crown Zellerbach, Hammermill, and St. Regis. However, Freedman and Jaggi (1988) included plants from these companies in their 1986 analysis of pollution performance. The pollution score in Table 2, therefore, includes all 15 pulp and paper companies. However, Tables 4B and 5 include only 12 pulp and paper firms in 1986.

REFERENCES

Arnold, P. 1990. The state and political theory in corporate disclosure research: A response to Guthrie and Parker. In *Advances in Public Interest Accounting*, Vol. 3, ed. M. Neimark, 177-182. Greenwich, CT: JAI Press.

Begley, S., and B. Larson. 1992. The grinch of Rio. *Newsweek* (June 15): 30.

Belkaoui, A. 1976. The impact of disclosure of the environmental effects of organizational behavior on the market. *Financial Management* (Winter): 26-31.

Belkaoui, A., and P.G. Karpik. 1987. Determinants of the corporate decision to disclose social information. *Accounting, Auditing and Accountability Journal* 2(1): 36-49.

Cannon, J. 1974. *Environmental Steel.* New York: Praeger.

Council on Economic Priorities. 1977a. *The Pollution Audit.* New York: Council on Economic Priorities.

———. 1977b. Environmental steel/update. *Newsletter* (September 26).

———. 1977c. The price of power/update. *Newsletter* (December 7).

Ellen, L., E.K. Kaufman, and J. Underwood. 1972. *Pollution in the Pulp and Paper Industry.* Boston, MA: MIT Press.

Freedman, M., and B. Jaggi. 1982. Pollution disclosures, pollution performance and economic performance. *OMEGA* (2nd Quarter): 167-176.

———. 1988. *Cleaning Up Their Act. Council on Economic Priorities Research Report (September). New York: Council on Economic Priorities.*

———. 1990. *A Mixed Cloud—Air Pollution and Electric Utilities* Council on Economic Priorities Research Report (July/August). New York: Council on Economic Priorities.

Freedman, M., and C. Wasley. 1990. The association between environmental performance and environmental disclosure in annual reports and 10Ks. In *Advances in Public Interest Accounting,* Vol. 3, ed. M. Neimark, 183-194. Greenwich, CT: JAI Press.

Gray, R., D.L. Owen, and K. Maunders. 1991. Accountability, corporate social regulating and the external social audits. *In Advances in Public Interest Accounting,* Vol. 4, ed. C. Lehman, 1-21. Greenwich, CT: JAI Press.

Guthrie, J., and L.D. Parker. 1990. Corporate social disclosure practice: A comparative international analysis. In *Advances in Public Interest Accounting,* Vol. 3, ed. M. Neimark, 159-176. Greenwich, CT: JAI Press.

Ingram, R., and K.B. Frazier. 1980. Environmental performance and corporate disclosure. *Journal of Accounting Research* (Autumn): 614-622.

Jaggi, B., and M. Freedman. 1982. An analysis of the information content of pollution disclosures. *Financial Review* (September): 142-152.

Kerlin, D., and D. Rabovsky. 1975. *Cracking Down Oil Refining and Pollution Control.* New York: Council on Economic Priorities.

Patten, D. 1992. Intra-industry environmental disclosures in response to the Alaskan oil spill: A note of legitimacy theory. *Accounting Organizations and Society* 17(5): 471-475.

Ramanathan, K. 1976. Toward a theory of corporate social accounting. *The Accounting Review* (July): 516-528.

Rockness, J. 1985. An assessment of the relationship between US corporate environmental performance and disclosure. *Journal of Business, Finance and Accounting* (Autumn): 339-354.

Shane, P., and B. Spicer. 1983. Market response to environmental information produced outside the firm. *Accounting Review* (July): 521-538.

Ullmann, A. 1985. Data in search of a theory: A critical examination of the relationship among social performance, social disclosure and economic performance of U.S. firms. *Academy of Management Review* (July): 540-557.

Wiseman, J. 1982. An evaluation of environmental disclosures made in corporate annual reports. *Accounting Organizations and Society* 7(1): 53-63.

AN EXAMINATION OF DIRECT AND INDIRECT GENDER EFFECTS IN PUBLIC ACCOUNTING

Eric N. Johnson, D. Jordan Lowe, and
Philip M.J. Reckers

ABSTRACT

This study applied an experimental approach to examine the effects of gender and explanation on peer evaluations of audit senior performance. One-hundred-and-five audit seniors from one Big Six public accounting firm evaluated the performance of a hypothetical audit senior on an audit engagement and also provided expectations of future performance. Audit senior gender and the senior's explanation for a significant time-budget overrun on the engagement were manipulated between subjects. Results revealed that subjects rated the current engagement performance lower, and indicated a lower likelihood of success on future engagements, when the hypothetical audit senior was described as female. Similarly, subjects rated the audit senior's current and future performance lower when the explanation for the budget overrun was family-related than when it was based on client factors. Implications of these findings for the public accounting profession and suggestions for future research are discussed.

Advances in Accounting, Volume 14, pages 179-192.
Copyright © 1996 by JAI Press Inc.
All rights of reproduction in any form reserved.
ISBN: 0-7623-0161-9.

INTRODUCTION

Women have been entering the public accounting profession in increasing numbers since the 1970s. In 1994, nearly 50 percent of all new hires entering public accounting were women (Hooks 1994). During the 1980s, the American Institute of Certified Public Accountants (AICPA) recognized the importance of assuring upward mobility for women as a major issue facing the profession (AICPA 1984) and established a special committee to study gender issues (AICPA 1988). Most recently, an AICPA survey of women's status and work and family issues (AICPA 1992) identified the recruiting and retention of women professionals as an important ongoing challenge to CPA firms. In particular, the higher turnover rate for women in public accounting, which was the subject of extensive study during the 1980s (e.g., AICPA 1984; Earnest and Lampe 1982; Gaertner et al. 1987; Pillsbury, Capozzoli, and Ciampa 1989), continues to be a major problem facing the profession in the mid-1990s (Collins 1993; Staff 1995).

Higher turnover among women public accountants may be due in part to discrimination against women, either directly or in connection with family issues (Gaffney and McEwen 1993; Reed and Kratchman 1990). Prior empirical research (Anderson et al. 1994) has documented that women auditors with children are perceived by their peers as less likely to experience career success. This study extends prior research by directly comparing family- versus client-related explanations for poor audit engagement performance across auditor gender. Results indicate that family-related explanations are perceived as less acceptable than client-related explanations as justification for poor auditor performance. Further, this effect is greater when the auditor is female.

This study uses peer evaluations of an audit senior's performance to test for gender- and family-related biases in performance evaluation. An audit senior's perceptions of the determinants of career success in public accounting are important because they reflect the organizational socialization processes of less-experienced public accountants.

BACKGROUND AND
THEORETICAL DEVELOPMENT

Organizational Socialization

Gaining an understanding of the elements of career success is an important part of the process of *organizational socialization* by newer employees in public accounting firms. Organizational socialization can be defined as the process in which individuals are shaped by the organization in which they aspire to gain full membership. Socialization has the effect of narrowing the range of individual behavior to be compatible with the organization. That is, individuals tend to conform to the characteristics of important elements of their environment by adopting the attributes of its membership. New employees tend to observe and then *mimic* the behavior of successful incumbents in order to achieve the results they aspire toward. Mimicry is also used for "defensive" purposes as individuals attempt to avoid organization censure associated with nonconformity (Fogarty 1992).

Related to public accounting, individuals learn to conform to their organizational environment (or terminate employment) in a number of ways. First, individuals change their behavior, values, and attitudes to perceived criteria for success in public accounting (*role modeling*). Second, individuals tend to rationalize observed behavior which subsequently guides their own actions (*diffusion*) (Fogarty 1992).

Gender Stereotype Effects

Women accountants may be perceived as less likely to achieve upward mobility and thus succeed in public accounting as a consequence of the profession being viewed as a male-stereotyped profession. Two potential sources of gender stereotypes and their negative effects on women public accountants are *person-centered* and *situation-centered* perspectives (Maupin 1993).

The person-centered perspective is based on Bem's (1974) Sex-Role Inventory which classifies personality traits as reflecting feminine, masculine, or neutral characteristics. Maupin and Lehman (1994) found that stereotypical "masculine-related" traits (e.g., aggressiveness, leadership, and competitiveness) increased directly with occupational level such that these traits were found to be lowest with audit juniors and highest with partners, *irrespective* of gender. Furthermore, they found that 100 percent of the women (and men) advancing to partnership levels had high stereotypic masculine characteristics. The authors interpreted these results to mean that exhibiting masculine-stereotyped behavior was one key to career satisfaction and success in public accounting.

The situation-centered perspective suggests that acceptance into the informal culture of a CPA firm (i.e., social and power structures) is an important factor with respect to professional development in public accounting. For instance, being assigned to prestigious client engagements is largely controlled by an individual's standing within the firm's power structure. This is particularly relevant given that assignment to valued clients has been identified as an important element in career success in public accounting (Maupin 1993).[1] Likewise, building networking and mentoring relationships with senior firm personnel is a function of embracing the firm's culture. Given that the culture of public accounting is largely defined along "patriarchal" values, females may be systematically restricted from gaining access to these opportunities (Collins 1993; Hooks 1992; Maupin and Lehman 1994).

This discussion suggests that both peer evaluations of engagement performance and estimates of future performance for female audit seniors will be influenced by negative gender stereotypes. Although gender biases may occur when rating a good performance (Crocker and McGraw 1984), rating a performance described as "substandard" should trigger an extended search for causal explanations to determine the reason(s) for the poor performance (DeNisi et al. 1984; Hunt and Messier 1995). If practicing audit seniors associate a male stereotype with acceptable performance in making performance evaluation judgments, gender is more likely to be viewed as a causal factor for substandard performance by a female auditor than by a male auditor. The following hypotheses are proposed:

Hypothesis 1A. Practicing auditors will rate a substandard engagement performance by a female audit senior lower than the same performance by a male audit senior.

Hypothesis 1B. Practicing auditors will judge a female audit senior's future performance lower than a male audit senior's future performance after the auditor has performed at a substandard level on an audit engagement.

Family-related Effects

Role conflict has been identified as another potential source of gender bias in public accounting (Gaffney and McEwen 1993; Hooks 1992). Role conflict occurs when an individual is unable to attend to all of his or her roles (i.e., work, social, family) completely. Gender plays an important part in role identity and therefore in role conflict. Prior research in sociology and psychology reports that women spend a disproportionate amount of time tending to family responsibilities (Cook 1988; Coverman and Shelley 1986; Krausz 1986; Yogev and Brett 1985). Thus, gender differences in role conflicts may be a function of family and child care responsibilities such that women feel greater role conflict than men when dealing with the competing demands of work and family.

Gaffney and McEwen (1993) examined career commitment among employees of two Big Six public accounting firms. Their results indicated that professional and organizational commitment was equal between childless men and women. Significant differences, however, were found between men and women with children, and these differences were consistent with a role conflict explanation. A national survey sponsored by the AICPA also suggests that family-based role conflicts are greater for female accountants than for male accountants:

> Women are less inclined than men to feel that parenting would be compatible with a successful career in accounting—whether it be at their current firm, at another public accounting firm, or in private industry. For example, while two out of every three of the male respondents feel that, should they become a parent or have another child, this would be very or somewhat compatible with a successful career at another public accounting firm, only 36 percent of the female respondents offered the same response (AICPA 1990, 135).

The role conflict model suggests that family and child care responsibilities are perceived to interfere with professional responsibilities more often for women than for men. Further, given the pervasive male stereotype for success in public accounting (Lehman 1990; Maupin 1990), family-related explanations for work disruptions (such as attending to the needs of an ill child) may be viewed as a less acceptable justification for "substandard" performance on an audit engagement. Trapp et al. (1989) provide some evidence of this: approximately one-quarter of the respondents to their survey of public accountants reportedly believed that special accommodations should not be made for females with primary responsibility for attending to sick children.

Work interruptions caused by child care issues may also affect audit seniors' perceptions of their peers' future performance. Audit seniors may have less confidence in the future ability and promotion prospects of their peers who miss work due to family illness than in those who miss work for other reasons (i.e., personal illness, physical disability).

Based on the foregoing discussion, it is predicted that assessments of an audit senior's current and future performance will be lower when the senior's explanation for the poor performance is based on work interruptions caused by a child's illness as opposed to non-family-related factors. A significant *explanation* effect in favor of a non-family-based excuse for substandard engagement performance will indicate the presence of an *indirect* bias against the female audit senior. That is, because working women bear primary responsibility for child care, as noted above, lower peer ratings in response to the family-based explanation will have a disproportionate effect on perceptions of the female's career success, ceteris paribus. These predictions are stated formally in the following hypotheses:

Hypothesis 2A. Practicing auditors will rate a substandard engagement performance by an audit senior lower when the senior's explanation for the substandard performance is family-related than when it is non-family-related.

Hypothesis 2B. Practicing auditors will rate an audit senior's future performance lower when the senior's explanation for substandard engagement performance is family-related than when it is non-family-related.

The traditional female role is more closely aligned with family responsibilities than is the traditional male role. As a result, the impact of the family-related explanation on performance evaluation might differ between the male and the female audit senior. We conjecture that a significant interaction will result such that the family-related explanation may be perceived as less viable for the female audit senior, leading to lower current and future performance evaluations.

METHOD

An experiment was conducted to test the above hypotheses. An experimental setting for research into gender effects offers the advantage of having control over extraneous factors (Hooks 1992). Control over these factors is difficult in a field study (e.g., survey); therefore, this study offers an alternative to much prior research. The experimental subjects, task, and independent, dependent, and control variables are described below.

Subjects

Subjects were practicing audit seniors representing one Big Six public accounting firm. One-hundred-and-fourteen subjects received the experimental materials as part of firm-wide training. Two of the 114 subjects failed a postexperimental manipulation check regarding the experimental treatment (described below). Seven additional subjects did not provide complete responses to the experimental materials. The responses of these nine subjects were deleted, leaving 105 observations for analysis. The 105 remaining subjects averaged 27 years of age, with approximately 43 months' auditing experience with their firm. Fifty of the 105 subjects were female.

Task

Each subject was given a scenario describing an audit senior's substandard performance on a recent audit engagement. The information contained in the base scenario was constant across cases, including information regarding the audit senior's performance on the current engagement. In addition, subjects were provided with the senior's performance ratings on nine audit engagements over the past year. All audit seniors were described as "average performers," having received five "at expectation" ratings, two "above expectation" ratings, and two "below expectation" ratings. In all cases, the scenario stated that the audit senior had significantly exceeded the audit time budget and failed to meet a client-imposed audit deadline. Time-budget and deadline failure were selected as the judgment criteria because they have been found to influence auditor performance appraisals (Kaplan and Reckers 1985, 1993; Wright 1980).

A brief description of the client's business (a manufacturer and retailer of electronic, audio and optical products, designed to represent a "typical" audit client) and relevant summarized financial information was also provided to subjects. After reading the questionnaire, subjects were subsequently directed to make performance appraisal judgments. The performance appraisals were followed by a debriefing questionnaire including standard demographic questions. As part of the debriefing, subjects were also given two manipulation checks which tested the subjects' recall of: (1) the audit senior's (ratee) gender, and (2) the audit senior's explanation for the substandard engagement performance. As noted above, the responses of two subjects were deleted from the analysis given that these subjects were unable to identify the audit senior's explanation correctly.

Independent Variables

Ratee Gender

The first independent variable was the audit senior's (ratee) gender (*RGEN-DER*). *RGENDER* was randomly assigned between subjects: 56 (49) subjects received the male (female) audit senior version of the case. The audit senior's gender was unambiguously described by his or her first name, and the senior's first name was repeated throughout the case.[2]

Explanation

The audit senior's explanation[3] for exceeding the time budget on the engagement (*EXPLAIN*) was also manipulated between subjects. The senior's explanation for the budget overrun was either family-related or client-related. In the family-related condition, the audit senior explained that the budget overrun was due to the senior's child becoming seriously ill during the engagement. The child's illness resulted both in loss of sleep and work time for the audit senior. In the client-related condition, the budget overrun was attributed to significant turnover in client personnel and major changes in the client's internal control structure from the previous year. These client-related changes required the senior to spend a significant amount of time performing audit tests and training inexperienced engagement staff. Subjects randomly received either the family-related ($n = 52$) or the client-related ($n = 53$) explanation for the time-budget overrun on the engagement.

Subject Gender

Subject gender (*SGENDER*) was included to examine the possible effects of raters' own gender on responses. Gender of the rater has been shown to influence performance ratings in some prior studies of performance evaluation, particularly when the ratee's performance was classified as substandard (Dobbins et al. 1983; Dobbins 1985).

Dependent Variables

Two dependent variables were elicited. The first variable was a formal evaluation of the audit senior's general performance on the engagement. Subjects responded to the statement, "Please indicate [the audit senior's] overall performance [on the engagement] using one of the following categories" (the categories were worded to correspond to the CPA firm's *own* performance evaluation form):

1. Rank *Above Expectation* and provide documentation.
2. Rank *At Expectation* and discuss individually unusual circumstances surrounding the engagement.

3. Rank *At Expectation* and discuss individually areas of improvement.
4. Rank *Below Expectation* and provide documentation relating to potential mitigating factors.
5. Rank *Below Expectation* citing specific areas of individual deficiency.

Although five performance categories were provided, no subject ranked the senior as performing "above expectation" on the engagement. Thus, responses to this scale were limited to the four remaining categories. Given the truncated range of this scale, subjects' responses were transformed into an indicator variable in which 0 = rank "below expectation" and 1 = rank "at expectation."

The second dependent variable assessed subjects' confidence "that the senior would perform *at or above expectation*" on future audit engagements. The process of organizational socialization suggests that less experienced members of an organization quickly determine what attributes are necessary for long-term success in the organization. Thus, this scale measured subjects' perceptions of how the audit senior's substandard performance on the current engagement would affect future performance as an audit senior with the firm. This variable was measured on a 10-point scale with endpoints anchored on 1 for "no confidence" and 10 for "complete confidence."

Control Variables

Two additional variables were included in the data analysis for control purposes, thereby providing a clearer understanding of the influence of the independent variables on the dependent variables. The first variable was each subject's rating of the audit senior's performance on his or her audit engagements over the past year (*PAST*). This assessment was measured on a 10-point scale anchored on 1 for "poor," and 10 for "outstanding." Inclusion of this variable controlled for the possible effects of subjects anchoring their ratings of the audit senior's engagement performance on his or her past performance (see Hunt and Messier 1995). The second variable was each subject's estimate of the percentage of audit seniors in their office who receive "below expectation" engagement performance ratings (*PCTBELOW*). This variable controls for differences in performance evaluation policies across offices of the firm as well as idiosyncracies in each subject's evaluation style.

RESULTS

Each of the two dependent variables was tested in a model that included the effects of the independent variables *RGENDER, EXPLAIN*, and *SGENDER*, the interaction between *RGENDER* and *EXPLAIN*, and the control variables *PAST* and *PCT-BELOW*. Different data analysis techniques were employed, depending on the distributional characteristics of the dependent variable being tested.

Table 1. Logistic Regression Results for Engagement Performance Evaluation

Variable	Coefficient	se	Wald Statistic	Significance
RGENDER (R)	−0.8130	.3307	6.0450	.0139
EXPLAIN (E)	−1.5112	.3999	14.2830	.0002
R X E	0.9423	.5122	3.3848	.0658
SGENDER	0.1724	.2427	.5046	.4775
PAST	0.6123	.2193	7.7929	.0052
PCT BELOW	−.0767	.0391	3.8461	.0499
Intercept	−2.3191	1.1760	3.8889	.0486

Model Chi-Square (6 d.f.) = 32.073; $p < .0001$

Current Engagement Performance

As discussed above, subjects' responses to the five-category engagement performance measure were transformed into a dichotomous (0,1) scale, in which 0 = rank "below expectation" and 1 = rank "at expectation." Logistic regression (logit) analysis was used to measure the effects of the independent variables on subjects' rankings of the audit senior's engagement performance. This analysis is shown in Table 1.

Table 1 indicates significant effects for *RGENDER, EXPLAIN, PAST,* and *PCT-BELOW,* as well as a marginally significant interaction between *RGENDER* × *EXPLAIN.* The negative regression coefficients for *RGENDER* and *EXPLAIN* indicate effects that are consistent with the hypothesized relationships. Subjects classified the female audit senior's performance lower than that of the male audit senior (Hypothesis 1A). Likewise, substandard performance based on the family-related explanation for the time-budget overrun was rated lower than the same performance accompanied by the client-related explanation (Hypothesis 2A).

In order to interpret the marginally significant interaction between *RGENDER* and *EXPLAIN,* cross-tabulations of category means were analyzed. When the explanation for the engagement budget overrun was family-related, the female audit senior was rated significantly lower than the male audit senior. However, no difference between senior gender was noted when the explanation was client-related. The direction of this interaction is consistent with our conjecture such that females with family responsibilities were rated lower than males with the same responsibilities.

Both control variables were significant. The positive coefficient for *PAST* indicates that subjects' evaluations of the audit senior's engagement performance were positively related to their preexperimental evaluations of his or her performance over the past year. The negative coefficient for *PCTBELOW* indicates that

***Table* 2.**   ANCOVA Results for Performance on Future Audit
Engagements

Panel A: ANCOVA Results

Source of Variance	SS	df	MS	F	Sig.	Reg. Coeff.
Covariates						
PAST	67.574	1	67.574	27.507	<.001	0.689
PCTBELOW	0.766	1	0.766	0.312	.578	−0.014
Main Effects						
RGENDER (R)	11.425	1	11.425	4.651	.034	
EXPLAIN (E)	16.076	1	16.076	6.544	.012	
SGENDER (S)	5.671	1	5.671	2.308	.132	
R X E	1.300	1	1.300	0.529	.469	
R X S	0.045	1	0.045	0.018	.893	
E X S	0.355	1	0.355	0.144	.705	
R X E X S	0.730	1	0.730	0.297	.587	
Error	233.383	95	2.457			

Panel B: Treatment Means (Standard Deviations)

RGENDER		EXPLAIN		SGENDER	
Female	*Male*	*Family-Related*	*Client-Related*	*Female*	*Male*
5.22	5.90	5.16	5.96	5.33	5.80
(1.80)	(1.74)	(1.78)	(1.72)	(1.78)	(1.82)

subjects' ratings reflected their own experiences: subjects from offices where a higher percentage of seniors are rated "below expectation" tended to rate the audit senior's engagement performance lower. Finally, subject gender (*SGENDER*) was not significantly related, directly or interactively, with evaluations of the audit senior's engagement performance.

Expectations of Future Performance

The second dependent variable measured subjects' confidence that the senior would perform at or above expectation on future audit engagements.[4] Because this dependent variable was measured on a continuous 10-point scale, analysis of covariance (ANCOVA) was considered to be appropriate for statistical analysis purposes. The results of the 2^3 ANCOVA are shown in Table 2.

The ANCOVA results indicate the same overall pattern of findings as the previous analyses. Subjects believed that the male audit senior was significantly more likely to perform at or above expectation on future audit engagements than the female audit senior (Hypothesis 1B). Likewise, audit seniors who gave a family-related explanation for exceeding the engagement time budget were judged as significantly less likely to receive good performance evaluations in the future than seniors who gave a client-related explanation for the budget overrun (Hypothesis 2B). The interaction of these factors, however, was not significant. Subject evaluation of the audit senior's *PAST* engagement performance was significant and positively related to judgments of future performance. Neither *SGENDER* nor *PCTBELOW* was significant in the future performance model.

SUMMARY AND DISCUSSION

One-hundred-and-five practicing auditors assessed the engagement and future performance of a hypothetical audit senior who had significantly exceeded the time budget on an audit engagement. The audit senior's gender and the senior's explanation for the budget overrun were manipulated between subjects. Across two dependent measures, subjects rated the female audit senior lower than the male audit senior, and the family-related explanation lower than the client-related explanation. The audit senior's past performance was significantly related to judgments of his or her current and future performance. Interestingly, subject gender was not significant in any of the analyses. This result is consistent with recent research (Anderson et al. 1994; Kaplan and Reckers 1992), suggesting that women making performance evaluation judgments do not rate other women differently than would men.

This study adds to existing literature in reporting experimental evidence of perceived biases regarding gender and family structure in public accounting. These results suggest both (1) a direct and (2) an indirect bias. The lower ratings assigned to the female auditor are evidence of *direct* gender bias. Subjects also rated the hypothetical audit senior lower when the explanation for the budget overrun was family-related than when it was based on client factors. The lower ratings given in response to the family-related explanation also indicate an *indirect* bias against the female auditor, because females continue to bear a disproportionate share of responsibility for family and child care issues (Gaffney and McEwen 1993).

The negative perceptions of female auditors and the demands of family are important findings irrespective of their accuracy. If they accurately portray bias in the profession, then corrective action is necessary. On the other hand, if they are inaccurate, then education to eradicate these erroneous perceptions is required. The accounting profession's failure to address the antecedent causes of these perceptions will carry heavy social costs. For example, as part of the basic socialization process, some young female accountants will pattern their lives to conform to perceived expectations (e.g., forego children). Alternatively, many highly qualified and expensively trained young female accountants may ultimately choose not to change themselves but to change their environment, by seeking employment outside the profession.

The accounting profession has begun to respond to charges that pervasive biases against women, including those involving family issues, are limiting the supply of qualified professionals for advancement. For example, one Big Six public accounting firm has initiated gender awareness training programs for partners, managers, and seniors in an effort to break down gender-related barriers to effective working relationships (AICPA 1992; Staff 1995). Other firms, large and small, are implementing flexible work schedules that will allow qualified individuals to remain on the "partner track" while working part-time through the manager level (Berton 1993; Cheramy 1993).

However, a particularly noteworthy aspect of these findings is that all subjects were at comparatively early stages of their careers in public accounting. Despite increasing acceptance by society toward women in the workplace, and the efforts that CPA firms have taken to reduce workplace biases against females, these results suggest that the male stereotype is deeply ingrained in CPA firm culture and is thus highly resistant to change (Maupin and Lehman 1994).

LIMITATIONS AND DIRECTIONS FOR FUTURE RESEARCH

The results of this study are subject to certain limitations. First, these findings provide evidence of only biased *perceptions* among audit seniors of a public accounting firm. Regardless of the accuracy of these perceptions, subjects in this study did not make actual performance evaluations of their peers. An obvious extension of this study would be to determine whether these biases are manifest among managers and partners who make actual evaluation and promotion decisions in practice. In addition, subjects were all drawn from a single Big Six public accounting firm, which further limits the generalizability of these results.

Second, the possibility of demand effects in responses must be considered. To reduce the likelihood that the subjects could discern the objectives of the study, all experimental factors were varied between subjects. Still, to the degree that subjects might have perceived the purposes of the experimental manipulations, a predictable reaction would have been to provide "politically correct" responses. However, because significant biases *were* found, this suggests that the actual biases among practicing auditors may be even greater than those reported here.

A third limitation is that we presented only one of many family-related circumstances. Other factors could be varied which would provide additional information on the biases reported here. For instance, future research could consider varying factors such as flexible work schedules and parental leaves (Hooks 1992; Staff 1995).

Finally, actual auditor evaluations are not made in an information vacuum. The task did not allow for the raters' actual knowledge of the ratee and his or her performance over time; hence, a more realistic decision setting may have yielded more externally valid findings. This is another avenue for future investigation.

NOTES

1. Prior research has shown that job assignment is an area in which women have reportedly perceived discrimination in public accounting (Walkup and Fenzau 1980; Pillsbury et al. 1989; Trapp et al. 1989).

2. Alternatively, if we had stated the specific gender of the audit senior, we may have introduced demand effects in that subjects may have guessed the purpose of our study.

3. Auditors use explanations or excuses in an attempt to mitigate poor performance. Since much of an audit senior's work is unobserved, superiors may rely on the ratee's explanation for problems that occur in the audit (Hunt 1995).

4. A similar dependent measure was given which assessed subjects' support for the senior in future audit engagements. Results were substantially the same as those reported for the second dependent measure.

REFERENCES

American Institute of Certified Public Accountants. 1984. *Major Issues for the Profession and the CPA.* New York: AICPA.

_____. 1988. *Upward Mobility of Women Special Committee Report to the AICPA Board of Directors.* New York: AICPA.

_____. 1990. *MAP Committee Survey on Professional Staff.* New York: AICPA.

_____. 1992. *How the Accounting Profession Is Addressing Upward Mobility of Women and Family Issues in the Workplace.* Report of the AICPA Upward Mobility of Women Committee. New York: AICPA.

Anderson, J.C., E.N. Johnson, and P.M.J. Reckers. 1994. Perceived effects of gender, family structure, and physical appearance on career progression in public accounting: A research note. *Accounting, Organizations and Society* 19(6): 483-491.

Bem, S.L. 1974. The measurement of psychological androgyny. *Journal of Consulting and Clinical Psychology* 42(2): 155-162.

Berton, L. 1993. Deloitte wants more women for top posts in accounting. *The Wall Street Journal* (April 28): B1, B4.

Cheramy, S.J. 1993. The impact of diversity on the accounting profession. Unpublished speech, Tempe, AZ, February.

Collins, K.M. 1993. Stress and departures from the public accounting profession: A study of gender differences. *Accounting Horizons* 7(1): 29-38.

Cook, A.H. 1988. Unions: Are they keeping up with women. Paper presented at the Women, Work, and Family Life Conference, New York, July.

Coverman, S., and J.F. Shelley. 1986. Changes in men's housework and child-care time, 1965-1975. *Journal of Marriage and the Family* 48: 413-422.

Crocker, J., and K.M. McGraw. 1984. What's good for the goose is not good for the gander: Solo status as an obstacle to occupational achievement for males and females. *American Behavioral Scientist* 27(3): 357-369.

DeNisi, A.S., T.P. Cafferty, and B.M. Megliano. 1984. A cognitive view of the performance appraisal process: A model and research propositions. *Organizational Behavior and Human Performance* 33(3): 360-396.

Dobbins, G.H. 1985. Effects of gender on leaders' responses to poor performers: An attributional interpretation. *Academy of Management Journal* 28(3): 587-598.

Dobbins, G.H., E.C. Pence, J.A. Orban, and J.A. Sgro. 1983. The effects of sex of the leader and sex of the subordinate on the use of organizational control policy. *Organizational Behavior and Human Performance* 32(3): 325-343.

Earnest, K.R., and J.C. Lampe. 1982. Attitudinal differences between male and female auditors. *The Woman CPA* 44(3): 13-20.

Fogarty, T.J. 1992. Organizational socialization in accounting firms: A theoretical framework and agenda for future research. *Accounting, Organizations and Society* 17(2): 129-149.

Gaertner, J.F., P.E. Hemmeter, and M.K. Pitman. 1987. Employee turnover in public accounting: A new perspective. *The CPA Journal* 57(8): 30-37.

Gaffney, M.A., and R.A. McEwen. 1993. Gender effects on commitment of public accountants: A test of competing sociological models. In *Advances in Public Interest Accounting*, Vol. 5, ed. C. Lehman, 45-73. Greenwich, CT: JAI Press.

Hooks, K.L. 1992. Gender effects and labor supply in public accounting: An agenda of research issues. *Accounting, Organizations and Society* (3/4): 343-366.

———. 1994. Facts and myths about women CPAs. *Journal of Accountancy* 178(4): 79-86.

Hunt, S.C. 1995. A review and synthesis of research in performance evaluation in public accounting. *Journal of Accounting Literature* 14: 107-139.

Hunt, S.C., and W.F. Messier. 1995. Auditor performance evaluation: Factors affecting information search and the rating decision. Unpublished working paper.

Kaplan, S.E., and P.M.J. Reckers. 1985. An examination of auditor performance evaluation. *The Accounting Review* 60(3): 477-487.

———. 1992. An examination of the effects of gender discrimination and role conflicts on auditors' performance evaluations. Unpublished working paper.

———. 1993. An examination of the effects of accountability tactics on performance evaluation judgments on public accounting. *Behavioral Research in Accounting* 5: 101-123.

Krausz, S.L. 1986. Sex roles within marriage. *Social Work* 31(6): 457-464.

Lehman, C.R. 1990. The importance of being ernest: Gender conflicts in accounting. In *Advances in Public Interest Accounting*, Vol. 3, ed. M. neimark, 137-157. Greenwich, CT: JAI Press.

Maupin, R.J. 1990. Sex role identity and career success of certified public accountants. In *Advances in Public Interest Accounting*, Vol. 3, ed. M. Neimark, 97-105. Greenwich, CT: JAI Press.

———. 1993. How can women's lack of upward mobility in accounting organizations be explained? *Group and Organizational Management* 18(2): 132-152.

Maupin, R.J., and C.R. Lehman. 1994. Talking heads: Stereotypes, status, sex-roles and satisfaction of female and male auditors. *Accounting, Organizations and Society* 19(4/5): 427-437.

Pillsbury, C.M., L. Capozzoli, and A. Ciampa. 1989. A synthesis of research studies regarding the upward mobility of women in public accounting. *Accounting Horizons* 3(1): 63-70.

Reed, S.A., and S.H. Kratchman. 1990. The effects of changing role requirements on accountants. In *Advances in Public Interest Accounting*, Vol. 3, ed. M. Neimark, 107-136. Greenwich, CT: JAI Press.

Staff. 1995. Women in the profession—1995: Progress varies by firm as initiatives take hold. *Public Accounting Report* (June 15): 1, 4.

Trapp, M.W., R.H. Hermanson, and D.H. Turner. 1989. Current perceptions of issues related to women employed in public accounting. *Accounting Horizons* 3(1): 71-85.

Walkup, M., and D. Fenzau. 1980. Women CPAs: Why do they leave public accounting? *The Woman CPA* 42(4): 3-6.

Wright, A. 1980. Performance appraisal of staff auditors. *The CPA Journal* 50(11): 37-43.

Yogev, S., and J. Brett. 1985. Patterns of work and family involvement among single- and dual-earner couples. *Journal of Applied Psychology* 70(4): 754-768.

A REEXAMINATION OF AUDITORS' INITIAL BELIEF ASSESSMENT AND EVIDENCE SEARCH

Jeffrey J. McMillan and Richard A. White

ABSTRACT

Auditing research suggests that confirmation proneness may not be as prevalent among auditors as other individuals and may be dependent on hypothesis framing and auditing experience. The primary purpose of this study was to investigate whether auditors' initial evidence search is characterized by confirmatory, conservative, or balanced behavior. In addition, we investigated the effect experience had on auditors' initial belief assessments and on their evidence search. The investigation of these effects was accomplished by replicating and extending Kaplan and Reckers (1989), by studying a much wider range of audit experience and creating a wider range of initial material error assessments. Consistent with their findings, the results of this study reveal that preliminary audit evidence and experience effected auditors' initial assessments of material error. However, in this study, experienced auditors had higher material error assessments than inexperienced auditors while Kaplan and Reckers found that inexperienced auditors were more conservative. With regards to

Advances in Accounting, Volume 14, pages 193-208.

evidence search, the current study found that only staff auditors exhibited confirmatory evidence search strategies while more experienced auditors (i.e., seniors and managers/partners) demonstrated balanced search behavior. This finding is somewhat different from Kaplan and Reckers, as their results suggested senior auditors may be prone to confirmatory search behavior.

INTRODUCTION AND MOTIVATION

Psychological research has demonstrated that people in general engage in confirmation-prone information search strategies (i.e., prefer seeking information that proves their beliefs are correct rather than seeking information that proves their beliefs are incorrect) (Snyder and Swann 1978; Fischoff and Beth-Marom 1983; Klayman and Ha 1987, 1989). However, research in auditing suggests that confirmation proneness may not be as prevalent among auditors as other individuals and may be dependent on hypothesis framing (Kida 1984) and auditing experience (Kaplan and Reckers 1989).

While examining hypothesis-testing strategies, Kida (1984) found that audit managers and partners who were asked to determine whether a firm would fall into bankruptcy, selected more failure information items than the auditor group which was asked to determine whether the firm would remain viable. Nevertheless, the latter group also selected more failure information items than viable information items. Since only the former group exhibited confirmatory behavior, Kida (1984) concluded that his results provided mixed evidence that experienced auditors may engage in confirmation prone behavior. However, after later review, Smith and Kida (1991) argue that Kida's (1984) viable subjects were actually exhibiting a conservative bias (i.e., a desire to ensure that material error possibilities are addressed). Anderson and Maletta (1994) concluded that their auditor subjects also seemed to exhibit conservative-prone behavior when asked to evaluate the internal controls of a sales accounting system. On the other hand, Kaplan and Reckers (1989) concluded that their investigation of belief assessment and information search showed that inexperienced auditors demonstrated confirmation-prone tendencies.

The primary purpose of this study was to investigate whether auditors' initial evidence search is characterized by confirmatory, conservative, or balanced behavior. In addition, the effect experience had on initial belief assessments and on evidence search was also investigated. An ancillary objective was to study the relationship between an auditor's initial belief assessment and the auditor's experience and preliminary evidence received (i.e., analytical review results and a brief report of last year's internal control investigation). The objectives were accomplished by replicating and extending the work of Kaplan and Reckers (1989).

Replication and extension of the Kaplan and Reckers (1989) study is important for several reasons. First, their study investigated two important decisions made during the initial stages of the audit process which affect the efficiency and effectiveness of the audit investigation: (1) the initial assessment of the relative likelihood of material error, and (2) the information search strategy used to investigate initial beliefs. Biggs and Mock (1983) found that information acquisition occupied a significant portion (approximately 30-50 percent) of auditors' decision processes, and Bedard and Mock (1992) indicated that although information search has been linked to decision accuracy, it has received little attention from auditing researchers. Additional information about how decision biases affect auditors' initial belief assessments and their information search strengthens the profession's understanding of this critical function of the audit process.

Second, in the current study, the subjects' hypothesis commitment was enhanced by requiring the auditors to first identify the hypothesis frame that they thought was more likely and then assign a likelihood assessment to it. Previous research has demonstrated that auditors who are committed to a hypothesis are more likely to engage in confirmatory behavior (Church 1991). Kaplan and Reckers (1989) had subjects allocate 100 relative likelihood points between two mutually exclusive causes of ratio fluctuations uncovered by analytical review procedures. The current study's experimental method resulted in a greater percentage of subjects initially favoring the material error hypothesis frame (i.e., assigned a likelihood assessment over 50 percent) than the percentage in the Kaplan and Reckers (1989) study. This allowed an examination of evidence search strategies across a greater range of error assessment scores.

Third, there have been significant environmental changes since the Kaplan and Reckers study which may have influenced auditors' initial belief assessments and evidence search behavior. For example, SAS 56 (AICPA 1988b), which involves the evaluation of internal control, was issued near or after the time the data was collected for the Kaplan and Reckers (1989) study. For the current study, the data was collected after the issuance of SAS 56. In addition, legal liability concerns of the accounting profession have continued to increase. With escalating legal and liability insurance costs, auditors may be more sensitive to internal control issues and material errors then ever before.

Fourth, it is important to investigate the behavior of staff auditors because they perform a large portion of the field work in an audit (Libby and Frederick 1990). Kaplan and Reckers (1989) indicated that auditors (i.e., seniors) with less than six years of experience were more prone to confirmatory behavior than auditors with more experience. Their less experienced group included seniors but not staff auditors. Libby and Frederick (1990) note that since experienced auditors explain and interpret the results of procedures performed by staff auditors, their interpretations could indirectly be affected by decision biases exhibited by staff auditors. In addition, an extension of the Kaplan and Reckers (1989) study to staff personnel may help explain the results found in the study by Anderson and Maletta (1994). Both studies found that less experienced subjects' evidence search was different from more experienced subjects' behavior. However, Kaplan and Reckers (1989) found that as the level of experience deceased, so did the propensity to engage in confirmatory behavior. Anderson and Maletta (1994) found that inexperienced subjects' attitudes were characterized as attending more to negative information than positive information. This was interpreted as conservative proneness. Caution should be made in comparing the results of the two studies because the two "inexperienced" groups were dissimilar. Kaplan and Reckers' (1989) subjects consisted primarily of auditors with four or more years of experience while Anderson and Maletta's (1994) most experienced subject group averaged three years experience. By including staff as well as more experienced subjects in the current study, a more accurate comparison of the two studies can be made.

Although not investigated in the current study, it should be noted that task knowledge may account for some of the difference in the results of the above two studies. Bonner (1990) notes that task-specific knowledge may aid the performance of experienced auditors in some components of judgment. For example, the results of the Bonner (1990) study demonstrated that experience played a more important role in analytical risk assessment than on control risk assessment.

EXPERIMENTAL TASK AND HYPOTHESES

The experimental materials and task used in this study were modeled after Kaplan and Reckers (1989). A contact person in each office randomly distributed a packet of printed materials detailing the preliminary audit information and a computer diskette to each subject.[1] For this study, the experimental task was integrated into a computer program which was designed to be user friendly and maintain experimental control (e.g., the task had to be completed in one sitting, the program could not be reactivated once completed, and each subject's response time was monitored automatically.)

The preliminary audit information was composed of background, financial, and nonfinancial information describing a hypothetical client. The financial information consisted of two years of summary data from the client's balance sheet and income statement, and a financial ratio profile. The ratio profile consisted of a quick ratio, a current ratio, and a gross margin ratio for the prior year (audited) and the current year (unaudited). All subjects received information in which the client's quick and current ratios increased from the prior year to the current year by amounts over 10 percent (1.04 to 1.25 for the quick ratio and 2.43 to 2.72 for the current ratio) while the change in the gross margin ratio was minuscule (26.1 to 26.3). Per SAS 55 (AICPA 1988a), comparative industry financial data and financial projections are sources auditors should consider when developing initial expectations. Thus, current year industry and projected figures for the three ratios were also provided. The nonfinancial information consisted of a description of the clients' internal control environment. Internal control environment was substituted for the management integrity factor used by Kaplan and Reckers (1989)

Consideration of internal control is prescribed by SAS 56 (AICPA 1988b) and should be more closely associated with material errors.

Consistent with Kaplan and Reckers (1989), the purpose of the preliminary audit evidence was to generate a diversity of initial beliefs from which the subjects would base their initial evidence search strategy. Therefore, a full factorial manipulation of the preliminary information was not germane to the goals of the study. Two sets of preliminary audit information were created by combining different ratio profiles with different descriptions of the client's internal control environment. One-half (83) of the subjects randomly received a portrayal of strong internal control and industry and projected ratios which were substantially the same as the client's current year ratios (strong/similar treatment). The other 83 subjects received a portrayal of a weak internal control environment and industry and projected ratios that differed from the client's current year ratios (weak/dissimilar treatment).

After studying the preliminary audit information, Kaplan and Reckers (1989) had their subjects allocate 100 relative likelihood points between an environmental frame (i.e., changes in economic, market conditions, or company policy) and a material error frame as the most likely explanation for the fluctuation in the current year's unaudited financial statement ratios. The subjects in the current study were first asked to select the cause that "most likely" identified the source of the ratio fluctuation, and then they were asked to indicate the likelihood, ranging from 0 percent (no chance) to 100 percent (completely certain), that the cause they selected represented the true state. As discussed earlier, it was believed that sequencing the task in this manner enhanced the subjects' focus and commitment on the cause (i.e., hypothesis frame) they felt was most likely. It was expected that the subjects who received the weak/dissimilar treatment would form higher material error assessments than the subjects who received the strong/similar treatment. This can be stated in the following alternative hypothesis:

Hypothesis 1.   Auditors who receive the weak/dissimilar treatment will have higher error assessments than auditors who receive the strong/similar treatment.

In the Kaplan and Reckers (1989) study, auditors with less experience tended to make stronger error assessments. On the other hand, Libby and Frederick (1990) argue that as auditors gain experience, they gain a greater understanding in the set of potential financial statement errors and error occurrence rates and therefore, are more able to generate a larger number of plausible hypotheses than less experienced auditors. Their results showed that the more experienced subjects generated more plausible hypotheses and less implausible hypotheses than the less experienced subjects across all three levels of experience. In the current study, this would suggest that for the auditors who received the weak/dissimilar treatment, the experienced auditors should assign higher error assessments than the inexperienced auditors.

Hirst and Koonce (forthcoming) report that 23 of the 26 auditors they interviewed indicated that analytical review procedures are usually performed by the senior and then reviewed by the manager. Therefore, a possible explanation for making different error assessments in the current study may be that staff members may not have the requisite knowledge to adequately assess the analytical review information. The subjects also were provided a portrayal of internal control strength. This information may partially offset any lack of knowledge effects in the analytical review assessment. Note that the "correct" error assessment score was not as critical to this study as receiving a wide range of assessment scores. Based on the above conflicts, the hypothesis testing the relationship between experience and auditors' initial beliefs was stated in the null form.

Hypothesis 2.   The auditors' initial error assessments will not be affected by experience.

After indicating their initial beliefs, the subjects were asked to review a "menu" of sixteen audit questions provided in the audit packet. Two types of audit questions were randomly positioned in the menu—eight environmental questions and eight error questions.[2] Kaplan and Reckers' (1989) original menu of questions contained two additional environmental and two additional error questions. From their list of 20 questions, they had subjects select the 10 questions to which they would initially seek answers in an effort to explain the change in the financial ratios and to rank-order the first six questions. However, based on their results, Kaplan and Reckers (1989) suggested that auditors may focus on a relatively short list of questions at any one point in time and that they may have added noise to their dependent measures by having the subjects consider so long a list. As a result, our study dropped the two environmental and error questions which were selected the least often by the subjects in Kaplan and Reckers (1989). In addition, the subjects in the current study were asked to select only eight questions and to rank order only their first four choices. After the subject completed the experimental task, the experimental materials were returned to the contact person.

Since the hypothesis that most accurately represents the true state is not known a priori for any given audit engagement, a balanced search strategy may be the most appropriate in the long run. However, the findings of Kaplan and Reckers (1989) suggest that less experienced auditors may be inclined to employ confirming behavior during their initial evidence search. As in the case of the Kaplan and Reckers (1989) study, the following interaction was hypothesized:

Hypothesis 3.   Experienced auditors will have more conservative (less confirmatory) search strategies than less experienced auditors.

Subjects

The results of this study are based on the responses of 166 professionals who participated in a field experiment. The sample group was comprised of 50 staff, 50 seniors, and 66 managers/partners. Thirty-seven percent of the subjects were female and 63 percent were male. Seventy-eight percent held undergraduate degrees while the remaining 22 percent had completed graduate degrees. All the subjects held full-time auditing positions in five regional CPA firms (18 percent) and three Big-Six CPA firms (82 percent).[3] Six cities in five different states participated and a minimum of two offices for each Big-Six firm were used.

DATA ANALYSIS AND RESULTS

Initial Belief Assessment

Consistent with Kaplan and Reckers (1989), analysis of covariance (ANCOVA) was used to analyze the subjects' initial likelihood assessments. The dependent variable in the ANCOVA model was the subjects' likelihood assessment that the change between the current and last year's financial ratios was due to material error. The two levels of the preliminary evidence manipulation served as the independent variable and years of audit experience functioned as the covariate.

An alternative model, where audit experience was categorized into three levels (staff, seniors, and managers/partners), also was analyzed. This model was constructed for two reasons. First, number of years alone may not represent an accurate measure of an individual's expertise. Some auditors are promoted to senior in less than two years while others are not promoted to senior until more than three years. Similarly, a partner with many years (e.g., 30 years) of experience may not have a great deal more expertise in assessing error rates than a partner with much less (e.g., 12 years) experience. Thus, classifying individuals by expertise levels may be more appropriate than by years of experience for this particular experiment. Second, Neter and colleagues (1985) indicate that if there is doubt about the nature of a statistical relationship, an analysis of variance (rather than regression or ANCOVA) should be employed. The relationship between experience, error assessment, and evidence search behavior has not been clearly established in the literature. Accordingly, experience level was analyzed as a discrete variable as well as a continuous variable.

Table 1 compares the ANCOVA results for this study's experiment (Panel A) with the results of the Kaplan and Reckers (1989) study (Panel B). The results are similar. As expected, the preliminary evidence treatment had a significant effect ($p < .0001$) on the subjects' assessment that material error was responsible for causing the ratio fluctuations.

Table 1. ANCOVA Analysis of Material Error Assessment

Model: F-value = 26.78,   p-value = .0001

Independent Variable	d.f.	SS	MS	F	p-value
Panel A: Current Study					
Preliminary evidence[1]	1	16380.7	16380.7	51.2	.0001
Years of experience	1	917.7	917.7	2.9	.0907
Error	163	51659.4	316.9		
Panel B: Kaplan and Reckers (1989)					
Preliminary evidence[1]					
Management integrity	1	3138.8	3138.8	9.65	.003
Industry average	1	1357.4	1357.4	4.17	.045
Years of experience	1	2710.1	2710.1	8.33	.005
Error	64	20815.2	325.2		

Note: [1]Internal control and financial information were used together to create the weak/dissimilar and the strong/similar treatment used in the current study while Kaplan and Reckers (1989) utilized a full factorial manipulation of their two-level preliminary evidence variables.

Panel A of Table 2 shows that the mean error assessment score assigned by the subjects that received the material error (weak/dissimilar treatment) preliminary evidence was significantly greater (48.68) than the mean error assessment score assigned by the subjects who received the environmental (strong/similar treatment) preliminary evidence (28.81). While the preliminary evidence in our study is not the most competent (i.e., strongest) type of evidence gathered during an audit, it significantly influenced the subjects' likelihood assessment of material error. Thus, Hypothesis 1 is supported.

Panel B of Table 2 presents the mean error assessments for each experimental treatment used in the Kaplan and Reckers (1989) study. The findings of the current study combined with those of Kaplan and Reckers (1989) appear to reveal that auditors have a preference for choosing to begin the audit judgment process favoring an environmental hypothesis frame. In the current study, 90 percent of the subjects (nearly equal across experience levels) who received the environmental preliminary evidence favored the environmental frame while only 44 percent of the subjects (20 percent lower for staff) given the error preliminary evidence favored the error frame. While there is some concern that staff may not have the knowledge to properly evaluate analytical review information, the above results do not indicate that task knowledge had a dramatic impact on error assessments, particularly for the subjects who received the strong/similar treatment.

The preceding results showed that the experimental task was effective in creating a wide range of error assessment levels. In terms of the percentage of variance

Table 2. Treatment Means and Standard Deviations for
Material Error Assessment

Treatment[1]	Mean	Standard Deviation
Panel A: Current Study		
Weak IC/Dissimilar financial	48.68	18.46
Strong IC/Similar financial	28.81	17.33
Panel B: Kaplan and Reckers (1989)		
Management integrity: low	36.10	21.40
Management integrity: high	23.15	14.97
Industry average: similar	24.98	13.82
Industry average: dissimilar	34.60	22.60

Note: [1]Internal control and financial information were used together to create the weak/
dissimilar and the strong/similar treatment used in the current study while
Kaplan and Reckers (1989) utilized a full factorial manipulation of their two-level
preliminary evidence variables.

in the dependent variable explained by the preliminary evidence independent variable (known as the eta-squared statistic), the percentage explained in the current study was approximately 24 percent compared to 16 percent in the Kaplan and Reckers (1989) study. In addition, the overall mean error assessment score of the current study was about 38 compared to about 29 in Kaplan and Reckers (1989) and there was nearly a 20 percentage point difference between the two levels (48.68 versus 28.81). Thus, a greater percentage of this study's subjects assigned error assessment scores above 50 percent compared to the subjects in Kaplan and Reckers (1989). This may be due to the first task of our experiment (committing to a hypothesis frame) or due to the different manipulation (manipulation of internal control rather than management integrity). Irrespective of the reason, the experimental procedure was successful in expanding the range of error assessment levels for which to test for confirmatory search strategies.

With respect to experience effects on initial error assessments, Panel A of Table 1 shows that years of experience as a covariable was marginally significant ($p < .0907$). This compares with the highly significant experience effect found in Kaplan and Reckers (1989) (Panel B of Table 1). The slope estimate for experience in the current study was 0.37, which implies that as years of experience increased, the subjects' error likelihood assessments also increased. In other words, as experience increased, so did conservative prone tendencies (i.e, the sensitivity to the possibility of material error).

Table 3. Material Error Assessment by Experience Level

Panel A: ANOVA Results

Model: F-value = 19.34, p-value = .0001

Independent Variable	d.f.	SS	MS	F	p-value
Preliminary evidence	1	16380.7	16380.7	52.3	.0001
Work experience	2	1801.2	900.6	2.9	.0594
Error	162	50775.9	313.4		

Panel B: Experience Level x Preliminary Evidence

	Evidence Treatment		
	Strong/Similar	Weak/Dissimilar	Overall
Staff	24.8	43.2	35.8 A
Senior	28.7	51.9	38.5 AB
Manager/Partner	31.1	51.7	41.1 B
Overall[1]	28.8 A	48.7 B	

Note: [1]Different letters denote significant differences at a .05 level of significance.

Table 3 presents the ANOVA results using the discrete experience level independent variable. The effect of preliminary evidence was unchanged ($p < .0001$) while the effect of experience level was somewhat improved ($p < .0594$). Although there was no significant experience by preliminary evidence interaction ($p < .8062$), examination of the mean error assessments by experience level and preliminary evidence provides additional insights. Panel B of Table 3 reveals that the mean error assessment of the manager/partners (41.14) was significantly greater than those of the staff (35.82) but not statistically greater then those of the seniors (38.50). These subgroup means are consistent with the positive slope estimate generated by the ANCOVA analysis. Based on the results reported in Tables 1 and 3, Hypothesis 2 is rejected. Experience does play a moderate role in affecting the initial error assessments of auditors.

The results of this study seem to support the notion that experienced auditors are more prone to generate conservative likelihood assessments tendencies than inexperienced auditors. At first glance, this appears to be in conflict with the findings of Kaplan and Reckers (1989) which found that their less experienced subjects made the strongest (i.e., most conservative) initial error assessments. However, one must remember that the subjects in Kaplan and Reckers (1989) inexperienced group consisted primarily of very experienced seniors (of the 29 subjects in this group, only one subject had two years of experience or less, eight had three years, nine had four years, and 11 had five years of experience). In contrast, most of the inexperienced subjects in the current study had less than two years of audit experience.

Evidence Search

Consistent with Kaplan and Reckers (1989), "raw" and "ranked" dependent measures were used to assess the subjects' initial evidence search behavior. The raw error score was based on the number of error questions selected by each subject. The maximum possible raw error score was eight and the minimum score was zero. The ranked error score was based on the four questions rank ordered by each subject. Each question was weighted by the ranking it received—the first question was assigned a weight of four, the second a weight of three, and so forth. The rank weights of error questions were summed making the maximum ranked error score possible ten and the minimum possible score zero.

The raw and ranked measures of information search were analyzed using separate regressions. The three independent variables for each raw and ranked regression model were the auditors' error assessment, years of audit experience, and the interaction of these two variables. Panel A of Table 4 reveals that all three independent variables had a major influence on the number of error questions selected and also on the importance the subjects placed on error questions. For the raw measure, the subjects' error assessment ($p < .0001$), years of experience ($p < .0001$), and interaction term ($p < .0001$) all were highly significant. Results for the ranked measure also were significant—error assessment ($p < .0001$), years of experience ($p < .0049$), and interaction term ($p < .0174$).[4]

Table 4. Multiple Regressions for Evidence Search

Independent Variable	Raw Measure			Ranked Measure		
	SRC	t-value	p-value	SRC	t-value	p-value
Panel A: Current Study—Years of Experience						
Error assessment	0.11	10.21	.0001	0.13	6.92	.0001
Years experience	0.17	5.17	.0001	0.16	2.85	.0049
Interaction	−0.02	3.78	.0001	−0.02	−2.40	.0174
Multiple R (R^2)			.78			.60
Panel B: Kaplan and Reckers (1989)—Years of Experience						
Error assessment	0.49	1.92	.06	0.76	3.08	.003
Years experience	0.38	1.65	.11	0.51	2.32	.02
Interaction	−0.39	−1.44	.15	−0.62	−2.42	.02
Multiple R (R^2)			.27			.39

When comparing the evidence search results of the current study (Panel A of Table 4) with those of Kaplan and Reckers (1989) (Panel B of Table 4), several points can be made. First, neither the experience nor the interaction term was significant for the raw measure in the Kaplan and Reckers (1989) study. Second, the sign of the coefficients for the independent variables under both evidence search measures were the same for both studies. Third, the Multiple R (R^2) for the current study is considerably higher for both measures (.78 versus .27 for the raw measure and .60 versus .39 for the ranked measure).

The extension of the experience ranges covered in this study allowed a more detailed examination of the effect of experience on the subjects' evidence search. Table 5 presents the results of a multiple regression where the years of experience variable is replaced with three levels of experience (staff, senior, and manager/partner). As discussed earlier, while these two variables are highly correlated, experience level may be a better indication of expertise than years of experience. Panel A of Table 5 reveals that the results essentially are the same as Panel A of Table 4, and the p-values and R^2 values are somewhat improved.

Because of the significant interaction between error assessment and experience level, separate regressions were performed for each experience level (Panels B, C, and D). The results indicate that only the staff auditors' information search was affected by their initial error assessments (raw $p < .0039$; ranked $p < .0034$). Note that the more experienced auditor groups selected an average of approximately four (3.96 for seniors and 4.22 for managers/partner) error questions. The error assessment coefficients and p-values imply that their initial error assessments did not significantly influence their initial evidence search (i.e., the slope coefficient was flat). As indicated by the mean search scores (where a 0 represents a perfectly balance behavior), the two more experienced levels essentially adopted a balanced search strategy. On the other hand, the staff auditors started with a base of 2.84 (1.43 ranked score) error questions and increased the number of error questions by 4.5 percent (8.3 percent ranked score) for each one point increase in error assessment score. The positive means score of .84 and 3.68 for the raw and ranked measures, respectively, also suggest that only staff auditors' evidence search appears to have been influenced by confirmatory tendencies. Thus, Hypothesis 3 is supported.

IMPLICATIONS AND FUTURE RESEARCH

The results of this study indicate that audit experience affects both the initial assessment of material errors and the initial search for audit evidence. With respect to material error assessment, the study found that conservative assessment tendencies tend to increase with experience. A possible explanation for this outcome may be that more experienced auditors are more familiar with analytical review procedures and make judgments that are more consistent with the evidence provided by

Table 5. Multiple Regressions of Evidence Search For Experience Level as a Class Variable

Independent Variable	Raw Measure			Ranked Measure		
	SRC	t-value	p-value	SRC	t-value	p-value
Panel A: Overall Model						
Error assessment	0.09	12.09	.0001	.11	6.55	.0001
Experience level	1.66	14.46	.0001	1.46	5.93	.0001
Interaction	−0.00	−8.97	.0001	−0.03	−4.04	.0001
Multiple R (R^2)			.89			.66
Panel B: Staff Auditors						
Error assessment	0.045	3.03	.0039	0.083	1.33	.0034
Intercept	2.84			1.43		
Multiple R (R^2)	.14			.15		
Mean search score	0.84			3.68		
Panel C: Senior Auditors						
Error assessment	0.005	0.60	.5538	0.013	0.58	.5667
Intercept	3.96			3.96		
Multiple R (R^2)	.01			.01		
Mean search score	−.04			0.68		
Panel D: Manager/Partner Auditors						
Error attribution	0.006	0.66	.5129	0.025	1.34	.1849
Intercept	4.22			3.70		
Multiple R (R^2)	.01			.01		
Mean search score	−.36			1.12		

the analytical review (Bonner 1990; Hirst and Koonce forthcoming). Our overall results suggest that auditors more likely begin their evidence search believing that differences between current unaudited financial information and prior year's audited financial information are caused by environmental variations rather than material error. This result is consistent with Libby and Frederick's (1990) findings that experienced auditors realize that the occurrence of material errors is not that high and the contention of Kaplan and colleagues (1992) that experienced auditors initially focus more on environmental issues than on error issues.

Because this study included staff auditors and more experienced auditors from several firms, its findings are more generalizable than studies which have restricted their sample to one firm or one office within a firm (e.g., Kaplan and Reckers 1989). Our results suggest that an auditor's error assessment may not just be a function of the training of one firm but more of a function of the experience gained from auditing. If staff auditors have initial error assessments which differ from more experienced auditors, the type of evidence sought and how it is evaluated could affect the efficiency and effectiveness of the audit.

The implications of the above findings depend on whether the preliminary assessment rate affects other decisions during the audit process such as the selection of audit evidence. Examination of experience level by error assessment interactions revealed that only staff auditors were influenced by their error assessment. On the other hand, Kaplan and Reckers (1989) findings suggested that senior auditors may have a propensity to engage in confirmatory behavior. A possible explanation of why the seniors in this study behaved more like managers and partners than those in Kaplan and Reckers' (1989) study is, perhaps, that because seniors spend a great deal of time evaluating internal controls, they were more comfortable with the internal control manipulation used in this study than the management integrity manipulation (often the province of managers and partners) used by Kaplan and Reckers (1989). Since senior auditors are a vital part of most audit engagements, future research should continue in this area to determine how evidence search by senior auditors is affected by their initial beliefs. In addition, further research can enhance the development of training materials to help staff auditors mitigate the confirmatory tendencies they seem to bring with them when they enter the profession.

In this study, the senior and manager/partner groups selected nearly an equal number of error and environmental explanations during their evidence search. Thus, while experienced auditors may enter an investigation favoring environmental explanations as to the cause of ratio fluctuations, they appear to adopt a balanced or somewhat conservative evidence search strategy. These findings clearly support the practice of leaving the design of audit programs in the hands of experienced seniors and managers. Nevertheless, staff auditors perform the bulk of the compliance and substantive work during audits and they often have to make program adjustments in the field. Their confirmatory tendencies may result in underweighting or failing to investigate items that would have been considered important and investigated by more experienced auditors. As a result, seniors, managers, and partners need to be aware of the confirmatory nature of their staff personnel when reviewing their work. In addition, staff training should make more of an effort to emphasize the potential dangers of acting too confirmatory during an audit. Last, experienced auditors need to work with staff auditors to help them temper confirmatory tendencies.

Further research should be conducted which examines whether the strength of audit evidence is dependent on the results of the investigation. That is, the negative nature of an item could increase its salience beyond just a question relating to investigating whether the control exists or not. Of course, if the particular evidence cue is not investigated (perhaps due to confirmatory search strategies), its increased competence level will not be attained. Thus, the investigation of auditors' information search strategies and the perceived strength of audit evidence before and after the evidence is collected and evaluated could be fruitful. Similarly, it could be beneficial to ascertain whether auditors with different experience levels have different perceptions concerning the competence of audit evidence. Finally, the information set provided in Kida (1984) and Anderson and Maletta (1994) consisted of results of audit inquiries, while the information set provided in the our study and Kaplan and Reckers (1989) were audit inquiries yet to be answered. Perhaps results of audit inquiries carry more weight than inquiries concerning error possibilities. The effects of differing information content warrant further study.

ACKNOWLEDGMENTS

The authors would like to thank the editor and the two anonymous reviewers for their insightful comments and suggestions. The quality and contribution of this manuscript was greatly enhanced by their efforts.

NOTES

1. A letter from each office's audit partner asking the subjects to complete the research project in a timely manner was included in each packet. A brief set of instructions informed the subjects how the materials were to be used and that the study examined strategies used by auditors and identified characteristics of audit decision making. Pretests were performed before the instruments were distributed.

2. Two randomized versions of the questions menu were randomly distributed among the subjects. Statistical tests revealed no evidence of order effects; thus, the subjects' responses were pooled for analysis purposes. See McMillan and White (1993, Table 5) for a listing of the actual audit questions.

3. Results based on just the Big Six responses were not significantly different from results which included the subjects from the regional firms. Thus, the results based on all the subjects is reported. In addition, information concerning gender, education level, and completion time of test instrument were included in the statistical models to see if they had any confounding effects. None had a significant effect on the results reported.

4. Following the methodology in Kaplan and Reckers (1989), the interaction effects were studied by performing separate regressions for subjects with less than six years of experience ($n = 102$) and those with six or more years of experience ($n = 64$). The results were consistent with the findings of Kaplan and Reckers (1989) in that the information search behavior of the less experienced subjects was positively correlated with their error assessment [raw $p < .0136$; ranked $p < .0156$ compared with a ranked p of $< .013$ in Kaplan and Reckers (1989). The raw measure was not tested in Kaplan and Reckers]. Furthermore, the error assessment of auditors with six or more years of experience did not affect their evidence search behavior [raw $p < .5129$; ranked $p < .1849$ compared with a ranked p of $< .847$ in Kaplan and Reckers (1989)].

REFERENCES

American Institute of Certified Public Accountants (AICPA). 1988a. *Statement on Auditing Standards No. 55: Consideration of the Internal Control Structure in a Financial Statement Audit.* New York: AICPA.
_____. 1988b. *Statement on Auditing Standards No. 56: Analytical Procedures.* New York: AICPA.
Anderson, B.H., and M. Maletta. 1994. Auditor independence and positive information: The effect of experience-related differences. *Behavioral Research in Accounting* 6: 1-20.
Bedard, J., and T.J. Mock. 1992. Expert and novice problem-solving behavior in audit planning. *Auditing a Journal of Practice and Theory* 11(Supplement): 1-20.
Biggs, S.F., and T.J. Mock. 1983. An investigation of auditor decision processes in evaluation of internal controls and audit scope decisions. *Journal of Accounting Research* 21(Autumn): 234-255.
Bonner, S.E. 1990. Experience effects in auditing: The role of task-specific knowledge. *The Accounting Review* 61(January): 72-92.
Church, B.K. 1991. An examination of the effect that commitment to a hypothesis has on auditors' evaluations of confirming and disconfirming evidence. *Contemporary Accounting Research* 7(Fall): 513-524.
Fischoff, B., and R. Beth-Marom. 1983. Hypothesis evaluation from a bayesian perspective. *Psychological Review* 93(July): 239-60.
Hirst, D.E., and L. Koonce. Forthcoming. Audit analytical procedures: A field investigation. *Contemporary Accounting Research.*
Kaplan, S.E., and P.M.J. Reckers. 1989. An examination of information search during initial audit planning. *Accounting, Organizations and Society* 14(5/6): 539-550.
Kaplan, S.E., P.M.J. Reckers, C.L. Moeckel, and J.D. Williams. 1992. Auditors' hypothesis plausibility assessments in an analytical review setting. *Auditing: A Journal of Practice and Theory* 11(Fall): 50-65.
Kida, T. 1984. The impact of hypothesis-testing strategies on auditors' use of judgment data. *Journal of Accounting Research* 22(Spring): 332-340.
Klayman, J., and Y.W. Ha. 1987. Confirmation, disconfirmation, and information in hypothesis testing. *Psychological Review* 96(April): 211-228.
Klayman, J., and Y.W. Ha. 1989. Hypothesis-testing in rule discovery: Strategy, structure, and content. *Journal of Experimental Psychology: Learning, Memory, and Cognition* 15(4): 596-604.
Libby, R., and D.M. Frederick. 1990. Experience and the ability to explain audit findings. *Journal of Accounting Research* 28(Autumn): 348-367.
McMillan, J.J., and R.A. White. 1993. Auditors' belief revisions and evidence search: The impact of hypothesis frame, confirmation bias and professional skepticism. *The Accounting Review* 68(July): 443-465.
Neter J., W. Wasserman, and M.K. Kutner. 1985. *Applied Linear Statistical Models,* 2nd edition. Homewood, Il: Richard Irwin.
Smith, J.F., and T. Kida. 1991. Heuristics and biases: Expertise and task realism in auditing. *Psychological Bulletin* 109(3): 472-489.
Snyder, M., and W.B. Swan. 1978. Hypothesis testing processes in social interactions. *Journal of Personality and Social Psychology* 36(November): 1202-1212.

THE INTERACTIVE EFFECT OF BUDGET-BASED COMPENSATION, ORGANIZATIONAL COMMITMENT, AND JOB INVOLVEMENT ON MANAGERS' PROPENSITIES TO CREATE BUDGETARY SLACK

Hossein Nouri and Robert J. Parker

ABSTRACT

The study examines the relationship between the propensity to create budgetary slack and three variables: budget-based compensation, organizational commitment, and job involvement. As hypothesized in the study, propensity to create budgetary slack will be highest when organizational commitment is low and job involvement and budget-based compensation are high. Propensity to create budgetary slack will be lowest when organizational commitment and job involvement are high and budget-based compensation is low. Survey results from a large U.S. company support

Advances in Accounting, Volume 14, pages 209-222.
Copyright © 1996 by JAI Press Inc.
All rights of reproduction in any form reserved.
ISBN: 0-7623-0161-9.

the hypothesized relationships. Implications for organizations that seek to minimize budgetary slack are discussed.

INTRODUCTION

In many organizations, subordinates submit estimates of future operating conditions to aid in the development of the organizational budget. If performance evaluation is based upon achieving budget, the subordinate may attempt to submit biased estimates to make the budget easier to achieve—that is, the subordinate may attempt to introduce slack into the budget (Waller 1988). The presence of budgetary slack may decrease the effectiveness of the budget in organizational planning and control (Kren 1993; Lowe and Shaw 1968).

Many accounting studies have sought to examine factors which seem to affect budgetary slack. For example, the relationship between participative budgets and budgetary slack has been extensively explored (e.g., Dunk 1993; Lukka 1988; Merchant 1985; Onsi 1973; Young 1985). Other variables theorized to affect budgetary slack include: incentive system (Chow et al. 1988; Waller 1988), individual risk preference (Waller 1988; Young 1985), and information asymmetry (Chow et al. 1988; Dunk 1993; Young 1985). Nouri (1994) reports evidence that organizational commitment and job involvement interact to affect budgetary slack. The current paper extends prior research by proposing that another variable—budget-based compensation—affects the relationships reported by Nouri (1994). More specifically, in the creation of budgetary slack, the current paper proposes a three-way interaction between organizational commitment, job involvement, and budget-based compensation. This hypothesis is tested using survey data collected from managers of a large multinational firm. Regression analysis indicates that the three-way interaction is statistically significant. As predicted, the propensity to create budgetary slack is highest when organizational commitment is low, job involvement is high, and compensation is budget-based. The propensity to create slack is lowest when organizational commitment and job involvement are high, and compensation is not primarily budget-based.

THEORETICAL DEVELOPMENT

In many organizations, subordinates are asked to submit estimates of future operating conditions to aid in developing budget goals. Budgetary slack is defined as intentional submission of estimates that, if incorporated into the budget, make it easier for the subordinate to achieve the budget. For example, subordinates may attempt to create slack by understating expected revenues and overstating expected costs. Prior studies have used a similar conceptualization of budgetary slack (Dunk 1993; Lukka 1988; Merchant 1985; Schiff and Lewin 1970; Young 1985).

Budgetary slack may reduce the effectiveness of the organizational budget. In many organizations, budgets facilitate planning, coordination, and organizational control. To create an effective budget, managers need reliable estimates of future conditions. In the case of budgetary slack, subordinates submit biased estimates which could reduce budget effectiveness (Kren 1993; Waller 1988).

Subordinates may attempt to build slack into budgets for a number of reasons. Perhaps foremost among the motivations is the desire to secure favorable performance evaluations at the end of the budget period. If performance evaluation depends upon reaching budget, subordinates may attempt to make the budget goal easier to reach by creating slack (Christensen 1982; Lowe and Shaw 1968; Lukka 1988; Schiff and Lewin 1970; Waller 1988). Other motivations for subordinates to introduce budgetary slack include: (1) to increase leisure time at work by making budgets easier to accomplish (Antle and Eppen 1985); (2) to protect against uncertainty (Lukka 1988; Onsi 1973; Schiff and Lewin 1970); and (3) to increase organizational resources and therefore increase status (Hopwood 1974; Lukka 1988).

A stream of accounting research has sought to identify factors that affect budgetary slack (e.g., Chow et al. 1988; Dunk 1993; Kren 1993; Lukka 1988; Merchant 1985; Nouri 1994; Onsi 1973; Waller 1988; Young 1985). The current study attempts to contribute to this stream by examining the relationship between budgetary slack and three variables: organizational commitment, job involvement, and budget-based compensation. Each variable is subsequently discussed.

Organizational commitment is characterized by: (1) strong belief in and acceptance of the organization's goals and values, and (2) a willingness to exert considerable effort on behalf of the organization (Angle and Perry 1981; Porter et al. 1974). As Lincoln and Kalleberg (1990) argue, the highly committed employee will expend effort on behalf of the organization even when such effort does not directly contribute to the individual's compensation or career opportunities. Organizational commitment has been extensively studied in the organizational behavior and psychology literatures. Several studies have found that organizational commitment has a relationship with positive work outcomes such as low absenteeism, low turnover, and high job effort (for reviews, see Mathieu and Zajac 1990; Randall 1990).

Job involvement is defined as the degree of importance of one's job to one's self image—that is, the degree of psychological identification with one's job (Lawler and Hall 1970). According to Kanungo (1982), the job involvement of an individual depends upon "the perceptions he or she has about the need-satisfying potentialities of the job" (p. 342). Accordingly, individuals with high job involvement believe that their jobs provide opportunities to satisfy salient personal needs. Jobs potentially offer a variety of intrinsic and extrinsic rewards that may satisfy personal needs. Job related rewards include salary, promotions, security, recognition, a sense of achievement, and positive social interaction (Gorn and Kanungo 1980).

Nouri (1994) reports evidence that job involvement interacts with organizational commitment to affect budgetary slack. For individuals with high organizational commitment, the relationship between job involvement and slack is inverse—that is, the higher the job involvement, the lower the budgetary slack. For individuals with low organizational commitment, the relationship between job involvement and slack is positive—that is, the higher the job involvement, the higher the budgetary slack.

The pivotal role of organizational commitment may reflect differences in motivation between individuals with high and low organizational commitment. Individuals with high organizational commitment want the organization to succeed. If such individuals view budgetary slack as dysfunctional, they may seek to limit their attempts to introduce slack. Individuals with high job involvement (and high commitment) may be even more inclined to limit slack since the organization has provided them opportunities to meet personal needs—that is, having the opportunity to fulfil personal needs provides greater motivation to "serve" the organization by minimizing slack.

For individuals with low organizational commitment, the relation between job involvement and budgetary slack may differ. Individuals with low organizational commitment may be more interested in pursuing self-interest rather than organizational interest. Since budgetary slack may help them gain favorable performance evaluation (and, thus, organizational rewards), such individuals may be inclined to introduce slack. This inclination may increase when the individual has high job involvement. As discussed, high job involvement may indicate that the individual has job opportunities to fulfil personal needs. In the case of high job involvement, the individual (with low organizational commitment) has more incentive to create slack since favorable performance evaluations (resulting from slack) have greater potential for fulfilling personal needs. In other words, when the job provides opportunities to gain personal rewards (i.e., job involvement is high), the individual with low organizational commitment has greater incentive to introduce budgetary slack to maximize these rewards. In contrast, when job involvement is high for individuals with high organizational commitment, the individual's desire to serve the organization by reducing budgetary slack is magnified in appreciation of the opportunities.

The current study extends this analysis by exploring how budget-based compensation influences the relationships between budgetary slack, organizational commitment, and job involvement. Budget-based compensation is the degree to which meeting budget goals is important to an employee's compensation and promotions. As argued by prior researchers (Dunk 1993; Merchant 1985; Waller 1988), when compensation is based upon budget performance, the individual has motivation to introduce slack to secure favorable evaluations (and, thus, higher compensation). Consequently, individuals whose compensation is budget-based may be more inclined to introduce budgetary slack than individuals whose compensation is not budget-based.

The current study proposes that budget-based compensation interacts with organizational commitment and job involvement in the creation of budgetary slack. As discussed, evidence of a two-way interaction between organizational commitment and job involvement is reported by Nouri (1994), who found that budgetary slack is highest when organizational commitment is low and job involvement is high. The current paper proposes a three-way interaction that includes budget-based compensation. Accordingly, budgetary slack will be highest when organizational commitment is low, job involvement is high, and budget-based compensation is high (i.e., reaching budgets is important for compensation). Conversely, the current study proposes that budgetary slack will be lowest when organizational commitment and job involvement are high and budget-based compensation is low (i.e., reaching budgets is not important for compensation).

The hypothesis, stated in the alternative form, summarizes the preceding arguments:

Hypothesis 1. Organizational commitment, job involvement, and budget-based compensation interact to affect the propensity to create budgetary slack. The propensity to create slack will be lowest when budget-based compensation is low and organizational commitment and job involvement are high. The propensity to create slack will be highest when organizational commitment is low and job involvement and budget-based compensation are high.

METHODOLOGY

Data Collection

Data for the study was collected by a survey questionnaire administered to a sample of managers in a large multinational company. The firm primarily produces oil and chemical products. The company has a highly formal management control system. Managerial evaluation is, in part, based upon: teamwork, developing subordinates, and achieving budget. In the three years preceding the survey, the company had experienced moderate growth in revenues and income. Managerial layoffs or major reorganizations had not occurred.

Initially, survey questionnaires were distributed to executives who were members of a company-wide, long-term planning committee. The divisional managers on the committee were requested to personally complete a questionnaire and to forward questionnaires to nine others in their respective organizations. In selecting participants, managers were asked to choose individuals with budget responsibilities. Participants were chosen from different functional areas in the United States.

Included with each questionnaire was a cover letter explaining the importance of the research, an endorsement letter from top management encouraging cooperation in the study, and written instructions to complete the task. To minimize response bias, respondents were asked to complete the questionnaire independently and to return the questionnaire directly to the researchers in postage-paid return envelopes. The instructions accompanying the instrument stressed confidentiality.

One-hundred-and-thirty-nine questionnaires were returned for a response rate of 68.5 percent.[1] With regard to the management level of the respondents, 6 percent were top management, 49 percent were middle management, 20 percent were lower management, 11 percent were first-level supervisors, and 14 percent were senior staff employees. The average respondent had 38 employees under him or her in the organizational hierarchy. On average, the respondents were 44 years old, had been employed by the company for 20 years, and had been in their current position for three years. The long length of company service is consistent with the companies in the study of Levering, Moskowitz, and Katz (1985). Based upon employee interviews, they rated the work environments of the largest U.S. companies. For the 100 firms with the best work environments (the firm surveyed in this study is among the 100), 46 percent of the employees had been with the firm for 15 years or longer.

Measures

The variables measured in the questionnaire included propensity to create budgetary slack, organizational commitment, job involvement, and budget-based compensation.

To measure the propensity to create budgetary slack, the current study employed Onsi's (1973) four-item instrument, which has been used in several prior accounting studies (e.g., Merchant 1985). A sample item in the scale is: "To protect himself/herself, a manager submits a budget that can safely be attained." The response format was a seven-point Likert-type scale ranging from one (strongly disagree) to seven (strongly agree). The Cronbach alpha for the current study was 0.75.

To assess organizational commitment, the current study employed the nine-item (short form) scale of the Mowday et al. (1979) instrument. A sample item in the scale is: "I really care about the fate of this organization." The response scale was a seven-point Likert-type scale ranging from one (strongly disagree) to seven (strongly agree). Acceptable levels of reliability and validity of the scale have been reported in prior studies (Angle and Perry 1981; Blau 1987; Price and Muller 1981). In the current study, the Cronbach alpha coefficient was .86.

Job involvement was measured using Kanungo's (1982) 10-item instrument. Blau (1985) determined that the Kanungo scale best operationalized the job involvement construct. A sample item in the Kanungo scale is: "Most of my personal life goals are job-oriented." The response format for the scale was a seven-point Likert-type scale ranging from one (strongly disagree) to seven (strongly agree). The Cronbach alpha coefficient for the current study was 0.77.

Budget-based compensation was measured using a four-item instrument developed by Searfoss (1976). The instrument asks participants whether their compen-

Table 1. Descriptive Statistics

Variable	Mean	Standard Deviation	Theoretical Range	Actual
Propensity to create slack	14.83	4.60	4-28	4-25
Organizational commitment	46.42	8.76	9-63	25-63
Job involvement	37.29	9.18	10-70	17-59
Budget-based Compensation	13.07	5.13	4-28	4-28

Note: n = 139

Table 2. Matrix of Intercorrelations

	Propensity to Create Budgetary Slack Y	Budget Based Compensation X1	Job Involvement X2	Organizational Commitment X3
Y	1.00			
X1	-0.03	1.00		
X2	-0.08	0.10	1.00	
X3	-0.36**	0.19*	0.29**	1.00

Notes: One-tail significance:
$*p < .05.$
$**p < .01.$

sation is related to their budget performance. A sample item is: "Budget variances in the division are mentioned by my superiors as factors in considering me for pay raises." The response format was a seven-point Likert-type scale ranging from one (strongly disagree) to seven (strongly agree). In the current study, the Cronbach alpha coefficient for the scale was 0.81.

To measure budget-based compensation, this study used individual perceptions rather than more objective types of evidence. This resulted from management's insistence that respondent anonymity be strictly safeguarded. The use of perceptions has the potential disadvantage that the perceptions of some individuals may be distorted. However, the advantage of using perceptions is that perceptions influence individual behavior.

Table 3. Regression Results

Variable	Coefficient	Value	S.D.	t	p
Constant	b0	−42.399	27.895	−1.52	n.s.
Budget-based compensation (X1)	b1	4.005	2.137	1.87	<.10
Job Involvement (X2)	b2	1.736	0.677	2.56	<.05
Organizational commitment (X3)	b3	1.231	0.593	2.08	<.05
Interaction (X1*X2)	b4	−0.105	0.523	−2.01	<.05
Interaction (X1*X3)	b5	−0.086	0.452	−1.91	<.10
Interaction (X2*X3)	b6	−0.037	0.014	−2.64	<.01
Interaction (X1*X2*X3)	b7	0.002	0.001	2.08	<.05

Notes: R-squared = 19%; $F(7,131) = 4.42$; $p < 0.001$; $n = 139$.

RESULTS

Table 1 presents descriptive statistics and Table 2 presents the matrix of intercorrelations for the variables in the study. The study's hypothesis was tested using the following regression equation:

$$Y = b0 + b1\,X1 + b2\,X2 + b3\,X3 + b4\,X1\,X2 + b5\,X1\,X3 \\ + b6\,X2\,X3 + b7\,X1\,X2\,X3 + e \tag{1}$$

where: Y = propensity to create budgetary slack,
$X1$ = budget-based compensation,
$X2$ = job involvement,
$X3$ = organizational commitment,
$X1\,X2, X1\,X3, X2\,X3, X1\,X2\,X3$ = interaction terms,
e = error term.

The hypothesis predicts an interaction between budget-based compensation, organizational commitment, and job involvement; therefore, a significant coefficient $b7$ in Equation (1) would lead to the acceptance of the hypothesis. The results of the regression analysis using Equation (1) appear in Table 3. The results indicate that the coefficient $b7$ is statistically significant ($p < .05$).[2] Consistent with the hypothesis, the three independent variables interact.[3] To further analyze the interaction, Table 4 presents a three-way table of slack scores based upon the three independent variables (dichotomized at their mean). The information in Table 4 was used to graph the three-way interaction shown in Figure 1.

The results in Table 4 and the graphs in Figure 1 indicate that propensity to create slack is lowest when organizational commitment and job involvement are high and budget-based compensation is low. Propensity to create slack is highest when

Table 4. Mean Scores for Propensity to Create Budgetary Slack

	Budget-based Compensation	
	Low	High
Low organizational commitment		
Low Job Involvement	15.138	15.700
	(3.768)	(3.498)
	n=29	n=10
High job involvement	16.824	18.167
	(5.376)	(1.602)
	n=17	n=6
High organizational commitment		
Low job involvement	13.941	14.632
	(4.603)	(4.487)
	n=17	n=19
High job involvement	12.533	14.115
	(5.805)	(4.546)
	n=15	n=26

Note: Standard deviation is given in parentheses

organizational commitment is low and job involvement and budget-based compensation are high. A *t*-test of mean slack values indicates that these two groups differ significantly ($t = 3.45$; $p < .01$).

DISCUSSION

The results suggest that budgetary slack is affected by the interaction of three variables: organizational commitment, job involvement, and budget-based compensation. According to the survey results, budgetary slack is lowest when organizational commitment and job involvement are high and budget-based compensation is low.

The findings have potential implications for organizations that seek to minimize budgetary slack. Of the independent variables examined in the study, budget-based compensation may be the most easily controlled by top management. To minimize budgetary slack, management could reduce the importance of reaching budget for individual compensation.[4] Of course, the potential benefits of such a change (decreased slack) would have to be weighed against potential costs (e.g., motivation to reach budget may decline).

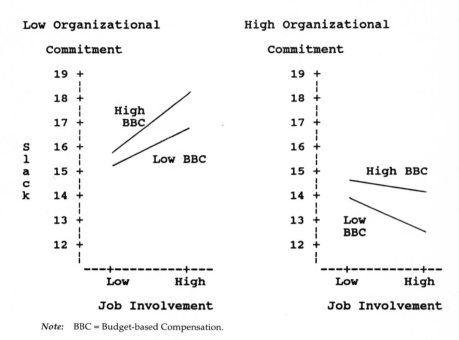

Figure 1.   Three-way Interaction

Whereas top management may be able to directly control budget-based compensation, top management's ability to control the study's other independent variables—organizational commitment and job involvement—may be more limited. Nevertheless, to decrease budgetary slack, management may consider attempting to increase the organizational commitment of their employees. According to Ouchi (1981), U.S. organizations may be able to increase employee commitment by imitating Japanese practices such as increasing the involvement of employees in decision making, providing long-term employment, and fostering egalitarianism within the organization. Ogilvie (1986) discusses how human resource management practices can influence the organizational commitment of employees. For example, for high commitment, Ogilvie (1986) argues that companies must adopt compensation policies that directly tie organizational rewards to performance.

Job involvement may be more difficult to control than organizational commitment. The job involvment of an individual hinges on whether the job provides opportunities to meet personal needs and individuals differ as to their needs (Gorn and Kanungo 1980). Jobs can meet personal needs by providing opportunities for (among other things): adequate salary, promotions, recognition by others, autonomy, and personal achievement. Individuals differ as to the importance of these factors. A further complication in controlling job involvement is that the effect of job involvement on budgetary slack is dependent upon the level of organizational commitment. For example, increasing job involvment could decrease or increase budgetary slack depending upon whether organizational commitment is high or low. In view of these difficulties, management may be better served in utilizing its scarce resources to control organizational commitment rather than job involvement.

Given the pivotal role of organizational commitment in explaining budgetary slack in the current study and the paucity of prior research in the area, perhaps future research should examine the relationship between organizational commitment and budgetary slack in more depth. For example, researchers could compare budgetary slack in high and low commitment organizations while controlling for other variables that may influence budgetary slack such as job involvement and budget-based compensation. Of particular interest may be budgetary slack in so-called "new" work organizations that are characterized by high organizational commitment (Applebaum and Batt 1994; Osterman 1994).

The current study is subject to several limitations. First, the study was conducted within a single organization, which may limit the generalizability of the findings. Second, since there was minimal control over the selection of respondents, the sample was not strictly random. Third, given the complexity of budgetary slack, the study could not control all possible independent variables.

Despite the limitations, the present paper reports on an important interaction that has not been investigated in previous research on budgetary slack—the interaction of organizational commitment, job involvement, and budget-based compensation. This study shows that these variables are important in the study of the budgetary slack.

ACKNOWLEDGMENT

The authors would like to thank Alan Dunk, Penelope Greenberg, Larissa Kyj, Leslie Richeson, and Heibatollah Sami for their many helpful comments and suggestions. We are also indebted to the associate editor and anonymous reviewers for their useful suggestions on earlier drafts of the paper. Thanks also to Temple University Graduate School for its financial support and to Stephen Fogg and Stanley Ross for their assistance in data collection.

NOTES

1. Several types of response biases were considered to assure that thoughtful responses were obtained from the respondents. These biases include extremity, content-related, initiation, fatigue, and routine biases (Alreck and Settle 1985). Analyses indicates that none of the biases appears to be present in any of the measures used in the study. In addition, the possibility of a social desirability response bias was investigated using the regression approach recommended by Ganster, Hennessey, and Luthans (1983). The analysis indicates that the bias did not occur.

2.   Two observations should be noted with respect to the use of the multiplicative model. First, except for the coefficient of the three-way interaction term ($b7$), the other coefficients ($b1$-$b6$) in Equation (1) are not interpretable since they can be altered by shifting the origin points of $X1$, $X2$, and $X3$ (Allison 1977; Southwood 1978). Second, the use of multiplicative terms in regression analysis may cause multicollinearity problems (Althauser 1971; Blalock 1979). To check this, the regression analysis was rerun with $X1$, $X2$, and $X3$ rescaled so that each variable had a mean value of zero (Cronbach 1987; Jaccard, Turrisi, and Wan 1990). Since no changes in results were observed, the original results, based upon unscaled values, are reported in the paper.

3.   Prior research indicates a link between hierarchial level and organizational commitment (e.g., Mathieu and Zajac 1990; DeCotiis and Summers 1987). As discussed in the data collection section, individuals in this study self-reported their hierarchial level (top management, middle management, lower management, first-level supervisors, senior employees). The correlation between hierarchial level and organizational commitment was .04 and was not statistically significant.

To assess the impact of hierarchial level on the hypothesized relationships, Equation (1) was modified to include hierarchial level as an additional independent variable. The three-way interaction predicted in the hypothesis remained statistically significant ($p<.05$).

4.   Technically, since budget-based compensation is measured using individual perceptions (see Methodology section), management should be concerned about the perceived importance of reaching budget. This study discusses the actual importance of reaching budget rather than perceived importance under the assumption that most organizational members accurately perceive the extent to which their compensation is based upon reaching budget.

REFERENCES

Allison, P.D. 1977. Testing for interaction in multiple regression. *American Journal of Sociology* :144-153.

Antle, R., and G.D. Eppen. 1985. Capital rationing and organizational slack in capital budgeting. *Management Sciences* (February) :163-174.

Alreck, P.L., and R.B. Settle. 1985. *The Survey Research Handbook*. Homewood, IL: Irwin.

Althauser, R.P. 1971. Multicollinearity and non-additive regression models. In *Causal Models in the Social Sciences*, ed. H.M. Blalock, 453-472. Chicago: Aldine.

Angle, H.L., and J.L. Perry. 1981. An empirical assessment of organizational commitment and organizational effectiveness. *Administrative Science Quarterly* (March): 1-14.

Applebaum, E., and R. Batt. 1994. *The New American Workplace* Ithaca, NY: ILR Press.

Blalock, H.M. 1979. *Social Statistics*, 2nd edition. New York: McGraw-Hill.

Blau, G.J. 1985. A multiple study investigation of dimensionality of job involvement. *Journal of Vocational Behavior* 27: 19-36.

_____. 1987. Using a person-environment fit model to predict job involvement and organizational commitment. *Journal of Vocational Behavior* 30: 240-257.

Chow, C.W., J.C. Cooper, and W.S. Waller. 1988. Participative budgeting: Effects of a truth-inducing pay scheme and information on slack and performance. *The Accounting Review* (January): 111-122.

Christensen, J. 1982. The determination of performance standards and participation. *Journal of Accounting Research* (Autumn): 589-603.

Cronbach, L. 1987. Statistical tests for moderator variables: Flaws in analysis recently proposed. *Psychological Bulletin* 102(3): 414-417.

DeCotiis, T.A., and T.P. Summers. 1987. A path analysis of a model of the antecedents and consequences of organizational commitment. *Human Relations* 40: 445-470.

Dunk, A. 1993. The effect of budget emphasis and information asymmetry on the relation between budgetary participation and slack. *The Accounting Review* (April): 400-410.

Ganster, D.C., H.W. Hennessey, and F. Luthans. 1983. Social desirability response effects: Three alternative models. *Academy of Management Journal* (26): 321-331.

Gorn, G.J., and R.N. Kanungo. 1980. Job involvement and motivation: Are intrinsically motivated managers more job involved? *Organizational Behavior and Human Performance* 26: 265-277.

Hopwood, A. 1974. *Accounting and Human Behaviour*. London: Haymarket Publishing.

Jaccard, J., R. Turrisi, and C.K. Wan. 1990. *Interactive Effects in Multiple Regression*. Beverly Hills, CA: Sage.

Kanungo, R.N. 1982. Measurement of job and work involvement. *Journal of Applied Psychology* 67(3):341-349.

Kren, L. 1993. Control system effects on budget slack. In *Advances in Management Accounting*, Vol. 2, ed. M.J. Epstein, 109-118. Greenwich, CT: JAI Press.

Lawler, E., and D. Hall. 1970. Relationship of job characteristics to job involvement, satisfaction, and intrinsic motivation. *Journal of Applied Psychology* 54(4): 305-312.

Levering, R., M. Moskowitz, and M. Katz. 1985. *The 100 Best Companies to Work for in America*. New York: New York Library.

Lincoln, J.R., and A.L. Kalleberg. 1990. *Culture, Control, and Commitment*. Cambridge, UK: Cambridge University Press.

Lowe, E.A., and R.W. Shaw. 1968. An analysis of managerial biasing: Evidence from a company's budgeting process. *Journal of Management Studies* (October): 304-315.

Lukka, K. 1988. Budgetary biasing in organizations: Theoretical framework and empirical evidence. *Accounting, Organizations and Society* 13: 281-301.

Mathieu, J.E., and D.M. Zajac. 1990. A review and meta-analysis of the antecedents, correlates, and consequences of organizational commitment. *Psychological Bulletin* 108: 171-194.

Merchant, K.A. 1985. Budgeting and the propensity to create budgetary slack. *Accounting, Organizations and Society* 10(2): 201-210.

Mowday, R., R. Steers, and L. Porter. 1979. The measurement of organizational commitment. *Journal of Vocational Behavior* 14: 224-247.

Nouri, H. 1994. Using organizational commitment and job involvement to predict budgetary slack: A research note. *Accounting, Organizations and Society* 19(5): 289-295.

Ogilvie, J.R. 1986. The role of human resource management practices in predicting organizational commitment. *Group and Organizational Studies* (December): 335-359.

Onsi, M. 1973. Factor analysis of behavioral variables affecting budgetary slack. *The Accounting Review* (July): 535-548.

Osterman, P. 1994. How common is workplace transformation and who adopts it? *Industrial and Labor Relations Review* 47: 173-188.

Ouchi, W.G. 1981. *Theory Z*. New York: Avon.

Porter, L.W., R.M. Steers, R.T. Mowday, and P.V. Boulin. 1974. Organizational commitment, job satisfaction, and turnover among psychiatric technicians. *Journal of Applied Psychology* 59(5): 603-609.

Price, J.L., and C.W. Muller. 1981. *Professional Turnover: The Case of Nurses*. New York: Spectrum.

Randall, D.M. 1990. The consequences of organizational commitment: methodological investigation. *Journal of Organizational Behavior* 11: 361-378.

Searfoss, D.G. 1976. Some behavioral aspects of budgeting for control: An empirical study. *Accounting, Organizations and Society* (1): 375-385.

Schiff, M., and A.Y. Lewin. 1970. The impact of people on budgets. *The Accounting Review* (April): 259-268.

Southwood, K.E. 1978. Substantive theory and statistical interaction: Five models. *American Journal of Sociology* (March): 1154-1203.

Waller, W.S. 1988. Slack in participative budgeting: The joint effect of truth-inducing pay scheme and risk preferences. *Accounting, Organizations and Society* 13(1): 87-98.

Young, S.M. 1985. Participative budgeting: The effects of risk aversion and asymmetric information on budgetary slack. *Journal of Accounting Research* (Autumn): 829-842.

AN EMPIRICAL ANALYSIS OF THE TIMING OF WRITEDOWN DISCLOSURES

Srinivasan Ragothaman and Bruce Bublitz

ABSTRACT

Large writedowns during the 1980s and early 1990s have generated considerable interest and controversy in the financial press. Consequently, the Financial Accounting Standards Board (FASB 1990, 1993) reconsidered the accounting rules with regard to writedown recognition, timing, and measurement and issued a new statement on asset writedowns in March 1995 (FASB 1995). We investigate whether the market acts as if it is aware of the management's incentives with regard to the timing of writedown disclosures and whether the reaction to writedown announcements is associated with the fiscal quarter of the announcement.

This study examines the effects of unexpected writedowns and unexpected earnings on unexpected returns. The results for a sample of 110 NYSE firms indicate that the signs and magnitude of writedowns and earnings are associated with unexpected returns. On average, writedown announcements made in earlier quarters are accompanied by less negative stock price reaction when compared with the writedown

Advances in Accounting, Volume 14, pages 223-240.
Copyright © 1996 by JAI Press Inc.
All rights of reproduction in any form reserved.
ISBN: 0-7623-0161-9.

announcements in the fourth quarter. Managers have some discretion with regard to timing decisions and appear to take writedowns in the earlier quarters when they have some positive news to convey. This positive news may dampen the negative news that is normally contained in an impairment disclosure.

INTRODUCTION

There was a knave who, when condemned to die by the King, convinced the King that if given a year's reprieve, he would teach the King's horse to talk in return for his life. The King agrees with this temporary reprieve. As the knave is being led off, his astonished friends ask how he could make such a bold promise. The knave replies: "Within a year anything could happen: the King could die, the horse could die or the horse could even learn to talk!"

—Verrecchia (1983)

The moral of the above story is that a manager may delay the disclosure of "bad news," hoping that in the interim some "good news" which would offset it might occur. We investigate whether stock prices react differently to writedown announcements made in the fourth quarter vis-à-vis those made in the earlier quarters. Such a differential reaction is consistent with the market being aware of the motives of management with regard to the timing of writedown disclosures. Elliott and Shaw (1988) suggest that managers exercise discretion with regard to the timing and quantification of writedowns. Penman (1987) and Kalay and Lowenstein (1986) have documented that managers delay the release of bad news—for example, bad earnings news and bad dividend news. Managers have incentives to manage bad news and delay writeoff announcements until the fourth quarter, when annual audits occur.[1]

The frequency and magnitude of asset writedowns increased significantly during the 1980s and the early 1990s. Pearson and Okubara (1987) report that over $26 billion in writedown charges were announced by public corporations during 1985-86. In 1988, AT&T wrote off $6.72 billion for obsolete network equipment. The S&P 500 companies took writedown charges totalling $46 billion in 1993 (Myers 1995). These large and frequent writedowns have generated considerable interest in the financial press. Consequently, the Financial Accounting Standards Board (FASB 1990, 1993) reevaluated the accounting rules for writedown recognition and measurement and issued a new standard on asset writedowns in March 1995 (FASB 1995).

Ronen (1977) examines managers' incentives under the insider trading rules to disclose positive versus negative information. He argues that managers have incentives to suppress bad news or to delay the production of information anticipated to be negative. On the other hand, managers have incentives to disseminate good news quickly. Hence, writedowns announced in earlier quarters may be considered better news than writedowns announced in the fourth quarter. Fried, Schiff, and Sondhi (1989) report that over 60 percent of the writeoffs in their sample of 870 were disclosed in the fourth quarter and another 21 percent in the third quarter. They suggest that perhaps annual audits cause writeoffs to be reported more often in the fourth quarter. Zucca and Campbell (1992, 33) make the same suggestion:

> However, the preponderance of fourth quarter writedowns ... may be due to the more intensive review which firms undergo at year end. Both the annual budgeting review process and the external audit process tend to occur in the fourth quarter or after the fiscal year end.

In addition, they note that many of these discretionary writedowns are associated with "big baths." Management is probably in a better position to determine whether a "big bath" is appropriate in the fourth quarter. It is possible that earlier quarter writedowns imply aggressive managerial action in the form of writedowns which signal cost savings, tax benefits, better prospects for higher earnings in the future, and downsizings.

Waymire (1988) argues that delayed writeoffs could sometimes lead to lawsuits against managers and auditors. In the wake of class action lawsuits under select provisions of the federal securities laws, audit firms are under increased pressure to weigh the legal risk of overstating the value of assets when they are clearly impaired.[2] Feroz, Park, and Pastena (1991) examine 224 Accounting and Auditing Enforcement Releases by the Securities and Exchange Commission (SEC) and report that 12.3 percent of the errors (29 of 239) are overstatements of long-lived assets, and another 55 percent of the errors (132 of 239) are overstatements of receivables and inventories. In an earlier study, St. Pierre and Anderson (1984) examined 334 accounting errors found in 129 court cases and concluded that none of the suits related to errors in undervaluing assets, and many of the errors were overstatements of assets or revenue. Thus, it is clear that auditors are interested in the timely recognition of asset impairments through writedowns or some other disclosure mechanism.

Chambers and Penman (1984) argue that early earnings announcements are characterized by good news and inordinately delayed reports often contain bad news. Givoly and Palmon (1982) report that the finding of delayed "unfavorable news" is robust to different definitions of expected earnings and timeliness. Sinclair and Young (1991) confirm the management tendency to delay bad news. In a similar vein, we suggest that writedowns announced during the first three quarters perhaps signal "good news" that the impairment problem is firmly tackled. Statman and Sepe (1986) argue that managers, acting under the sunk cost fallacy, sometimes deploy assets beyond the point which the market believes is prudent. Hence, when managers decide to cut their losses early and downsize by taking writedowns, the market may consider such writedowns to be favorable news.[3]

We hypothesize that the market reactions to non-fourth-quarter writedown announcements will be less negative when compared to reactions to fourth quarter writedown announcements. The writedown announcements made in earlier quarters could imply that the impairment problem is being successfully addressed. Early release of writedown news could imply that the future prospects for increased operating income are good. The results for a sample of 110 NYSE firms indicate that the signs and magnitude of writedowns and earnings are associated with unexpected returns. On average, writedown announcements made in earlier quarters are accompanied by less negative stock price reaction when compared with the writedown announcements in the fourth quarter. The results provide indirect evidence on signaling implications of writedown announcements made in the first three quarters. We use market reactions to writedown announcements to provide evidence about the timing of writedowns. The remainder of this paper is organized as follows. The second section describes the motivation for the study; the third section develops the hypothesis; the fourth section describes the model and the data collection procedures; the fifth section analyzes the results; and the sixth section provides a summary.

MOTIVATION

Theories of voluntary disclosure suggest that managers suppress or delay public disclosure of unfavorable information (Verrecchia 1983; Dye 1985; Jung and Kwon 1988). In the Verrecchia model (1983), the manager may disclose or withhold information. However, if the manager decides to disclose the information, there is a cost associated. Disclosure costs include preparation and dissemination costs as well as other indirect costs associated with the use of information by competitors, employees, lenders, stockholders, and so forth. For example, if favorable sales and income data are reported, employees may demand a higher bonus. Verrecchia (1983) calls these disclosure-related costs proprietary costs. The existence of a proprietary cost, when information is withheld by managers, prevents investors from inferring that the withheld information is really bad news. This occurs when withheld information is good news, but not good enough to persuade the managers to incur the proprietary cost.[4] Verrecchia (1983) goes on to show that "the proprietary cost is a continuous, decreasing function of time." For example, current information may have a substantial proprietary cost associated with it, but as information becomes dated and old, proprietary costs may approach zero. This would explain delayed release of bad news and is consistent with investors exhibiting rational expectations about withheld information.

Dye (1985) argues that when investors are not sure whether managers are endowed with private information, partial disclosure by managers is possible. When managers have not made any public disclosure, investors are uncertain as to the reason for this withholding/delay. Investors may wonder if the nondisclosure/

delay is due to absence of information or due to unfavorable information. This uncertainty prevents investors from inferring the worst (adverse selection) and leads to partial disclosure by management in equilibrium. Dye (1985) suggests that if disclosing a piece of information would result in the incurrence of direct or indirect costs, full disclosure by managers should not be expected. Jung and Kwon (1988) analytically show that if investors believe that the probability of managers receiving information increases as time elapses, unfavorable news is contained in late announcements. These three theoretical analyses suggest that writedown announcements made in the first three quarters could be associated with less negative market reactions than writedown announcements made in the fourth quarter.

In Accounting Series Release 177, the SEC states that a major motivation for involving public accountants in the quarterly reporting process is the desire to prod management to disseminate negative information. SEC release 5092 (1970) stresses that management has an obligation to announce all material information on a timely basis. Report Form 8-K must be filed with the SEC within 10 days after the close of the month in which any of the following events occurs: acquisition or disposition of assets, *extraordinary item charges* and credits, *other material charges*, and *other material provisions for losses*. Accounting Series Release 138 (ASR 138) supports the position of the SEC on the timely disclosure of "incipient problems" and asserts that:

> registrants should make special efforts to recognize incipient problems that might lead to ... charges and to identify them clearly at the earliest possible time in financial statements and other forms of disclosure, including public reports filed with the Commission, so that public investors may recognize the risks involved.

Lurie and Pastena (1975) argue that Item 10(a) of Report Form 8-K was designed to help investors with relevant decision making information on a timely basis. By examining all Standard & Poors 500 companies that filed 8-Ks, 10-Ks, and 10-Qs in the year 1973, they determined the degree to which management complied with the requirements of ASR 138. They find that "almost 59 percent of the favorable filings occurred in the first half of the registrant's fiscal year. Only 22 percent of the unfavorable filings occurred in that period, however, and more than 38 percent of all unfavorable filings occurred in the twelfth month of the registrant's fiscal year."

The late disclosure of negative information is contrary to the spirit of many accounting pronouncements and other SEC rulings that require the dissemination of potentially unfavorable information such as anticipated writeoffs, asset impairments, and anticipated losses from discontinuations as early in the fiscal year as possible. Pastena and Ronen (1979) find that managers act as if they attempt to delay the disclosure of negative information and disseminate negative information essentially after such information can no longer be withheld. Early writedown announcements can signal that an asset impairment problem has been aggressively addressed. Especially when there is no pressure from external auditors in the first three quarters, management taking a writedown can signal that value enhancing restructurings are around the corner. Hence, one could expect that the market would react less negatively to earlier quarter writedown announcements.

The writedown disclosure itself can convey new information to the market about the decline in the economic value of the assets. Writedown announcements could suggest that assets have become impaired and that the future cash flow expectations are low. These low expectations would then lead to a negative stock price reaction.[5] For example, the huge $2.1 billion General Motors writeoff in 1990 suggested that product demand had declined, automobile prices had failed to keep up with costs, and prospects for future profits were low. By definition, writedowns imply that the expected future cash flows associated with the asset are less than the carrying value of the asset.

HYPOTHESIS DEVELOPMENT

Based on the preceding discussion, writedown announcements made during the first three quarters could be expected to cause either a positive or a negative market reaction. Managers use their expectations about repairs, warranty costs, advertising costs, and so forth for the entire fiscal year to estimate costs for the first three interim reports. Managers can partially hide bad earnings signals by interim cost estimates. Mendenhall and Nichols (1988) state that generally accepted accounting principles for interim reports allow managers to exercise some control in adjusting non-fourth-quarter earnings reports.

APB Opinion 28 selected the integral theory as the primary theory of interim reporting. The integral theory views an interim period as an installment of an annual period. Under this view, expenses that would normally be charged to an annual accounting period could be deferred and expensed in several interim periods. The allocations could be based on expected sales volume, production levels, or some other discretionary basis. In a rational market, investors would expect managers to exercise control over writedowns in the first three quarters and, hence, would react more positively to non-fourth-quarter writedowns. Earlier quarter writedowns are voluntary, and it is likely that managers would voluntarily release good news early. We hypothesize that writedown announcements in earlier quarters will have a less negative effect on stock returns than fourth quarter writedown announcements.

Hypothesis H0.   Ceteris paribus, the market reaction to 4th quarter writedown announcements is not different (same sign and magnitude) from the market reaction to writedown announcements in the earlier three quarters.

Hypothesis HA.   Ceteris paribus, the market reaction to 4th quarter writedown announcements is more negative than the market reaction to writedown announcements in the earlier three quarters.

THE MODEL AND DATA

Because the writedown is usually announced with overall earnings, the reaction to any unexpected earnings could confound the writedown effect. We therefore construct a test similar to Mendenhall and Nichols (1988) to test the hypothesis. They find that the market reacts more negatively to unexpected negative earnings in the first three quarters than in the fourth quarter. They hypothesize that, because management has a greater ability to delay bad news in the first three quarters, the release of bad news in these quarters is interpreted more negatively. The situation, thus, is seen as so bad that management could not delay disclosure. To control for the effects of unexpected earnings, we include an unexpected income variable in our model.

Size is another factor that could confound the writedown effect. Prior research suggests that stockholders have more information about large firms than small firms and that they react differently to accounting information releases for small and large firms (Collins et al. 1989). Chen, Roll, and Ross (1986) argue that "size may be the best theory we now have of expected returns." To control for this effect, we include a size variable (log of total assets) in our model.

The security market reaction to writedown announcements is examined using an ordinary least squares regression with a binary variable ($C1$) indicating the fourth quarter:

$$CAR_{jt} = \beta_0\,INT1 + \beta_1\,(UWD_{jyq}) + \beta_2\,(CUWD_{jyq}) + \beta_3\,(UE_{jyq})$$
$$+ \beta_4\,(CUE_{jyq}) + \beta_5\,(LTA_{jyq}) + \beta_6\,C1 + e_{jt} \qquad (1)$$

where: CAR_{jt} = Cumulative abnormal return for firm j for writedown announcement days 0 and -1, where day 0 is the day writedown news appeared in *The Wall Street Journal*.[6]

$INT1$ = Intercept deflated by sales per share,

UWD_{jyq} = Unexpected writedown scaled by sales per share for firm j, year y, and quarter q,

$C1$ = 1, if q = non-fourth quarter; 0 otherwise,

$CUWD_{jyq}$ = $C1 * UWD_{jyq}$,

UE_{jyq} = Unexpected earnings before writedowns scaled by sales per share for firm j, year y, and quarter q,

CUE_{jyq} = $C1 * UE_{jyq}$,

LTA_{jyq} = Log of total assets (a size measure).

Deflation by sales is a heteroscedasticity adjustment and has been suggested by Shalit and Sanker (1977) and Landsman (1986).[7] Sales is a factor-neutral measure of firm size—that is, it is not affected by writedown charges, unlike total assets. Landsman (1986) argues that sales is a better measure of firm size because it is less dependent on capital structure or the size of a firm's pension plan. The slope coefficient β_2 measures the difference in market reaction between fourth quarter writedowns and writedowns announced in the other three quarters. If β_2 is statistically significant, then the null hypothesis can be rejected. Differences in market reaction in the fourth quarter could be in terms of slope or intercept. We include both in the model for completeness. The intercept dummy variable ($C1$) in the model allows for a changing intercept. If β_6 is statistically significant, then the null hypothesis also can be rejected. We employ a naive earnings expectation model to compute unexpected earnings—fourth differences in quarterly earnings are measured as earnings surprises. O'Brien (1988) has shown that forecast errors from a naive earnings expectations model provide better predictions of abnormal stock returns than analysts' forecast errors. She concludes that analysts do not provide a better model of "market expectation" than mechanical models. Foster, Olsen, and Shevlin (1984) show that an earnings expectation model using a seasonal component yields virtually the same result as an earnings expectation model that uses a seasonal and an adjacent quarter-to-quarter component.

We selected the sample from all writedown announcements disclosed by *The Wall Street Journal Abstract* compiled by NEXIS. The final sample consists of 110 announcements made during 1983 through 1988 for which full data are available.[8] The sample includes 56 firms making writedown announcements in the first three quarters and 54 firms making writedown announcements in the fourth quarter. We

Table 1.   Descriptive Statistics for Key (Undeflated) Variables:
(Quarterly Data—$ Millions—Number of observations in parenthesis)

Variables	Mean	Std. Dev	Med	Minimum	Maximum
Panel A: Descriptive Data for Writedowns in First Three Quarters:					
Sales (56)	1095.20	1878.90	361.7	3.38	9278.00
Cogs (45)	908.71	1445.48	301.5	2.63	6551.00
Writedown (56)	231.07	421.93	83.0	1.16	1900.00
Income (56)	152.58	292.62	24.6	−100.39	1113.88
Total assets (56)	5412.14	8226.93	2137.5	42.02	37471.01
Panel B: Descriptive Data for Writedowns in The Fourth Quarter:					
Sales (54)	1191.56	2136.81	461.3	3.08	13341.00
Cogs (45)	1113.29	2362.25	438.0	0.78	15063.00
Writedown (54)	296.06	916.46	78.6	2.20	6720.00
Income (54)	139.78	493.85	12.9	−169.02	3378.00
Total assets (54)	5152.31	7763.80	2405.8	22.68	35152.01

Notes: Sales = Sales per quarter.
Cogs = Cost of goods sold per quarter.
Writedown = Writedown charge in the writedown quarter.
Income = Income per quarter before writedown.
Total assets = Total assets per quarter.

obtained stock returns from CRSP and other variables from COMPUSTAT. Writedown amounts were obtained from *The Wall Street Journal Abstract*. A naive measure of expectations is computed for unexpected writedowns. Because writedowns are an unusual event, we assume that the expected writedown is zero (as in Elliott and Shaw 1988).

EMPIRICAL RESULTS

The sample firms are large, as evidenced by mean sales ($1.14 billion) and total assets ($5.28 billion). The average writedown (for all four quarters) is also rather large at $263 million. The average sales are $1.09 billion and writedowns are $231.1 million for firms that took writedowns in the first three quarters. The corresponding mean sales are $1.191 billion and writedowns are $296.1 million for firms that took writedowns in the fourth quarter. However, *t*-tests for differences in group means indicate no statistically significant difference between the means of these variables for the two groups. Descriptive data for undeflated variables are provided in Table 1.

Manufacturing firms made the bulk of writedown announcements. The sample contains 110 writedown announcements from 30 SIC two-digit industries. The average number of firms per two-digit industry is 3.6, and the range is from 1 to 21. Bernard (1987) argues that cross-sectional dependence in stock return data can bias OLS-based statistics toward the rejection of the null hypothesis of a zero slope. Because this study employs only two-day CARs, the probable bias in this study is not as strong as in studies using annual return metrics. Moreover, Bernard's results suggest that when the number of sample firms per industry is small, the bias is likely to be small. Because the mean number of firms per two-digit industry is only 3.6, we do not believe that this bias is a serious problem. Table 2 provides descriptive data for the sample firms in terms of industry groupings.

Electric, gas and other services are most frequently represented in the sample with 21 firms. The machinery and equipment industry experienced 13 writeoffs; the petroleum refining industry had nine announcements; and chemicals, automobiles, and oil and gas each had seven writedowns. These industries were closely followed by iron and steel foundries, electrical and electronics, railroads, and telecommunication.[9]

Table 3 provides descriptive statistics for the deflated independent variables and *CAR*. Distributional characteristics of *UWD* and *UE* are dissimilar. The mean of *UWD* in the first three quarters is smaller than the mean of the fourth quarter *UWD*. However, the mean of two-day CAR for the first three quarters is larger than the mean of two-day CAR for the fourth quarter writedowns. *T*-test results for differences in group means indicate no significant difference between the means of any of the three variables for the two groups. There are more positive cumulative unexpected returns in the first three quarters than negative ones. However, in the

Table 2.   Frequency Distribution of Writedown
Announcements by Industry

		Writedowns	
Two-digit SIC Code	Industry	Fourth Quarter	Non-Fourth Quarter
10	Metal mining	1	–
13	Oil and gas	1	6
15	General building	1	–
16	Construction—nonbuilding	1	–
26	Paper and allied products	1	–
27	Printing and publishing	1	1
28	Chemicals	4	3
29	Petroleum refining	5	4
30	Rubber and miscellaneous plastics	1	1
32	Flat glass	1	1
33	Iron and steel foundries	4	1
34	Hardware and tools	–	1
35	Machinery and equipment	8	5
36	Electrical and electronics	1	4
37	Automobiles	3	4
38	Engineering lab	1	2
40	Railroads	1	4
44	Water transport	1	–
45	Air transport	–	1
48	Telecommunication	3	1
49	Electric, gas, and other services	10	11
50	Wholesale—durables	1	–
51	Wholesale—parts	–	1
58	Retail—eating	1	–
61	Personal business credit	1	–
65	Real estate	–	1
73	Computer services	–	1
79	Amusement services	–	2
80	Health services	1	–
87	Engineering consulting	1	–
30	Total	54	56

fourth quarter, more market reactions are negative than positive. Chi-squared test
reveal that the positive and negative results are not equally distributed over the
quarters.

Table 4 presents Pearson product moment correlations for *CAR* and all explan
atory variables. This table indicates that explanatory variables are moderately cor
related with each other. Because multicollinearity could be present in the data

Table 3. Descriptive Statistics for Deflated Forecast Errors
(Number of observations in parenthesis)

Variables		Mean	Std. Dev.	Minimum	Maximum
Panel A:	**All Writedowns**				
UWD	(110)	0.777	1.406	0.005	10.14
UE	(110)	−0.108	0.882	−5.013	5.38
CAR	(110)	0.009	0.062	−0.179	0.41
Panel B:	**Writedowns in the First Three Quarters:**				
UWD	(56)	0.748	1.493	0.005	10.14
UE	(56)	−0.109	0.825	−5.013	2.02
CAR	(56)	0.011	0.073	−0.088	0.41
Panel C:	***Writedowns in the Fourth Quarter:***				
UWD	(54)	0.807	1.322	0.014	5.49
UE	(54)	−0.108	0.944	−2.937	5.38
CAR	(54)	0.006	0.050	−0.179	0.14

Notes: UWD = Writedown forecast error deflated by sales per share.
UE = Earnings forecast error deflated by sales per share.
CAR = Cumulative abnormal stock price return.

diagnostic measures of collinearity, specifically condition indexes based on Belsley and colleagues (1980) are obtained. The degree of collinearity appears to be too small to degrade the estimation results.[10]

We use the conventional event-time technique to estimate the valuation effects of writedown announcements. We assume that the security returns are distributed multivariate normal. The market model is used to compute abnormal returns:

$$AR_{jt} = R_{jt} - (\hat{a}_j + \hat{b}_j R_{mt}),$$

where AR represents the abnormal returns; $\hat{a}_j$ and $\hat{b}_j$ are the ordinary least-squares estimates of the intercept and slope of the market model regression, respectively; R_{mt} is the rate of return for day t on the equal-weighted CRSP index; and R_{jt} is the continuously compounded rate of return on security j for day t. The 120-day estimation period is from 210 days before to 91 days before the writedown announcement day ($t = 0$). We compute the two-day announcement period abnormal return by adding the prediction errors for day −1 and day 0.

Table 5, Panel A, gives regression results for a specification in which the intercept and slope coefficients for the explanatory variables do not differ across quarters. In this specification, the dependent variable is the two-day announcement period excess return, and the explanatory variables are unexpected writedowns and unexpected earnings for the writedown quarter. The slope coefficient for unex-

Table 4.   Pearson Correlation Coefficients

	UWD	UE	CUWD	CUE	INT1	CAR
UWD	1.000					
UE	0.326	1.000				
	(0.000)					
CUWD	0.706	0.199	1.000			
	(0.000)	(0.035)				
CUE	0.221	0.683	0.318	1.000		
	(0.018)	(0.000)	(0.000)			
INT1	0.464	−0.015	0.170	−0.074	1.000	
	(0.000)	(0.869)	(0.071)	(0.434)		
CAR	−0.016	0.067	0.031	−0.007	0.201	1.000
	(0.864)	(0.486)	(0.741)	(0.938)	(0.027)	

Notes: Significance level shown in parentheses.
   UWD   = Deflated writedown forecast error per share.
   UE   = Deflated earnings forecast error per share.
   CUWD = C1 * UWD.
   CUE   = C1 * UE.
   C1   = 0, for fourth quarter; 1, otherwise
   INT1 = Deflated intercept.
   CAR   = Cumulative abnormal returns for day 0 and -1.
   The deflator used is the sales per share.

pected writedowns is −0.008, which is statistically significant at the 0.10 level. Thus, the relative size of the unexpected writedown helps explain the cross-sectional abnormal returns. The negative sign of the coefficient supports the bad news hypothesis and is consistent with Elliott and Shaw (1988). The slope coefficient for unexpected earnings is 0.01, which is statistically insignificant. The positive sign of the coefficient for earnings is as expected and is consistent with prior research. The adjusted R^2 is 0.065.

Our conjecture and prior research suggest that writedown coefficients for the first three quarters may be different from the fourth quarter coefficients. In addition to unexpected writedowns and earnings, we now include an intercept dummy ($C1 = 1$ if non-fourth quarter, and $C1 = 0$ for fourth quarter) and two additional explanatory variables, $C1$ times the unexpected writedown and $C1$ times the unexpected earnings. The estimate of the slope coefficient, β_2, measures the difference in market reaction between the fourth quarter writedowns and writedown disclosures in other three quarters. If β_2 is statistically significant, then the null hypothesis that the market reaction to writedowns is identical in the fourth quarter as in earlier three quarters can be rejected. The results are reported in Table 5, Panel B. The adjusted R^2 increases from 0.065 to 0.066.

The deflated intercept is 0.057 and is statistically significant. The slope coefficient for unexpected writedowns is −0.019 and is statistically significant at the 5

Table 5. Regression of Announcement Period Abnormal Returns on Unexpected Writedowns and Unexpected Earnings (N=110)

$$CAR_{jt} = \beta_0\, INT1 + \beta_1\,(UWD_{jyq}) + \beta_2\,(UE_{jyq}) + e_{jt}$$

Variable	Coefficient Estimate	Std. Error	P*
Panel A:			
INT1	0.051	0.016	0.002
UWD	−0.008	0.005	0.087
UE	0.010	0.007	0.153

Adjusted $R^2 = 0.065$

PANEL B:

$$CAR_{jt} = \beta_0\, INT1 + \beta_1\,(UWD_{jyq}) + \beta_2\,(CUWD_{jyq})$$
$$+ \beta_3\,(UE_{jyq}) + \beta_4\,(CUE_{jyq}) + \beta_5\,(LTA_{jyq}) + \beta_6\, C1 + e_{jt}$$

INT1	0.057	0.017	0.001
UWD	−0.019	0.008	0.011
CUWD	0.017	0.009	0.069
UE	0.017	0.009	0.067
CUE	−0.013	0.014	0.353
LTA	0.001	0.001	0.408
C1	−0.007	0.013	0.586

Adjusted $R^2 = 0.066$

Notes:
UWD = Deflated writedown forecast error per share.
UE = Deflated earnings forecast error per share.
C1 = 0, if quarter is fourth; 1, otherwise.
CUWD = C1*UWD; CUE = C1 * UE.
LTA = Log of total assets (a size measure).
CAR = Cumulative abnormal return for day 0 and -1.
INT1 = Deflated intercept term.
(Deflator used here is the sales per share).

*Two-tailed significance probability.

percent level. β_2 (0.017, standard error = 0.008) is statistically significant at the 10 percent level, implying that the market reaction to writedowns is more negative in the fourth quarter than in the earlier three quarters. β_3, the slope coefficient for unexpected earnings, is 0.017, and is statistically significant at the 10 percent level. Because β_3 is significant in this regression, one can infer that it is better specified than the previous regression (see Table 5, Panel A). β_4 is statistically insignificant, suggesting that the market reaction to unexpected earnings in this sample is not different between quarters. β_5, the slope coefficient for the size variable, is 0.001 and not statistically significant at conventional levels. This suggests that the other explanatory variables are not proxying for firm size. β_6, the coefficient for the intercept dummy variable (C1), is -0.007 and is not statistically significant, suggesting that there is not a shift in the intercept in the fourth quarter.

The coefficient of unexpected writedowns for first three quarters is β_1 plus β_2, or -0.002, which is statistically different from the fourth quarter coefficient (-0.019). This difference is significant at the 10 percent level (i.e., the p-value for CUWD is 0.067). The results are consistent with the hypothesis that the market perceives writedowns in the earlier quarters[11] to be better news than writedowns taken in the fourth quarter.

SUMMARY

This study examines the effects of unexpected writedowns on unexpected returns. Unexpected announcement period returns are calculated over a two-day (day 0 and day -1 relative to *The Wall Street Journal* announcement) event period. The results for a sample of 110 NYSE firms indicate that the signs and magnitudes of writedowns and earnings are associated with unexpected returns. We further investigate whether there is a differential market reaction to fourth quarter writedowns vis-à-vis writedowns recorded in the first three quarters. Our results indicate that writedown announcements made in earlier quarters are associated with fewer negative returns compared with writedown announcements in the fourth quarter.

The coefficient of unexpected writedowns announced during the first three quarters is statistically more positive (at the 10 percent level) than that of the fourth quarter writedown announcements. Managers have some discretion about the timing of writedowns. The results indicate that the market views writedowns announced in the first three quarters as more positive than fourth quarter writedowns. Earlier writedowns may indicate some positive news such as cost savings, tax benefits, better prospects for operating income, or other value-enhancing restructurings. This positive news may dampen the negative news that might otherwise be contained in an impairment disclosure.

In the way of limitations, it should be noted that data constraints affected sample selection procedures. Because the sample consists of data from the COMPUSTAT PST tape only, the results are not generalizable to all firms. The COMPUSTAT PST tape only includes data from large firms and, hence, the results from this study may not apply to small firms. We are also unable to differentiate between our explanation and the alternative explanation that good news writedowns are randomly distributed across all quarters while there are more bad news writedowns in the fourth quarter. In this case, we would expect a more negative reaction to the fourth quarter writedowns due to their information content per se. Another limitation of this study is that we have no control for the "type" of writedown in our regression. For example, asset impairments are different from abandoning unprofitable projects. Unfortunately, it is very difficult to have a control variable for "type" of writedowns, because of inadequate disclosures. Fried and colleagues (1989) examine 870 writedown disclosures and conclude that firms tend to *group writedowns across different types of writedowns*, different valuation methods, and the nature of costs involved.

Our results suggest that sophistication of market participants should be considered by the FASB before imposing additional regulatory burdens. For example, the FASB Exposure Draft (FASB 1993) considered three options for measurement timing.[12] Because impairments of long-lived assets are somewhat infrequent, it may not be necessary to require impairment tests annually or every reporting period. Rather, it may be enough to recognize that managers are aware of the events or changes in circumstances that indicate impairment and that the market apparently prefers timely writedowns. The FASB decided not to impose periodic (say, quarterly or annual) impairment tests and, instead, limited impairment testing to "whenever events or changes in circumstances indicate that the carrying amount of an asset may not be recoverable" (see FASB 1995, 2). This paper provides evidence in support of the FASB's decision: if managers do not take these writedown charges on a timely basis, the stock market punishes (or at least recognizes the motivation of) those firms with negative stock returns.

ACKNOWLEDGMENT

This paper is based on the dissertation thesis of the first author completed at the University of Kansas. Helpful comments by two anonymous referees, an associate editor and the editor, and by Mike Ettredge, Jim Waegelein, Bill Salatka, Maurice Joy, Richard Metcalf, Paul Koch, and the workshop participants at Kansas, Connecticut, South Carolina, St. Louis, Nebraska (Omaha), and South Dakota, and participants at the Midwest AAA meeting are acknowledged. The usual disclaimer applies. This research was partially supported by the Clifford Graese/KPMG Peat Marwick Grant awarded to the first author.

NOTES

1.   Following Elliott and Shaw (1988), Fried, Schiff, and Sondhi (1989), and Lindahl and Ricks (1989), writedowns are defined broadly to include: impairment of long-lived assets, writeoffs of idle or excess manufacturing capacity, discontinuations, restructurings, and plant closings. The terms "writedowns" and "writeoffs" are used synonymously in this paper.

2.   Ampex Inc. in its annual report for 1970 reported an income of $12 million. Later, in its annual report for 1972, Ampex reported a loss of $90 million, including various writedowns totalling $58.7 million. The firms' auditors withdrew certification for 1971, and refused to certify the 1972 financial statements, because they were uncertain whether the 1972 loss was solely attributable to that year. Investors who purchased Ampex shares in the timespan of 27 months between the release of 1970 and 1972 annual reports sued Ampex, its officers, and its auditors in a class action for violating section 10(b) of the Securities Exchange Act of 1934. The plaintiffs won this case against Ampex in the appeal at the Federal Court of Appeals (9th circuit) and the U.S. Supreme Court denied certiorari. Further details are available in *Blackie vs. Barrack* (524 F2d 891 (1975)) and 429 U.S. 816.

3.   For example, Texas Instruments announced on Friday, June 10, 1983, that it expected a $100 million loss in the second quarter because of a drop in the sales of home computer models and extensive price cutting (*The Wall Street Journal*, June 13, 1983). On Monday, June 13, the stock price tumbled 25 percent to $118-1/4 from the previous Friday's closing price. Again, on another Friday, October 28, 1983, Texas Instruments announced its decision to quit the home computer business and disclosed more losses (*The Wall Street Journal*, October 31, 1983). On Monday, October 31, the share price shot up 22 percent, from $101-3/4 to $124-1/2.

4.   Investors observe actions of other managers in competing firms in the industry. These competitors' actions could cause investors to suspect that managers of firms in which they are interested are withholding information.

5.   Strong and Meyer (1987) report a negative but statistically insignificant market reaction to writedown announcements by 78 firms during 1981-1985. Elliott and Shaw (1988) report similar results, and the market reaction to 223 writedowns during 1982-1985 is significantly negative. While Strong and Meyer use the market model to compute the abnormal announcement period returns, Elliott and Shaw use the industry-adjusted returns methodology.

6.   We assume that the writedown news hits the stock exchange floor the day before it appears in the *Wall Street Journal*.

7.   To test the robustness of the deflation scheme, other deflators are used. The alternative deflators are the stock price at the beginning of the quarter and the stock price at the end of the quarter. The results are available from authors on request and are similar to those reported in the paper.

8.   The sample of writedown firms was selected from *The Wall Street Journal Abstract*, available on the NEXIS database. This abstract contains selected news items from *The Wall Street Journal*. A keyword search was conducted for 1983 through 1988 and the key words were writedown, writedown, and writeoff. Many data points were eliminated because they referred to the same event. Announcements related to litigation losses, bank loan writeoffs, inventory writeoffs, receivables writeoffs, writeoffs related to capital stock expenses, debenture issuance costs, and notes receivables were excluded. After these filters, a sample of 144 firms remained that had returns on CRSP. Of these 144, complete data for analysis were available on COMPUSTAT PST for 110 writedown announcements.

9.   Some firms from regulated industries (such as Electric, Oil & Gas, Petroleum, etc.) are in our sample and, in our opinion, this should not create any difficulties in interpreting the results. Writedowns have been frequent in these industries and all earlier papers on writedowns have included these types of industries. For example, Strong and Meyer (1987, 647) indicate that their sample had strong representation among natural resource firms. Unfortunately, they do not give any more details. Zucca and Campbell (1992, 33) report that 22.4 percent of their sample of 67 firms comes from the transportation and utilities and natural resource industries. Lindahl and Ricks (1989), in their asset writedown sample of 194 firms, included 42 oil and gas writedowns. King and Lippman (1990), in their writeoff sample of 120 firms, included 21 "electrical, petroleum, and utilities" firms.

10.   Belsley and colleagues (1980) suggest that condition indexes in excess of 30 indicate moderate to strong dependencies among explanatory variables. The largest condition index observed in the regression is 4.57. This suggests that collinearity is not a problem in this study.

11.   We also constructed a three-day CAR (days −1, 0, and +1) to account for news releases that occurred after the close on day 0, and we used the three-day CAR as the dependent variable and reperformed the regression. When we used the three-day CAR, we found that the coefficient of unexpected writedowns in the first three quarters was still less negative (−0.004) than the fourth-quarter writedown coefficient (−0.011), as hypothesized. However, the difference is not statistically significant at conventional levels.

12.   The three options considered by the FASB with regard to the measurement timing issue are: (1) every reporting period, (2) when events or circumstances indicate, and (3) annually.

REFERENCES

Belsley, D.A., E. Kuh, and R.E. Welsch. 1980. *Regression Diagnostics: Identifying Influential Data and Sources of Collinearity*. New York: Wiley.

Bernard, V.L. 1987. *Cross-sectional dependence and problems in inference in market-based accounting research*. Journal of Accounting Research (Spring): 1-45.

Chambers, A., and S. Penman. 1984. Timeliness of reporting and the stock price reaction to earnings announcements. *Journal of Accounting Research* (Spring): 21-46.

Chen, N., R. Roll, and S. Ross. 1986. Economic forces and the stock market. *Journal of Business* (July): 383-404.

Dye, R.A. 1985. Disclosure of nonproprietary information. *Journal of Accounting Research* 23(1, Spring): 123-145.

Elliott, J.A., and W.H. Shaw. 1988. Write-offs as accounting procedures to manage perceptions. *Journal of Accounting Research* (Supplement): 91-119.

Feroz, E.H., K. Park, and V. Pastena. 1991. The financial and market effects of SEC's accounting and auditing enforcement releases. *Journal of Accounting Research* (Supplement): 107-142.

Financial Accounting Standards Board (FASB). 1990. *Discussion Memorandum: An Analysis of Issues Related to Accounting for the Impairment of the Long-Lived Assets and Identifiable Intangibles*. Stamford, CT: FASB.

_____. 1993. *Exposure Draft: Accounting for the Impairment of the Long-Lived Assets*. Stamford, CT: FASB.

_____. 1995. *SFAS 121: Accounting for the Impairment of the Long-Lived Assets and for Long-Lived Assets to be Disposed Of*. Stamford, CT: FASB.

Foster, G., C. Olsen, and T. Shevlin. 1984. Earnings releases, anomalies, and the behavior of security returns. *The Accounting Review* (October): 574-603

Fried, D., M. Schiff, and A. Sondhi. 1989. *Impairments and Writeoffs of Long-Lived Assets*. Montvale, NJ: National Association of Accountants.

Givoly, D., and D. Palmon. 1984. Timeliness of annual earnings announcements: Some empirical evidence. *The Accounting Review* (October): 486-508.

Jung, W., and Y. Kwon. Disclosure when the market is unsure of information endowment of managers. *Journal of Accounting Research* 26(1, Spring): 146-153.

Kalay, A., and U. Lowenstein. 1986. The informational content of the timing of dividend announcements. *Journal of Financial Economics* (July): 373-388.

King, R.D., and E. Lippman. 1990. Accounting writeoffs and the big bath and smoothing hypotheses. Working Paper, University of Oregon, January.

Landsman, W. 1986. An empirical investigation of pension funds property rights. *The Accounting Review* (July): 662-691.

Lurie, A., and V. Pastena. 1975. How promptly do corporations disclose their problems. (October): 55-62.

Lindahl, F.W., and W.E. Ricks. 1989. Market reactions to announcements of writeoffs. Working paper, Duke University.

Mendenhall, R.R., and W.D. Nichols. 1988. Bad news and differential market reactions to announcements of earlier-quarters versus fourth quarter earnings. *Journal of Accounting Research* (Supplement): 63-86.

Myers, R. 1995. Much ado about write-offs. *CFO: The Magazine for Senior Financial Executives* (March): 61-64.

O'Brien, P.C. 1988. Analysts' forecasts as earnings expectations. *Journal of Accounting and Economics* (January): 53-83.

Pastena, V., and J. Ronen. 1979. Some hypotheses on the pattern of management's disclosures. *Journal of Accounting Research* (Autumn): 550-564.

Pearson, M.W., and L.L. Okubara. Restructurings and impairment of value: A growing controversy. *Accounting Horizons* (March): 35-41.

Penman, S. 1987. The distribution of earnings news over time and seasonalities in aggregate stock returns. *Journal of Financial Economics* (June): 199-228.

Ragothaman, S. 1991. Economic implications of asset writedown disclosure policy. Unpublished Ph.D. dissertation, University of Kansas.

Ronen, J. 1977. The effect of insider trading rules on information generation and disclosure by corporations. *The Accounting Review* (April): 438-449.

St. Pierre, K., and J. Anderson. 1984. An analysis of the factors associated with lawsuits against public accountants. *The Accounting Review* (April): 242-263.

Securities and Exchange Commission. 1983. Income statement presentation of restructuring charges. Staff Accounting Bulletin No.67. In *SEC Accounting Rules*. Chicago: Commerce Clearing House Inc.

Shalit, S.S., and U. Sanker. 1977. The measurement of firm size. *Review of Economics and Statistics* (August): 290-298.

Sinclair, N., and J. Young. 1991. The timeliness of half-yearly earnings announcements and stock returns. *Accounting and Finance* (November): 31-51.

Statman, M., and J.F. Sepe. 1986. The disposition to throw good money after bad: Evidence from stock market reaction to project termination decisions. Working Paper, Leavey School of Business and Administration, University of Santa Clara.

Strong, J.S., and J.R. Meyer. 1987. Asset writedowns: Managerial incentives and security returns. *Journal of Finance* (July): 643-661.

Verrecchia, R. 1983. Discretionary disclosure. *Journal of Accounting and Economics* (December): 179-194.

Waymire, G. 1988. Discussion of write-offs as accounting procedures to manage perceptions. *Journal of Accounting Research* (Supplement): 120-126.

Zucca, L.J., and D.R. Campbell. 1992. A closer look at discretionary writedowns of impaired assets. *Accounting Horizons* (September): 30-41.

THE RELATIONSHIP OF CAREER STAGE TO JOB OUTCOMES AND ROLE STRESS:
A STUDY OF EXTERNAL AUDITORS

James E. Rebele, Ronald E. Michaels, and
Renee Wachter

ABSTRACT

Career development theory suggests that individuals progress through four stages over the course of their careers. Empirical studies have shown that career stage is associated with certain job-related attitudes, behaviors, work needs, and motivation. This study investigated whether external auditors' job outcomes (satisfaction, performance, tension, work alienation, and organizational commitment) and role stress (role ambiguity and role conflict) differ across the four career stages identified by Super. The results indicate that career stage is significantly related to external auditors' job outcomes and role stress. For example, auditors in the earliest career stage were found to have the lowest levels of job satisfaction and organizational commitment and the highest level of work alienation. Auditors in the final career stage were

Advances in Accounting, Volume 14, pages 241-258.
ISBN: 0-7623-0161-9.

found to have the highest level of job performance, indicating that performance levels for auditors in the more advanced career stages should not be expected to decline. Implications of the general career stages model and the results of this study for both auditing practitioners and researchers are discussed.

INTRODUCTION

A career has been characterized as a sequence of experiences which a person goes through over the course of his or her life's work (Hall 1971). Research in both sociology and vocational psychology demonstrates that any explanation of an individual's relationship to his or her job must consider how that person might change over time (Van Maanen and Schein 1979; Morrow and McElroy 1987). One career stage model, developed by Super (1957), proposes that individuals progress through four distinct career stages: exploration, establishment, maintenance, and disengagement.

The interest of researchers in examining the relationship between the auditing work environment and auditors' job-related attitudes and behaviors has increased recently (Rasch and Harrell 1990; Snead and Harrell 1991; Harrell, Chewning, and Taylor 1986; Senatra 1980; Bamber, Snowball, and Tubbs 1989; Rebele and Michaels 1990; Pasewark, Strawser, and Wilkerson 1994). The objective of this study is to examine the relationship between auditors' career stage and job outcomes and role stress.

CAREER STAGES: BACKGROUND
AND HYPOTHESES

A fundamental premise of career stage research is that individuals pass through several distinct stages during their careers. Each stage becomes a cognitive frame of reference which provides guidance, meaning, and interpretative value to the individual (Isabella 1988). Although a number of career stage models have been proposed, one which has received significant support in the literature (Sonnenfeld and Kotter 1982; Whiston 1990; Smart and Peterson 1994) is Super's model of career stages.

Super's concept of career stage focuses on an individualistic perspective—one which assumes that many factors (e.g., physical, social, and psychological) determine a person's current career stage. A major tenet of the theory is that individuals of similar ages can cognitively be positioned in different career stages because they may have very different career priorities, goals, and attitudes. A brief description of each of Super's (1957) four career stages follows.

Exploration

A primary concern of individuals in the exploration stage of their careers is finding an occupation in which they are comfortable and which they believe will afford them the opportunity to be successful. A fundamental question asked during this stage is, "What do I want to do with the rest of my life?" Loyalty to a particular occupation or organization on average is relatively low.

Establishment

Individuals at this stage of their careers have settled on a particular occupational field, and their efforts are directed at establishing a secure place within the organization. Individuals in the establishment stage have usually learned the fundamental requirements of a job and can now focus on using these skills to produce superior results. More often than not, the desire for promotion to more advanced levels within an organization is high for people in this career stage.

Maintenance

Individuals in the maintenance stage of their careers are generally very concerned with preserving their present position, status, and performance levels, which are usually relatively high (Cron and Slocum 1986). People in the maintenance career stage tend to exhibit greater loyalty to their organizations. Such individuals often feel threatened by competition from younger employees, technological innovations, and new job assignments (Cron and Slocum 1986).

Disengagement

Finally, most individuals must make the transition from work to retirement. Reducing the pace of work as a person plans for retirement is an important part of the disengagement career stage. Some people often view retirement as a way of escaping a frustrating job, but for others it may also mean a loss of professional identity. Research (Cron and Slocum 1986) suggests that some people may psychologically disengage from their work long before reaching chronological retirement age.

Career Stage Research: Job Outcomes

In this section, we propose hypotheses about the relationship between career stage and several job outcomes. Prior empirical research is reviewed to provide background for each hypothesis.

Job Satisfaction

Research on job satisfaction has produced mixed results (Rhodes 1983). Studies by Slocum and Cron (1985), Cron and Slocum (1986), and Ornstein, Cron, and Slocum (1989) found that, in general, salespeople in the early stages of their careers were the least satisfied with most aspects of their jobs. Other studies report that job satisfaction either does not increase with time spent in the organization (Van Maanen and Katz 1976) or actually decreases over time (Churchill, Ford, and Walker 1976; Mount 1984).

In accounting-related research, Adler and Aranya (1984) found, for a sample of California CPAs, that both intrinsic and extrinsic satisfaction increased over the first three career stages and then declined in the preretirement stage. In contrast, Norris and Niebuhr (1983) found job level was unrelated to job satisfaction for a sample of accountants from one Big Eight firm. The limited existing research findings are therefore inconclusive. The following nondirectional hypothesis is therefore proposed:

Hypothesis 1.   There will be no significant difference in mean levels of job satisfaction across the exploration, establishment, maintenance, and disengagement career stages of external auditors.

Job Performance

In many occupations, performance may be expected to decline with age. Research focusing on professionals, however, has generally not found a negative relationship between age and performance (e.g., Hall and Mansfield 1975; Cron and Slocum 1986). Arguably, auditors in more advanced career stages may still be high performers because of their extensive auditing experience and strong client contacts. The following nondirectional hypothesis was tested in the study.

Hypothesis 2.   There will be no significant diminution in mean levels of performance at higher auditor career stages.

Job-Related Tension

Job-related tension is an employee's physiological or psychological response to an external event called a stressor (Matteson and Ivancevich 1982). In organizations, stressors arise from a number of sources: the physical environment, the individual, the work group, and/or the organization. All employees experience job-related tension to varying degrees during their work and careers; and in various ways, some more successful than others, individuals react, and adjust, to such stressors.

Individuals with more experience likely have developed personal strategies for managing different types of job-related tension. However, disengagement prospects may contribute new stressors. In our literature search, we found no empirical study that has investigated the relationship between career stage and job-related tension. Therefore, the following nondirectional hypothesis was tested:

Hypothesis 3. There will be no significant difference in mean levels of job-related tension across the exploration, establishment, maintenance, and disengagement career stages of external auditors.

Organizational Commitment

Organizational commitment may also be related to career stage. For example, a review of existing research on age-related differences in work attitudes and behaviors by Rhodes (1983) found that older workers were generally more committed to the organization than younger workers. People in the exploration stage are likely to be more critical of their organization because of unrealistically high aspirations and expectations (Hall 1976). Establishment and maintenance stage individuals, who may have received promotions and raises from the organization, are likely to perceive a more favorable work environment.

Research in accounting contexts has produced mixed results regarding the relationship between career stage and organizational commitment. For example, Adler and Aranya (1984) found that older accountants were generally more committed to their organizations than their younger colleagues, but Ferris (1981) found age to be unrelated to organizational commitment. Although Aranya and Ferris (1984) found a positive relationship between level in the organizational hierarchy and organizational commitment, Norris and Niebuhr (1983) found job level to be unrelated to organizational commitment. McGregor, Killough, and Brown (1989) found organizational commitment to be positively associated with organizational tenure for a sample of management accountants, while Harrell, Chewning and Taylor (1986) and Norris and Niebuhr (1983) found organizational tenure to be unrelated to organizational commitment for samples of internal auditors and public accountants, respectively. Thus, again, the existing evidence is mixed. The following hypothesis concerning the relationship between external auditors' career stage and organizational commitment was tested in this study:

Hypothesis 4. There will be no significant difference in mean levels of organizational commitment across the exploration, establishment, maintenance, and disengagement career stages of external auditors.

Work Alienation

Work alienation focuses on work itself and reflects a situation in which an individual cares little about the work, approaches work with little energy and ambition, and works primarily for extrinsic rewards (Dubin 1956; Moch 1980). In the ultimate sense of self-estrangement, work alienation represents the end point on a unidimensional continuum opposite job involvement (Kanungo 1979; Organ and Greene 1981; Lefkowitz, Somers, and Weinberg 1984). Our search of the literature revealed no prior study which has examined the relationship between work alienation and career stage. The following nondirectional hypothesis was therefore tested in this study:

Hypothesis 5.   There will be no significant difference in mean levels of work alienation across the exploration, establishment, maintenance, and disengagement career stages of external auditors.

Research Related to Role Stress

This section presents hypotheses on the relationship between career stage and role stress. Role conflict is the degree of incompatibility of expectations communicated by a role sender to a role incumbent, while role ambiguity refers to a lack of clarity concerning job expectations, methods for fulfilling known expectations, and/or the consequences of specific role performance (Kahn et al. 1964). Walker, Churchill, and Ford (1975) and Cron (1984) explain why both role ambiguity and role conflict should decrease across career stages. Role ambiguity should decline with experience on the job as employees gather information about expectations which other role set members have for them. Experience may also reduce the amount of perceived role conflict because (1) a more experienced person may learn how to resolve or cope with conflict; (2) over time, an individual may build up psychological defense mechanisms to screen out conflicting demands; and (3) people who are sensitive to conflict may change jobs. Still, Cron (1984) notes that although experience may reduce both role conflict and role ambiguity, conflict may be experienced over a longer period of time than ambiguity. For example, external auditors beyond the exploration stage of their careers may still perceive conflicting demands from family, clients and their firms.

The following hypotheses concerning role ambiguity and role conflict were tested in this study:

Hypothesis 6.   There will be no significant difference in mean levels of role ambiguity across the exploration, establishment, maintenance, and disengagement career stages of external auditors.

Hypothesis 7.   There will be no significant difference in mean levels of role conflict across the exploration, establishment, maintenance, and disengagement career stages of external auditors.

RESEARCH METHOD

Data Collection

Participants were obtained from the Midwestern offices of four international accounting firms. Questionnaires were distributed using each firm's office mail

Table 1. Characteristics of External Auditors within Each Career Stage

	Exploration $N = 37$	Establishment $N = 71$	Maintenance $N = 42$	Disengagement $N = 7$
Mean age	25.3	26.0	30.1	41.4
Mean firm tenure	2.5	3.3	6.1	16.8
Mean auditing experience	2.7	3.4	6.6	16.8
Frequencies[a]				
Sex:				
Male	25	47	35	7
Female	11	24	7	0
Position:				
Partner	0	4	6	5
Manager	6	12	11	2
Senior	10	16	17	0
Staff	18	38	6	0
Age Ranges				
22-25	22	46	14	0
26-30	12	16	14	1
31-35	1	6	6	0
36-40	0	2	5	3
41-45	0	0	1	1
45+	0	1	2	2

Note: [a]Column sums within each category may not equal total number of auditors because of missing responses.

system and were accompanied by a letter from the partner in charge of the office encouraging participation. The auditors completed the questionnaires during normal working hours and returned the questionnaires directly to the researchers using the self-addressed, postage-paid envelopes which had been provided. Of 211 questionnaires distributed, 168 were completed and returned to the authors, for a response rate of 79.6 percent.

Respondents were, on average, 28 years of age, had been with their firms for approximately five years, and had 4.9 years of auditing experience. Approximately 73 percent of the respondents were male. Approximately 40 percent were audit staff; 29 percent were seniors; 19 percent were managers, and 11 percent were partners.[1]

Table 1 presents selected characteristics of the respondents classified as exploration-, establishment-, maintenance-, and disengagement-stage auditors. Average

age, firm tenure, and auditing experience are presented at the top of the table and frequency distributions of sex, age, and position ranges within each career stage are shown at the bottom. Responses from 11 auditors were eliminated because their individual response patterns did not clearly indicate membership in one specific career stage.

Measures

Career Stages

An unsettled issue in career stages research is how best to operationalize career stage. Prior research has used what Dillard and Ferris (1989) classify as demographic variables (e.g., age, rank, organizational tenure, and position tenure) and cognitive/psychological factors (i.e., a perceptually based measure) to operationalize career stage. Although a study of professional women by Ornstein and Isabella (1990) found changing career attitudes to be a function of age rather than psychological stage, studies have generally shown that perceptual approaches to measuring career stage account for more variance in job attitudes than measures such as age, rank or position, position tenure, or job tenure (Rush et al. 1980; Cron and Slocum 1986; Ornstein et al. 1989; Chao 1990; Morrow et al. 1990).[2]

Dillard and Ferris (1989, 209) note that cognitive/psychological variables, not demographic variables, have the greatest effect on individual work behavior. This position is supported by Morrow and colleagues (1990) who provide evidence that Levinson's age-based model is better at explaining non-work attitudes and behaviors while Super's perceptual model provides a better explanation of work-related attitudes. Since the focus of this study was on the association between auditors' career stage and work-related attitudes and behaviors, we chose to use a career stage measure that is based on an individual's perception of career issues.

The Career Concerns Inventory (CCI) is a perceptual-based measure of career stage developed by Super, Zelkowitz, and Thompson (1981). As its title implies, the measure is constructed to ascertain what career concerns are most cogent to an employee, and then uses those current issues to categorize respondents into one of four career stages. This perceptual approach to classifying individuals into a specific career stage has been successfully used in several prior studies (e.g., Slocum and Cron 1985; Cron and Slocum 1986; Cron et al. 1988; Ornstein et al. 1989). The results of a recent study of 457 Australian workers (219 men and 238 women) support the factorial validity of the CCI and demonstrate its congruence with Super's hypothesized four stages (Smart and Peterson 1994, 253).

Consistent with expectations based on Super's (1984) model, the evidence in Table 1 demonstrates a great deal of variability of age, experience, and position attained within each career stage. Utilizing an a priori measure like age or position to classify individuals into a particular career stage is likely to produce classifications which are inconsistent with the respondent's own perceptions.

Job Outcome Measures

Job Satisfaction. Job satisfaction was assessed using Hoppock's (1935) four-item measure of job satisfaction. Hoppock's job satisfaction measure has been validated by McNichols, Stahl, and Manley (1978) in repeated studies involving more than 20,000 subjects. This measure has been used in accounting studies by Harrell and Stahl (1984), Harrell and Eickhoff (1988), and Rasch and Harrell (1990).

Job Performance. Self-rated job performance was measured using a 26-item scale constructed specifically for this study. A performance evaluation form used by a Big Six accounting firm was used to generate the initial inventory of performance items. The performance instrument was refined and finalized in a series of reviews and pretests with auditors from several firms.

Job-related Tension. Job-related tension was measured using an 11-item scale previously used by Lysonski (1985). This measure was developed by incorporating items from the Taylor Manifest Anxiety Scale (Taylor 1953) with items from House and Rizzo (1972). The scale items ascertain if respondents perceive their jobs as affecting their physical health in terms of tension, anxiety, stress, worry, and fatigue.

Organizational Commitment. Organizational commitment was measured using a 15-item scale from Mowday, Steers, and Porter (1979). Their Organizational Commitment Questionnaire uses a seven-point Likert-type scale to measure, among other things, an individual's loyalty to an organization, concern for the future of the organization, and willingness to exert a great deal of effort to help the organization succeed. This frequently used measure of organizational commitment has been utilized successfully in a number of accounting studies (e.g., Adler and Aranya 1984; Aranya and Ferris 1984; Harrell, Chewning, and Taylor 1986).

Work Alienation. Work alienation was measured using a five-item scale from Miller (1967). The scale items measure the level of pride in doing one's work, sense of accomplishment in doing a particular type of work, work being a rewarding experience, and like/dislike for the work itself.

Role Stress Measures

The role conflict and role ambiguity scales used in this study were developed by Rizzo, House, and Lirtzman (1970). Role conflict was assessed using a 13-item scale while role ambiguity was measured using a 10-item scale. These scales have been used by most researchers studying role stress (Van Sell, Brief, and Schuler 1981), including several in auditing (Senatra 1980; Bamber, Snowball, and Tubbs

Table 2. Scale Means, Standard Deviations, Ranges,
Number of Items, and Reliabilities

Scale	Mean	SD	Range	Items[a]	Alpha
Job Outcomes					
Job satisfaction	4.97	.90	2.00-6.50	4	.91
Job performance	5.19	.73	3.60-6.80	15	.89
Job-related tension	4.03	.88	1.75-5.88	8	.80
Organizational commitment	5.24	1.01	2.50-6.93	14	.90
Work alienation	3.08	1.28	1.20-7.00	5	.87
Role Stress					
Role ambiguity	2.86	.89	1.00-5.38	8	.82
Role conflict	3.04	.92	1.11-6.44	9	.80
Career Stages					
Exploration	3.12	1.01	1.33-5.00	15	.95
Establishment	3.16	.77	1.13-5.00	15	.94
Maintenance	2.79	.78	1.13-5.00	15	.92
Disengagement	1.69	.64	1.00-4.73	15	.92

Notes: The job-related tension scale is scored from 1 = low to 6 = high; each career stage from 1 = low to 5 = high and all other scales from 1 = low to 7 = high.
[a]After item analysis and scale refinement.

1989). Psychometric evaluations have shown these scales to be acceptable measures of role conflict and role ambiguity (Schuler, Aldag, and Brief 1977; Jackson and Schuler 1985; Gregson, Wendell, and Aono 1994).

Table 2 presents means, standard deviations, range of responses, number of items, and reliability estimates (Cronbach Alpha) for measures used in the study. Coefficients alpha ranged from .80 to .95, indicating sufficiently high levels of internal consistency reliability (Nunnally 1978).

Data Analysis Procedures

A three-step process was used to analyze the data. First, multivariate analyses of variance (MANOVA) were employed to assess the overall relationship between career stage and the five job outcomes and between career stage and the two components of role stress.[3] Second, if the MANOVA investigations in step one produced significant results, then univariate analyses of variance (ANOVA) were conducted. Contrasts were conducted when the ANOVA results were significant.

RESULTS

Table 3 presents MANOVA results which indicate that career stage is significantly related to both job outcomes ($F = 3.16$, $p < .001$) and role stress ($F = 2.78$, $p < .05$).

Table 3. MANOVA Results for Career Stages of External Auditors

	Exploration (EX)	Establishment (ES)	Maintenance (MA)	Disengagement (DN)	Univariate F-values	Significant Contrasts[1]
Job Outcomes						
Job satisfaction	17.2	20.0	21.4	22.6	12.73[a]	EX<ES,MA,DN
Job performance	75.3	76.4	80.8	90.3	5.78[a]	ES<MA,DN MA<DN
Job-related tension	34.2	31.9	30.8	29.3	2.09[d]	EX>MA,DN
Organizational commitment	66.8	73.4	76.4	81.9	4.38[b]	EX<ES,MA,DN
Work alienation	19.8	15.0	13.1	10.6	10.07[a]	EX>ES,MA,DN
Multivariate F (3, ½, 72) = 3.16[a]						
Role Stress						
Role ambiguity	25.3	23.0	21.4	17.3	3.73[c]	EX>MA<DN ES>DN
Role conflict	30.6	26.4	26.9	26.7	2.16[d]	EX>ES
Multivariate F (2, 0, 73½) = 2.78[c]						

Notes: [a] $p \leq .001$.
[b] $p \leq .01$.
[c] $p \leq .05$.
[d] $p \leq .10$.

[1]One can interpret contrasts, for example, EX < ES, MA, DN as the mean level of exploration being significantly less than establishment, maintenance, and disengagement. Only hypothesized, significant contrasts are reported.

[2]Numbers in the first four columns are mean sum scores for each variable in each career stage.

Table 3 also reports F-values from the univariate ANOVAs. The right-hand column of the table presents significant contrasts among the four career stages. In the following sections, only significant contrasts are reported.

Hypothesis 1:   Job Satisfaction

Table 3 reports that there are significant differences in the mean level of job satisfaction across the four career stages ($F = 12.73$, $p < .001$). Job satisfaction is significantly lower in the exploration career stage relative to the latter three stages. Job satisfaction also was significantly lower for auditors in the establishment career stage as compared with those auditors in the maintenance and disengagement stages.

Hypothesis 2:   Job Performance

Job performance was found to significantly vary across the four career stages ($F = 5.78$, $p < .001$). The level of job performance in the exploration career stage is significantly lower than the levels in the maintenance and disengagement stages. Job performance in the establishment career stage also was significantly lower than in the maintenance and disengagement stages. Auditors in the disengagement career stage exhibited the highest level of performance; significantly higher than for each of the other stages.

Hypothesis 3:   Job-Related Tension

Table 3 indicates that differences in levels of job-related tension across the four career stages are significant only at the marginal level of 0.10 ($F = 2.09$, $p < .10$). In the only significant contrast, the mean level of job-related tension was higher in the exploration stage than in the maintenance and disengagement stages.

Hypothesis 4:   Organizational Commitment

The level of organizational commitment reported in Table 3 differs significantly across career stages ($F = 4.38$, $p < .01$). The mean level of organizational commitment in the exploration stage is significantly lower than in each of the latter three career stages.

Hypothesis 5:   Work Alienation

The results also reveal a significant difference in the mean level of work alienation across the four career stages ($F = 10.07$, $p < .001$). In the only significant contrast, exploration stage auditors experience significantly higher levels of work alienation than auditors in the other stages.

Hypothesis 6: Role Ambiguity

As shown in Table 3, the level of role ambiguity for external auditors varies significantly across the four career stages ($F = 3.73$, $p < .05$). The level of role ambiguity in the exploration stage is significantly higher than in the maintenance and disengagement stages. Role ambiguity also is significantly lower in the disengagement career stage relative to the exploration and establishment stages.

Hypothesis 7: Role Conflict

Differences in the mean level of role conflict across career stages are significant only at the .10 level ($F = 2.16$, $p < .10$). With the exception that auditors in the exploration stage have higher levels of role conflict than those in the establishment stage, there were no significant differences.

DISCUSSION AND CONCLUSIONS

The public accounting profession has certainly not escaped the competitive challenge that is confronting all industries and types of business entities. Accounting firms are restructuring and changing their hiring practices in order to meet clients' ever-changing needs in a more efficient and effective manner. As noted by Hermanson and colleagues (1995), firms that are able to develop and retain their high-performing staff will have an advantage in this new competitive environment. Firms can no longer afford to commit significant resources to training staff auditors who, after a few years, leave and take their expertise with them. This is especially true now that firm employees have received more specialized training and may not be replaced as easily as in the past (Hooks and Cheramy 1994).

An understanding of career development theory, and a recognition of its importance for career counseling, may prove beneficial to both individual auditors and accounting firms. For example, this study used a career stages framework to demonstrate that job outcomes and role stress are significantly related to auditors' career stage. Perhaps most significantly, auditors in the exploration stage of their career exhibited the lowest levels of job satisfaction and organizational commitment and the highest levels of work alienation and role ambiguity. Clearly, accounting firms face a challenge in creating a work environment that auditors early in their careers find desirable and rewarding.

Hermanson and colleagues (1995) report that the changes most desired by staff accountants relate to work environment issues, not to issues of, for example, compensation. Although our study did not specifically address this issue, our results seem to support the idea that auditors early in their careers would benefit from more satisfaction in, and involvement with, their job. Our findings for exploration-stage auditors illustrate the importance of following the suggestion to offer more challenging job assignments early in an auditor's career (Elliott 1991).

Although efforts at improving the work environment of auditors can be directed at groups (e.g, staff auditors), firms must also address career development issues at the individual level. The career stages model can be used for individual career counseling purposes by demonstrating to auditors how their own career concerns relate to the sequential career development milestones that are encountered throughout working life (Smart and Peterson 1994). For example, auditors in the exploration stage can be shown how their concerns are characteristic of most others in this career stage. Recognizing this similarity of experiences may help some auditors avoid the high cost of leaving a position for the wrong reasons; that is, changing organizations may not necessarily provide a solution to someone who is dissatisfied with accounting as a career.

Most present theories of career development are based on the study of males (Morrow et al. 1990; Ornstein and Isabella 1990). Because women's careers are often characterized by discontinuous or alternative activities, women may not adhere to the traditional career development model (Ornstein and Isabella 1990). More research describing the career experiences of women is needed to determine if career development models developed for males are generalizable to females.

Career development for women is an especially important issue in public accounting where females and males enter the profession in equal numbers but where a smaller percentage of women advance to the point that they are considered for admission to the partnership (Hooks and Cheramy 1994). To deal with this discrepancy between hiring and retention percentages and to retain talented individuals, accounting firms must understand and respond to differences in career concerns between men and women (Hooks and Cheramy 1994; Hermanson et al. 1995). It is clear, however, that accounting firms cannot respond to career issues that affect women differently without first identifying these issues.

An AICPA study on women and family issues found that gender-related turnover differences were most noticeable at the senior and senior-supervisor and manager ranks of the larger accounting firms (Hooks and Cheramy 1994, 81). This would suggest that this is a time when career issues become a particular concern for female auditors. As suggested by Whiston (1990), human resource counselors may find the CCI useful for helping individuals focus on their important career concerns. Career counselors in accounting firms can use the CCI to identify important career issues for women at those ranks where gender-related turnover differences have been found. By identifying the issues that are most important to a particular individual, counselors can work with that person to, for example, explore a different career path or to develop strategies for advancing within the firm.

The concept of career stage also has implications for auditing researchers. As noted by Van Maanen and Katz (1976), researchers studying the psychological and sociological differences among workers usually group individuals into categories without considering that they may exhibit significant individual differences. Constructing a sample of individuals from a variety of career development stages may bias and confound results because of the heterogeneity of the sample

(Cron 1984). Career stage theory suggests that employee attitudinal changes, such as changes in job satisfaction or organizational commitment, are systematic. Individuals therefore could, and should, be placed in more homogeneous groups according to career stage.

A possible limitation of this study is that all measures are self-reported. In addition, our sample contained only seven disengagement-stage individuals; accordingly, results concerning this stage should be viewed as tentative. Although not detected, fatigue factors because of the length of the data collection instrument remain a concern.

The results of this study suggest several other areas for future research on auditors' career stages. Future studies could examine the relationship between career stage and additional variables such as job involvement, job challenge, and motivation. The prior research conducted by Adler and Aranya (1984) on the relationship between career stages and work needs and attitudes could be replicated using Super's Career Concerns Inventory, instead of age, to measure career stage. More generally, a more extensive study of career development issues for auditors is needed. These studies should explore for differences in career development patterns and issues between male and female auditors.

ACKNOWLEDGMENT

The authors gratefully acknowledge the helpful comments provided by Jim Largay and Phil Reckers.

NOTES

1.   A comparison check across the four cooperating firms revealed no statistically significant differences in mean values for age, position tenure, firm tenure, public accounting experience, or auditing experience. Moreover, there were no significant differences across the four firms in mean level of the variables of interest in the study.

2.   Although Ornstein and Isabella (1990) found some support for Levinson's age-based career stage model, the results did not demonstrate the distinctive pattern of differences across age groups predicted by Levinson (p.14). The results, therefore, do not provide strong support for the superiority of the age-based career stage model over a perceptual model. Ornstein and Isabella do note that Super's model still holds promise, although it may need to be refined for women.

3.   A critical assumption of MANOVA is equality of covariance matrices across the four career-stage groups in this analysis. The hypothesis of equality of covariance matrices, tested using Box's M statistic, could not be rejected for the overall multivariate analyses of variance. Thus, this test indicates that the data meet this important underlying assumption. Moreover, the Pillai-Bartlett trace was chosen as the MANOVA test statistic for this study because it has been shown to be the most robust (relative to alternative test statistics) to violations of the assumptions underlying MANOVA (Bray and Maxwell 1985).

REFERENCES

Adler, S., and N. Aranya. 1984. A comparison of the work needs, attitudes, and preferences of professional accountants at different career stages. *Journal of Vocational Behavior* 25: 45-57.

Aranya, N., and K. Ferris. 1984. A reexamination of accountants' organizational-professional conflict. *The Accounting Review* (January): 1-15.

Bamber, E.M., D. Snowball, and R.M. Tubbs. 1989. Audit structure and its relation to role conflict and role ambiguity: an empirical investigation. *The Accounting Review* (April): 285-299.

Bray, J.H., and S.E. Maxwell. 1985. *Multivariate Analysis of Variance.* Beverly Hills, CA: Sage.

Chao, G.T. 1990. Exploration of the conceptualization and measurement of career plateau: a comparative analysis. *Journal of Management* 16: 181-193.

Churchill, G.A., N.M. Ford, and O.C. Walker. 1976. Organizational climate and job satisfaction in the salesforce. *Journal of Marketing Research* (November): 323-332.

Cron, W.L. 1984. Industrial salesperson development: A career stages perspective. *Journal of Marketing* (Fall): 41-52.

Cron, W.L., A.J. Dubinsky, and R.E. Michaels. 1988. The influence of career stages on components of salesperson motivation. *Journal of Marketing* (January): 78-92.

Cron, W.L., and J.W. Slocum. 1986. The influence of career stages on salespeople's job attitudes, work perceptions, and performance. *Journal of Marketing Research* (May): 119-129.

Dillard, J.F., and K.R. Ferris. 1989. Individual behavior in professional accounting firms: a review and synthesis. *Journal of Accounting Literature* 8: 208-234.

Dubin, R. 1956. Industrial workers' worlds: a study of the central life interests of industrial workers. *Social Problems* 3: 131-142.

Elliott, R.K. 1991. Improvements in the early employment experience. *Accounting Horizons* (September): 114-119.

Ferris, K.R. 1981. Organizational commitment and performance in a professional accounting firm. *Accounting, Organizations and Society* 6: 317-326.

Gregson, T., J. Wendell, and J. Aono. 1994. Role ambiguity, role conflict, and perceived environmental uncertainty: Are the scales measuring separate constructs for accountants? *Behavioral Research in Accounting* 6: 144-159.

Hall, D.T. 1971. A theoretical model of career subidentity development in organizational settings. *Organizational Behavior and Human Performance* 6: 50-76.

_____. 1976. *Careers in Organizations.* Pacific Palisades, CA: Goodyear.

Hall, D.T., and R. Mansfield. 1975. Relationships of age and seniority with career variables of engineers and scientists. *Journal of Applied Psychology* 60: 201-210.

Harrell, A., E. Chewning, and M. Taylor. 1986. Organizational-professional conflict and the job satisfaction and turnover intentions of internal auditors. *Auditing: A Journal of Practice & Theory* (Spring): 109-121.

Harrell, A., and R. Eickhoff. 1988. Auditors' influence-orientation and their affective responses to the "big eight" work environment. *Auditing: A Journal of Practice & Theory* 7: 105-118.

Harrell, A., and M.J. Stahl. 1984. McClelland's trichotomy of needs theory and the job satisfaction and work performance of CPA firm professionals. *Accounting, Organizations and Society* 9: 241-252.

Hermanson, R.H., J.V. Carcello, D.R. Hermanson, B.J. Milano, G.A. Polansky, and D.Z. Williams. 1995. Better environment, better staff. *Journal of Accountancy* (April): 39-43.

Hooks, K.L., and S.J. Cheramy. 1994. Facts and myths about women CPAs. *Journal of Accountancy* (October): 79-86.

Hoppock, R. 1935. *Job Satisfaction.* New York: Harper and Brothers.

House, R.J., and J.R. Rizzo. 1972. Role conflict and ambiguity as critical variables in a model of organizational behavior. *Organizational Behavior and Human Performance* (June): 467-505.

Isabella, L.A. 1988. The effect of career stage on the meaning of key organizational events. *Journal of Organizational Behavior* 9: 345-358.

Jackson, S.E., and R.S. Schuler. 1985. A meta-analysis and conceptual critique of research on role ambiguity and role conflict in work settings. *Organizational Behavior and Human Decision Processes* (August) 16-78.

Kanungo, R.N. 1979. The concepts of alienation and involvement revisited. *Psychological Bulletin* 86: 119-138.

Kahn, R.L., D.M. Wolfe, R.P. Quinn, D.J. Snoek, and R.A. Rosenthal. 1964. *Organizational Stress: Studies in Role Conflict and Ambiguity.* New York: Wiley.

Lefkowitz, J.M., M.J. Somers, and K. Weinberg. 1984. The role of need level and/or need salience as moderators of the relationship between need satisfaction and work alienation-involvement. *Journal of Vocational Behavior* 24: 142-158.

Lysonski, S. 1985. A boundary theory investigation of the product manager's role. *Journal of Marketing* (Winter): 26-40.

Matteson, M.T., and J.M. Ivancevich. 1982. *Managing Job Stress and Health.* New York: The Free Press.

McGregor, C.C., Jr., L.N. Killough, and R.M. Brown. 1989. An investigation of organizational-professional conflict in management accounting. *Journal of Management Accounting Research* (Fall): 104-118.

McNichols, C.W., M.J. Stahl, and T.R. Manley. 1978. A validation of Hoppock's job satisfaction measure. *Academy of Management Journal* (December): 737-742.

Miller, G.A. 1967. Professionals in bureaucracy: Alienation among industrial scientists and engineers. *American Sociological Review* (October): 755-768.

Moch, M.K. 1980. Job involvement, internal motivation, and employees' integration into networks of work relationships. *Organizational Behavior and Human Performance* 25: 15-31.

Morrow, P.C., and J.C. McElroy. 1987. Work commitment and job satisfaction over three career stages. *Journal of Vocational Behavior* 30: 330-346.

Morrow, P.C., E.J. Mullen, and J.C. McElroy. 1990. Review—vocational behavior 1989: The year in review. *Journal of Vocational Behavior* 37: 121-195.

Mount, M.K. 1984. Managerial career stage and facets of job satisfaction. *Journal of Vocational Behavior* 24: 340-354.

Mowday, R.T., R.M. Steers, and L.W. Porter. 1979. The measurement of organizational commitment. *Journal of Vocational Behavior* (April): 224-247.

Norris, D.R., and R.E. Niebuhr. 1983. Professionalism, organizational commitment and job satisfaction in an accounting organization. *Accounting, Organizations and Society* 9: 49-59.

Nunnally, J.C. 1978. *Psychometric Theory.* 2nd edition. New York: McGraw-Hill Book Company.

Organ, D.W., and C.N. Greene. 1981. The effects of formalization on professional involvement: a compensatory process approach. *Administrative Science Quarterly* 26: 237-252.

Ornstein, S., W.L. Cron, and J.W. Slocum, Jr. 1989. Life stage versus career stage: A comparative test of the theories of Levinson and Super. *Journal of Organizational Behavior* 10: 117-133.

Ornstein, S., and L. Isabella. 1990. Age vs. stage models of career attitudes of women: A partial replication and extension. *Journal of Vocational Behavior* 36: 1-19.

Pasewark, W.R., J.R. Strawser, and J.E. Wilkerson, Jr. 1994. An empirical examination of the relationships among leader behaviors, audit team performance, and staff satisfaction. In *Advances in Accounting*, Vol. 12, ed. B.N. Schwartz, 143-166. Greenwich, CT: JAI Press.

Rasch, R.H., and A. Harrell. 1990. The impact of personal characteristics on the turnover behavior of accounting professionals. *Auditing: A Journal of Practice & Theory* (Spring): 90-102.

Rebele, J.E., and R.E. Michaels. 1990. Independent auditors' role stress: antecedent, outcome, and moderating variables. *Behavioral Research in Accounting* 2: 124-153.

Rhodes, S.R. 1983. Age-related differences in work attitudes and behavior: a review and conceptual analysis. *Psychological Bulletin* 93: 328-367.

Rizzo, J.R., R.J. House, and S.I. Lirtzman. 1970. Role conflict and ambiguity in complex organizations. *Administrative Science Quarterly* 15: 150-163.

Rush, J.C., A.C. Peacock, and G.T. Milkovich. 1980. Career stages: A partial test of Levinson's model of life/career stages. *Journal of Vocational Behavior* 16: 347-359.

Schuler, R.S., R.J. Aldag, and A.P. Brief. 1977. Role conflict and ambiguity: a scale analysis. *Organizational Behavior and Human Performance* 20: 111-128.

Senatra, P.T. 1980. Role conflict, role ambiguity, and organizational climate in a public accounting firm. *The Accounting Review* (October): 594-603.

Slocum, J.W., and W.L. Cron. 1985. Job attitudes and performance during three career stages. *Journal of Vocational Behavior* (April): 126-145.

Smart, R.M., and C.C. Peterson. 1994. Super's stages and the four-factor structure of the adult career concerns inventory in an Australian sample. *Measurement and Evaluation in Counseling and Development* (January): 243-257.

Snead, K., and A. Harrell. 1991. The impact of psychological factors on the job satisfaction of senior auditors. *Behavioral Research in Accounting* 3: 85-96.

Sonnenfeld, J., and J.P. Kotter. 1982. The maturation of career theory. *Human Relations* 35: 19-46.

Super, D.E. 1957. *The Psychology of Careers.* New York: Harper and Brothers.

Super, D.E. 1984. Career and life development. In *Career Choice and Development,* eds. D. Brown and L. Brooks. San Francisco, CA: Jossey-Bass.

Super, D.E., R.S. Zelkowitz, and A.S. Thompson. 1981. *Career Development Inventory: Adult Form I.* New York: Teachers' College, Columbia University.

Taylor, J.A. 1953. A personality scale of manifest anxiety. *Journal of Abnormal Social Psychology*: 285-290.

Van Maanen, J., and R. Katz, 1976. Individuals and their careers: Some temporal considerations for work satisfaction. *Personnel Psychology* 29: 601-616.

Van Maanen, J., and E.H. Schein, 1979. Toward a theory of organizational socialization. In *Research in Organizational Behavior,* Vol. 1, ed. B. Staw, 209-264. Greenwich, CT: JAI Press.

Van Sell, M., A.P. Brief, and R.S. Schuler. 1981. Role conflict and role ambiguity: Integration of the literature and directions for future research. *Human Relations* 34(1): 43-71.

Walker, O.C., G.A. Churchill, and N.M. Ford, 1975. Organizational determinants of the industrial salesman's role conflict and ambiguity. *Journal of Marketing* (January): 32-39.

Whiston, S.C. 1990. Evaluation of the adult career concerns inventory. *Journal of Counseling and Development* 69: 78-80.

AN EXAMINATION OF THE FEATURE-POSITIVE EFFECT IN AUDITORS' EVALUATION OF ACCOUNTING ESTIMATES

Philip M.J. Reckers and Bernard Wong-On-Wing

ABSTRACT

The feature-positive effect refers to the greater difficulty in processing nonoccurrences (e.g., nonbehaviors) than occurrences (e.g., behaviors). This study examined the extent to which auditors are subject to the effect in assessing management's deviation from expectations. The results suggest that deviations resulting from management's nonbehaviors are perceived to be less extreme than equivalent deviations resulting from behaviors. These perceived deviations of management were found to be significantly associated with auditors' subsequent judgments in the areas where deviations were observed and in other separate audit areas.

Advances in Accounting, Volume 14, pages 259-268.
Copyright © 1996 by JAI Press Inc.
All rights of reproduction in any form reserved.
ISBN: 0-7623-0161-9.

INTRODUCTION

Auditors' expectations play an important role in influencing audit decisions. More specifically, the extent to which events deviate from expectations affects auditors' subsequent judgments. For example, in assessing the likelihood of Fraudulent Financial Reporting (FFR), the auditor would consider the extent to which management corrects existing observed weaknesses in internal control (NCFFR 1988, appendix F). Failure to correct weaknesses would deviate from auditors' expectations and lead to higher perceived risk of FFR. Similarly, the degree to which events deviate from expectations may influence auditors' investigation of the cause of the observed deviation (Anderson and Koonce 1995; Koonce and Phillips 1996).

The purpose of this study is twofold. First, given the importance of deviations from expectations, the present research examines whether deviations resulting from management's *nonbehavior* would be processed equivalently to deviations from management's *behavior*. Research studies in psychology have observed greater difficulty in processing nonoccurrences (e.g., nonbehaviors) than occurrences (e.g., behaviors) as positive cues for solving problems. Jenkins and Sainsbury (1970) have termed this phenomenon the feature-positive effect.

In the auditing context, management's nonbehavior in many instances should be as informative as management's behavior. For example, in assessing whether management's choice of accounting estimates deviates from expectations, management's failure to revise accounting estimates when the need is obvious, should be as informative as management's revision to accounting estimates when revisions are not justified. Other similar nonbehaviors which should be informative include management's failure to adequately write off obsolete inventory and management's failure to adopt a new Statement on Financial Accounting Standards (SFAS) early, where application would reduce income. If the feature-positive effect exists among auditors, inferences from management's nonbehavior may not be as normatively adequate as inferences from management's behavior.

A second objective of the present research is to examine the extent to which perceived deviations in one audit area is related to judgments in another audit area. SAS 53 states that if the auditor has determined that an adjustment is, or may be, an irregularity and has determined that the effect could be material or has been unable to evaluate potential materiality, the auditor should among other things, consider the implications for other aspects of the audit (AICPA 1988a, par. 25). One reason for auditors' failure to detect financial statement misstatement is their inability to recognize the possibility of pervasive fraud once a questionable situation has been identified (Groveman 1995).

The following section first reviews research on auditors' perceived deviation from expectations, and research on the feature-positive effect. The hypotheses and the study are then presented followed by a discussion of the results.

DEVIATIONS FROM EXPECTATIONS

SAS 53 (AICPA 1988a) and the recommendations of the NCFFR (1987) provide general guidelines on the assessment of the likelihood of errors and irregularities. These include a list of unexpected or unusual behaviors by management that should alert the auditor to the possibility of fraudulent acts. Examples of such behaviors that would be considered unexpected include the domination of management operating and financing decisions by a single person, management having an unduly aggressive attitude toward financial reporting, and management placing undue emphasis on meeting earnings projections (AICPA 1988, par. 10). A study by Wong-On-Wing, Reneau, and West (1989) found that as prescribed by these guidelines and consistent with research in psychology (see reviews by Ross and Fletcher 1985; Kelley and Michela 1980), auditors were generally sensitive to deviations resulting from unexpected management behavior.

In the study by Wong-On-Wing and colleagues, auditors were asked to make an inference about the reason for the sale of a fixed asset by management. The results showed that when the sale reflected high deviations from expectations, auditors attributed the transaction to management's disposition (i.e., something about management). Conversely, when the sale transaction did not deviate from expectations, auditors attributed it to situational factors. Low/high deviation from expectations were manipulated by indicating that the behavior by management (sale transaction) was consistent/inconsistent with (1) prior behavior in similar situations and (2) behavior of management of other firms in the same industry.

Several studies (e.g., Jenkins and Ward 1965; Ward and Jenkins 1965; Jenkins and Sainsbury 1970; Newman, Wolff and Hearst 1980; Fazio, Sherman and Herr 1982) have found that there is greater difficulty in processing nonoccurrences than occurrences as positive cues for solving problems. For example, Ward and Jenkins (1965) found that in making judgments of contingency, individuals estimate the level of contingency between an event and an outcome (e.g., cloud seeding and rain) mainly by the number of positive-confirming instances (i.e., cloud seeding followed by rain). Cases of cloud seeding without rain, rain without cloud seeding, and no seeding and no rain contribute far less. Similarly, Fazio and colleagues (1982) found that individuals inferred less extreme attitudes from the nonoccurrence of a behavior than from the occurrence of a behavior.

HYPOTHESES

The first part of the present study examines whether auditors are as sensitive to deviations resulting from management's nonbehavior as they are to those resulting from management's behavior. One would expect management to adopt a higher rate for estimating allowance for doubtful accounts if recent experiences obviously indicate significantly higher bad debts expenses. Management's continued use of the same (prior year's) rate, or its failure to adopt a higher rate, would constitute a nonbehavior which would be considered a deviation from expectations. Thus, the question is whether auditors perceive management's nonbehavior to be a deviation from expectations to the same extent that they would based on the behavior of management. Hence, the first three hypotheses are:

Hypothesis 1.   Auditor-subjects will perceive a deviation from expectations to be less extreme when the deviation results from management's nonbehavior than when it results from management's behavior.

Hypothesis 2.   The higher the perceived deviation from expectations, the higher will be the assessed inherent risk.

Hypothesis 3.   The higher the perceived deviation from expectations, the more reasonable auditors will assess the adjustment proposed by their staff.

The second part of this study examines the relationship between auditors' perceived deviation of management concerning a given accounting estimate and their judgments relating to another accounting estimate. Audit judgments relating to different accounting estimates, presumably, are not made independently of each other. For example, SAS 57 states that "if each accounting estimate included in the financial statements was individually reasonable, but the effect of the difference between each estimate and the estimate best supported by the audit evidence was to increase income, the auditor should reconsider the estimates taken as a whole" (AICPA 1988b, par. 14). Thus, the next three hypotheses are:

Hypothesis 4.   Perceived deviation of management from expectations relating to a given accounting estimate will be significantly and positively associated with perceived deviation relating to another accounting estimate.

Hypothesis 5.   The higher the perceived deviation from expectations relating to a given accounting estimate, the higher will be the assessed inherent risk related to another accounting estimate.

Hypothesis 6.   The higher the perceived deviation from expectations relating to a given accounting estimate, the more reasonable auditors will assess the adjustment proposed by their staff to another accounting estimate.

Finally, this study sought to determine whether auditors naturally assess and attend to deviations from expectations. In the present study, half of the auditors were specifically asked to assess the extent of management's deviation from expectations before their audit judgments, and the other half, after the audit judgments. One may infer that auditors naturally assess and attend to management's deviation from expectations if the deviation assessments and audit judgments of the two groups of subjects do not differ significantly (see Wong and Weiner 1981; Pyszczynski and Greenberg 1981). Hence, the last hypothesis is:

Hypothesis 7.   There will be no significant difference in judgments between subjects who assess management's deviation before making audit judgments and those who assess management's deviation after making audit judgments.

METHOD

Auditor-subjects were presented with one of two versions of a case describing a deviation by management. In the first version, the deviation resulted from management's behavior (application of a new lower rate for estimating bad debts) whereas in the second version, the deviation resulted from management's nonbehavior (application of the same old rate—that is, failure to apply a new rate). Subjects were asked to indicate the extent to which they perceived the use of the rate to be a deviation from their expectations. Half of the subjects were asked to assess management's deviation from expectations before making the audit judgments, and the other half made the deviation assessment after making the audit judgments. Subjects were randomly assigned to one of the four experimental conditions (see Table 1).

Subjects

Subjects were 76 audit seniors from various offices of a large public accounting firm. All, but one, had three or more years of audit experience. Seventy-three (97 percent) of the subjects indicated that it was common for them to assess the reasonableness of accounting estimates. Sixty-seven (89 percent) indicated that the case material was realistic. Subjects' age ranged from 23 to 40 with an average of 26. The research questionnaires were administered during one of the firm's advanced senior training programs.

Research Instrument

The case scenario related to the audit of a publicly traded retail corporation. Background information was provided including the client's comparative balance

Table 1.   Study Design

	Behavior	Nonbehavior
Order 1	18	19
Order 2	19	20

Notes: Order 1: Deviation Assessment made before audit judgments.
Order 2: Deviation Assessment made after audit judgments.

sheets and income statements. The case described two audit issues related to accounting estimates. Each description was followed by a set of questions. The first audit issue pertained to estimates of bad debts and allowance for doubtful accounts, and contained the behavior/nonbehavior manipulation (see next subsection). After reading this first issue, subjects responded to three questions (see Audit Judgments below). The second issue related to the allowance for obsolete inventory. This description was *identical across all four experimental conditions.* Again subjects were asked the three questions described below. The last section of the instrument inquired some demographic information about the subjects.

Behavior / Nonbehavior

Both the "behavior" and "nonbehavior" of management were made explicit as follows. In the "behavior" condition, it was stated that "the company has adopted a new rate for estimating bad debts and the related allowance for doubtful accounts." In contrast, the "nonbehavior" case stated, "the company has adopted the same rate . . . for estimating bad debts and the related allowance for doubtful accounts." Both conditions, however, reflected a comparable deviation from expectations. In other words, management used a (new/old) rate which was not supported by recent credit experiences and which was below the industry average.

Audit Judgments

As noted earlier, after reading each one of the two accounting estimate cases, subjects made three judgments. They were first asked to indicate, on an 11-point scale, the extent to which they considered management's use of the given rate to be a deviation from their expectations. The scale ranged from "not at all" (0) to "to a great extent" (10). The second judgment was to assess the inherent risk related to the accounting estimate using an 11-point scale labeled zero percent to 100 percent. Finally, subjects were asked to indicate the extent to which they believed that a staff-proposed adjustment to the estimate was reasonable. The scale used was identical to the one used for the first judgment (i.e., the deviation question).

Results

An analysis of variance was performed on the deviation scores with "behavior" (behavior versus nonbehavior) and "deviation assessment order" (before versus after audit judgments) as the independent variables. The results ($F(1, 72) = 5.86$, $p < 0.018$; see Table 2) support the first hypothesis. Auditors in the nonbehavior condition (6.28, $n = 39$, $s.d. = 2.45$) perceived management's deviation to be less extreme than auditors in the behavior condition (7.45, $n = 37$, $s.d. = 1.64$).[1]

Using Hartley's test (Kirk 1982), the variances of the two means were found to be significantly different ($F(2, 39) = 2.24$, $p < 0.05$). This suggests that there was

Table 2. Anova on Deviation Assessment

Source	SS	DF	F	P
Behavior (B)	25.41	1	5.86	0.0180
Order (O)	3.35	1	0.77	0.3819
B x O	11.37	1	2.62	0.1096
Error	312.02	72		

Table 3. Correlation Between Deviation and Audit Judgments

	r	p
Allowance for Doubtful Accounts		
Deviation from expectations	1.000	0.000
Inherent risk	0.326	0.004
Reasonableness of staff-proposed adjustment	0.259	0.023
Allowance for Obsolete Inventory		
Deviation from expectations	0.368	0.001
Inherent risk	0.349	0.002
Reasonableness of staff-proposed adjustment	0.281	0.014

relatively higher consensus among auditors in the behavior condition than among auditors in the nonbehavior case.

Table 2 also shows that the deviation assessments were not significantly different for the two "order" conditions ($F(1, 72) = 0.77$, $p < 0.38$). The mean scores for subjects who assessed management's deviation before and after the audit judgments were 7.08 ($n = 37$, s.d. = 2.03) and 6.64 ($n = 39$, s.d. = 2.29), respectively. This finding together with the test result of Hypothesis 7 (see below) suggests that auditors naturally assess and attend to deviation from expectations.

The next five hypotheses were tested using correlational analyses. Table 3 shows the results of the Pearson correlation tests between auditors' assessed deviation and the audit judgments studied.

As predicted, auditors' assessment of management's deviation from expectations was positively and significantly correlated with their assessment of inherent risk concerning the given accounting estimate ($r = 0.326$, $p < 0.004$), and the extent of their belief that a staff-proposed adjustment to the estimate was reasonable ($r = 0.259$, $p < 0.023$).

Similarly, subjects' perception of management's deviation relating to the first accounting estimate was positively and significantly associated with their perception of management's deviation relating to the second accounting estimate ($r = 0.368$, $p < 0.001$), their assessment of inherent risk relating to the second account-

Table 4. Effect of Order on Audit Judgments

	r	p
Allowance for Doubtful Accounts		
Deviation from expectations	0.77	0.3819
Inherent risk	1.14	0.2893
Reasonableness of staff-proposed adjustment	0.04	0.8352
Allowance for Obsolete Inventory		
Deviation from expectations	0.00	0.9684
Inherent risk	0.46	0.4978
Reasonableness of staff-proposed adjustment	0.30	0.5860

Note: Neither the behavior factor nor the interaction term was significant on any of the judgments except the first, as shown in Table 2.

ing estimate ($r = 0.349$, $p < 0.002$), and the extent of their belief that a staff-proposed adjustment to the second estimate was reasonable ($r = 0.281$, $p < 0.014$).

To determine whether the order in which the deviation assessments were made (i.e., before or after the audit judgments) had an effect on the audit judgments, separate ANOVA's with "behavior" and "order" as independent variables, were performed on each audit judgment. The results (see Table 4) show that none of the judgments were affected by the "order" factor. This suggests that auditors assessed and attended to the deviation of management from expectations whether or not they were explicitly instructed to do so.

DISCUSSION

Professional standards (e.g., AICPA 1988a, 1988b) prescribe that auditors should attend to deviations from expectations in making audit judgments. Research in psychology (Kelley and Michela 1980; Ross and Fletcher 1985) and in auditing (Wong-On-Wing, Reneau, and West 1989) provides evidence that individuals attend to deviations from expectations. The present research extends these prior studies by examining whether auditors perceive deviations resulting from management's behavior to be equivalent to those that result from management's nonbehavior. These preliminary results indicate that auditors perceived the deviation arising from management's nonbehavior to be less extreme than the deviation arising from management's behavior. This evidence is consistent with findings of research on the feature-positive effect in nonaccounting contexts (e.g., Jenkins and Sainsbury 1970; Newman et al. 1980). Moreover, it was observed that there was lower consensus among auditors in the nonbehavior condition than among those in the behavior condition irrespective of whether auditors were asked to assess management's deviation before or after making the audit judgments.

The present research also supports the prior findings of by Wong-On-Wing and colleagues (1989). With respect to the evaluation of accounting estimates, the results indicate that perceptions of management's deviation relating to a given estimate were related not only to the perceived inherent risk and reasonableness of a staff-proposed adjustment relating to that estimate but also to the perceived deviation of management, the inherent risk, and the reasonableness of a staff-proposed adjustment relating to another estimate.

Finally, the present study examined whether auditors naturally assess and attend to deviation from expectations. The evidence suggests that they do. This finding is consistent with studies by Wong and Weiner (1981), and Pyszczynski and Greenberg (1981).

The present research has limitations. The results have limited generalizability to the extent that they relate to a specific task involving particular issues performed by a specific group of senior auditors from a single firm. In addition, manipulation checks were not included that could have established whether subjects actually did perceive the manipulations as behavior and nonbehavior. Lacking these checks, one cannot definitively ascribe the results of the first part of the study to the feature-positive phenomenon. Future research must determine the extent to which the feature-positive effect is present and leads to suboptimal or nonnormative decisions in auditing. The present study represents only a first step in research in that direction.

ACKNOWLEDGMENT

Financial support was provided to the second author in part by the Accounting Development Fund at Washington State University.

NOTE

1. The assumption of homogeneity of error variance was not met. Kirk (1982, 79) notes that the F distribution is relatively unaffected by heterogeneity of variance. Nevetherless, a transformation (square) of the dependent measure was performed and it achieved relatively homogeneous variances. The results of the ANOVA using the transformed data were not significantly different ($F(1,72) = 5.43$, $p < 0.02$) from the results using the untransformed data ($F(1,72) = 5.86$, $p < 0.01$).

REFERENCES

American Institute of Certified Public Accountants (AICPA). 1988a. *Statement on Auditing Standards No. 53: The Auditor's Responsibility to Detect and Report Errors and Irregularities.* New York: AICPA.
_____. 1988b. *Statement on Auditing Standards No. 57: Auditing Accounting Estimates..* New York: AICPA.
Anderson, U., and L. Koonce. 1995. Explanation as a method for evaluating client-suggested causes in analytical procedures. *Auditing: A Journal of Practice and Theory* (Fall): 124-132.

Fazio, R.H., S.J. Sherman, and P.M. Herr. 1982. The feature-positive effect in the self-perception process: Does not doing matter as much as doing? *Journal of Personality and Social Psychology* 42(3): 404-411.

Groveman, H. 1995. How auditors can detect financial statement misstatement. *Journal of Accountancy* (October): 83-86.

Jenkins, H.M., and R.S. Sainsbury. 1970. Discrimination learning with the distinctive feature on positive or negative trials. In *Attention: Contemporary Theory and Analysis*, ed. D. Mostofsky. New York: Appleton-Century-Crofts.

Jenkins, H.M. and W.C. Ward. 1965. Judgment of Contingency Between Responses and Outcomes. *Psychological Monographs: General and Applied* (Whole No. 594).

Kelley, H.H., and J.L. Michela. 1980. Attribution theory and research. *Annual Review of Psychology* 31: 457-501.

Koonce, L., and F. Phillips. 1996. Auditors' comprehension and evaluation of client-suggested causes in analytical procedures. *Behavioral Research in Accounting* 8: 32-48.

Newman, J., W.T. Wolff, and E. Hearst. 1980. The feature-positive effect in adult human subjects. *Journal of Experimental Psychology: Human Learning and Memory* 6: 630-650.

Pyszczynski, T.A., and J. Greenberg. 1981. Role of disconfirmed expectancies in the instigation of attributional processing. *Journal of Personality and Social Psychology* 40(1): 31-38.

National Commission on Fraudulent Financial Reporting. 1987. *Report of the National Commission on Fraudulent Financial Reporting*. Washington, DC: NCFFR.

Ross, M., and G. Fletcher. 1985. Attribution and social perception. In *Handbook of Social Psychology*, Vol. 2, eds. G. Lindzey and E. Aronson, 73-122. Cambridge, MA: Addison-Wesley.

Ward, W.C., and H.M. Jenkins. 1965. The display of information and the judgment of contingency. *Canadian Journal of Psychology* 19: 231-241.

Wong, P.T.P., and B. Weiner. 1981. When people ask "why" questions, and the heuristics of attributional search. *Journal of Personality and Social Psychology* 40(4): 650-663.

Wong-On-Wing, B., J.H. Reneau, and S.G. West. 1989. Auditors' perception of management: Determinants and consequences. *Accounting, Organizations and Society* 14(5/6): 577-587.

Advances in Accounting

Edited by **Philip M. J. Reckers,** *School of Accountancy, Arizona State University*

Volume 13, 1995, 247 pp. $73.25
ISBN 1-55938-881-1

CONTENTS: The Determinants of Audit Delay, *Michael Aitken, Freddie Choo, Michael Firth, and Roger Simnett.* The Audit Review Process and Its Effect on Auditor's Assessments of Evidence from Management, *Urton Anderson, Lisa Koonce, and Gary Marchant.* Evidence of the Security Market's Ex Ante Assessment of Differential Management Forecast Accuracy, *Stephen P. Baginski, Allen W. Bathke, Jr., and John M. Hassell.* Assessing Accounting Doctoral Programs by Their Graduates' Research Productivity, *James R. Hasselback and Alan Reinstein.* An Investigation of the Feasibility of Using Statistically-Based Models as Analytical Procedures, *Kenneth S. Lorek, Stephen W. Wheeler, Rhoda C. Icerman, and David Fordham.* An Investigation of the Determinants of Accounting Method Choice Among Initial Public Offering Firms, *John D. Neill, Susan G. Pourciau, and Thomas F. Schaefer.* Examining the Dimensionality of the Ethical Decision Making Process of Certified Management Accountants, *R. Eric Reidenbach, Donald P. Robin, Thomas J. Phillips, Jr., and Steven M. Flory.* Additional Evidence of Auditor Changes: The Effects of Client Financial Condition, *Earl R. Wilson, Inder K. Khurana, and W. David Albrecht.* On the Use of Contingent Valuation Method to Estimate Environmental Costs, *Maribeth Coller and Glenn W. Harrison.* Accounting for Debt Conversions: Current and Future Alternatives, *Alan K. Ortegren and Thomas E. King.* Auditor Materiality Judgement and Consistency Modifications: Further Evidence from SFAS 96, *Michael L. Costigan and Daniel T. Simon.* Indirect Cash Flow Measures Versus Cash Flows Reported Persuant to SFAS No. 95, *Hanan ElSheika, Paul Munter, and Thomas Robinson.* The Relative Importance of Operating Cash Flows and Accrual Income in Explaining Stock Returns: A Cross-Sectional Approach, *Gary R. Freeman and Glen R. Larsen.*

Also Available:
Volumes 1-12 (1984-1994) $73.25 each

J A I P R E S S

Advances in International Accounting

Edited by **Timothy S. Doupnik,** *School of Accounting, University of South Carolina*

Volume 9, 1996, 264 pp. $73.25
ISBN 1-55938-991-5

CONTENTS: Accounting Standard-Setting Strategies and Theories of Economic Development: Implications for the Adoption of International Accounting Standards, *Robert K. Larson and Sara York Kenny.* The IASC Comparability Project: Examining the Outcomes Using Two Theoretical Models, *Stephen B. Salter and Clare B. Roberts.* Implementing the OCAM Plan: Two Contrasting Case Studies, *Charles Elad.* The Timeliness of Bahraini Annual Reports, *Jasim Y. A. Abdulla.* The Relationship Between Geographic Segment Information and Firm Risk, *Martha M. Pointer and Timothy S. Doupnik.* Evidence from the U.S. Market of the Association of Capitalized Non-Goodwill Intangibles to Firm Equity Value, *Mark G. McCarthy and Douglas K. Schneider.* Auditors' Reports: A Six Country Comparison, *Michael John Jones and Yusuf Karbhari.* Performance Evaluation in U.S.-Based Multinationals, *Linda F. Christensen.* The Impact of Company Size and Profitability on the Ability of Mexican Firms to Attract Foreign Investment: Some Evidence from the Mexican Stock, *Alejandro Hazera.* Physical Asset Valuation and Zakat: Insights and Implications, *Frank Clarke, Russell Craig, and Shaari Hamid.* A New Approach to Preparing International Cases Involving Student and Faculty, *Jayne Fuglister and Robert Bloom.* International Accounting Dissertation Abstracts, Compiled and Comments by *Frederick Niswander.*

Also Available:
Volumes 1-8 (1987-1995) $73.25 each

JAI PRESS INC.
55 Old Post Road No. 2 - P.O. Box 1678
Greenwich, Connecticut 06836-1678
Tel: (203) 661- 7602   Fax: (203) 661-0792

Advances in Accounting Information Systems

Edited by **Steven G. Sutton**, *KPGM Peat Marwick; Professor, Bryant College*

Volume 4, In preparation, Winter 1996
ISBN 1-55938-990-7   Approx. $73.25

TENTATIVE CONTENTS: Preface. Have We Lost the *Accounting* in AIS Research? The Need for Leadership in a Technology Driven Accounting and Audit Environment, *Steven G. Sutton.* PART I. INFORMATION SYSTEMS PRACTICE AND THEORY. The Effect of Socioeconomic Background on Computer Anxiety and Performance: Evidence from Three Experiments, *Dana Gibson and James E. Hunton.* The Effect of Socioeconomic Background on Computer Anxiety and Performance, *Somnath Bhattacharya.* An Integrative Model of Audit Expert System Development, *Kristi Yuthas and Jesse F. Dillard.* Response to an Integrative AES Model, *James C. Lampe.* User's Affective Response to an Information System: Conceptual Development and an Empirical Comparison of Four Operationalizations, *Jon B. Woodroof and George M. Kasper.* A Distributed Assumption-Based Truth Maintenance (DATMS) Approach to Communication Issues in Distributed Audit Contexts, *Gary V. Howorka and Cynthia A. Frownfelter.* PART II. INFORMATION SYSTEMS AND THE ACCOUNTING/AUDITING ENVIRONMENT. Articulating Accounting Database Queries: An Analysis of Actual and Perceived Effort, *Donald R. Jones and Martha M. Eining.* Memory Measure Differences in Fraud Risk Assessments: Implications for the Design and Use of Audit Decisions Aids, *Somnath Bhattacharya.* A Neural Network Approach to Financial Distress Analysis, *Harlan Etheridge and Ram Sriram.* Vendor and Staff Support and User Satisfaction: Microcomputer Accounting Packages, *William L. Hamby and Robert A. Leitch.* PART III. PERSPECTIVES ON INFORMATION SYSTEMS RESEARCH. Developing Intelligent Technologies that Improve Human Judgment and Decision Making: Compensating for Heuristic Biases, *Vicky Arnold.* Opportunities for Behavioral Research in AIS: The Matter of Expertise, *Marinus J. Bouwman.* Toward Effective Group Decision Making: Integrating Group Support Systems into the Accounting Environment, *Stephen C.Hayne and Steve G. Sutton.* The Role of Decision Aids in Accounting: A Synthesis of Prior Research, *Martha M. Eining and Darrell Brown.* Organizational Sociology and Accounting Information Systems Research, *Jesse F. Dillard.*

Also Available:

Volumes 1-3 (1992-1995) $73.25 each

Research on Accounting Ethics

Managing Editor: **Lawrence A. Ponemon,** *Center for the Study of Ethics and Behavior in Accounting, School of Management, State University of New York at Binghamton.*

Volume 2, 1996, 288 pp. $73.25
ISBN 1-55938-997-4

CONTENTS: Should Auditors Provide Nonaudit Services to their Audit Clients?, *Ronald A. Davidson and Craig Emby.* Applying Behavioral Models as Prescriptions for Ethics in Accounting Practice and Education: Revisiting Fish Out of Water and an Experiment, *Tom Tolleson, Barbara D. Merino, and Alan G. Mayper.* A Study of the Relationship Between Accounting Students' Moral Reasoning and Cognitive Styles, *Dann G. Fisher and Richard L.Ott.* Accounting Ethics: The Search for Truth in an Age of Moral Relativism, *C. Richard Baker.* The Litigation Crisis: Auditor Responsibility to the Public, *Bonita A. Daly and James R. Hamill.* Value Judgements Using Belief Functions, *Rajendra P. Srivastava.* Ethical Obligations of CPAs in Advertising and Solicitation: Public Interest Considerations, *Kathy S. Moffeit, Steven M. Mintz, and Ruth Lesher Taylor.* Integrating Ethics into Intermediate Accounting: An Experimental Investigation Incorporating Attribution Theory, *Sara York Kenny and Martha M. Einning.* The Impact of Ethics Education in Accounting Curricula, *James Lampe.* Commentary on "Integrating Ethics Exercises into Intermediate Accounting" and "The Impact of Ethics Education in Accounting Curricula", *Bruce L. Oliver.* Ethics for Business Faculty, *Raef A. Lawson.* Ethics Violations in the Accounting Profession: An Empirical Investigation, *C. William Thomas and Samuel L. Seaman.* On Serving the Public's Going-Concern Report Modifications, *Marshall G.A. Geiger, K. Raghunandan, and D.V. Rama.*

Also Available:
Volume 1 (1993) $73.25

JAI PRESS INC.
55 Old Post Road No. 2 - P.O. Box 1678
Greenwich, Connecticut 06836-1678
Tel: (203) 661- 7602   Fax: (203) 661-0792